The
State of
Working
America

The State of Working America

1990–91
Edition

Lawrence Mishel
David M. Frankel
Economic Policy Institute

M. E. Sharpe, Inc.
Armonk, New York
London, England

Copyright © 1991 by M. E. Sharpe, Inc.
80 Business Park Drive, Armonk, New York 10504

Available in the United Kingdom and Europe from M. E. Sharpe Publishers, 3 Henrietta Street, London WC2E 8LU.

ISSN: 1054-2159

ISBN: 0-87332-812-4 (cloth)   0-87332-813-2 (paper)

Printed in the United States of America

MV   10   9   8   7   6   5   4   3   2

For Julia and Eli

L.M.

To Sheldon and Roberta

D.F.

TABLE OF CONTENTS

PREFACE

T his second biennial issue of *The State of Working America* provides us with the latest series of statistical snapshots showing how those who work for a living and their families have been doing in today's economy.

The erosion of living standards that we reported two years ago in our first issue continues. Real wages—reflecting the actual value received for an hour or a week of labor—are still declining. Family incomes remain relatively stable, but only because more people in the family have gone to work. In fact, all of the increase in incomes of married couples with children since 1979 has been contributed by working mothers. One result is that both men and women are working more hours on the job and at home, leaving less time for leisure, family, and community.

There is also less money available for what might be called the economic foundations, or "infrastructure," of family life. The number of homeowners is still dropping, education is becoming less available, and both the extent and quality of health care coverage are deteriorating for large numbers of workers and their families.

The decline in real wages and the accompanying increase in inequality have finally worked their way into the nation's consciousness. We are becoming aware that the experiment called Reaganomics failed in its promise to bring long-term prosperity to the average American. Compared with previous economic recoveries, the income gains during the most recent one have been very small or negative for the vast majority of American families. These same families have been left holding the bill (in the form of higher taxes and reduced public services) for the fiscal and trade deficits, the bailout of a recklessly deregulated banking system, and the other costs of a decade in which the redistribution of income in favor of the rich was the principal goal of economic policy. Only through increased earnings can workers prevent the further deterioration of their living standards. But because of the inadequate level of investment in skills, capital goods, and infrastructure over the past decade, America's working people are now less competitive in the international marketplace than they were ten years ago.

The numbers tell us that real wages have been falling throughout most of the past decade. Until recently, however, this reality was ignored by pundits and dismissed by

The experiment called Reaganomics failed in its promise to bring long-term prosperity to the average American.

In 1987 a male
high school
graduate with 1-5
years work
experience was
earning 18% less
than his
counterpart in
1979.

"experts." Conventional wisdom held that wages were lower because of the enlarged supply of baby boomers entering the workforce. Time, we were told, would solve the problem. We know now that conventional wisdom was wrong; the smaller post-baby boom generation has now entered the labor force and their incomes are even lower than those of the baby boomers! One of the most dramatic statistics in these tables tells us that in 1987 a male high school graduate with 1-5 years work experience was earning 18% less than his counterpart in 1979.

The slowdown in productivity since 1973 would be a more credible explanation for the slowdown of wage growth. Over the long run, there is little doubt that the real income of an economy depends on its productivity. Yet even here, the case is not so simple. From 1979 to 1989 U.S. hourly productivity *grew* about 12%, while real hourly wages and benefits *fell*. Clearly, the *kind* of productivity growth we have had—based upon shrinking the industrial sector, undermining trade unions, and out-sourcing production to areas of the world where labor is cheap—does not translate into higher living standards in the United States. Indeed, the shift of workers from high- to low-paying industries has undercut optimistic forecasts that job "upskilling" would mean increased wage growth. Employment projections now suggest that by the year 2000 American workers may need more education to qualify for jobs that will pay less.

The tables in this volume provide additional detailed information about what is happening. There has been a shift of capital from productive investment to financial speculation. This shift is reflected, on the one hand, by the expansion in the share of income derived from ownership of capital gains, interest, and dividends, and by the shrinkage of the share coming from wages and salaries and farm and small business income on the other. Since ownership of financial assets is concentrated among the rich, it is no surprise that they have done proportionally better than workers, farmers, and small businesspeople.

For much of our modern history, a function of American government has been to counterbalance the natural tendency of the private market to generate inequality. But beginning in the late 1970s, the federal government reinforced inequality by shifting the tax burden downward. Between 1977 and 1990, federal tax rates declined for the richest 5% of taxpayers and rose for everyone else. During the past decade payroll taxes—which are regressive and fall entirely on labor income—rose faster than any other federal tax.

In the last few years, tax policy has begun to react to the erosion of market incomes. Our data show that the Tax Reform Act of 1986 has helped reverse the upward redistribution of income. And the long debate over the federal budget deficit recently has exposed smoldering citizen outrage over tax unfairness.

But whatever tax policies are adopted, current trends suggest that underlying market forces will put further pressure on the living standards of working people. For example, real wages continued to drop through the first half of 1990 and will be reflected in future Census reports on family earnings. The recent slowdown in economic growth will also manifest itself later as reduced incomes.

Another ominous sign is the increasingly higher poverty rate for children: 19% in 1989 compared with 16% and 14% at the peak of the last two business cycle peaks. The rates have risen for children of all races. Given the proven connection between poverty and school and work performance, we are currently sowing the seeds for a future harvest of low productivity, low wages, and low incomes.

When the Economic Policy Institute first began to report on these disturbing trends in the mid-1980s, America was in the midst of a financial boom fueled by policies that encouraged the wealthy to use their money for short-term speculation rather than for investment in new products and more efficient production. At that time, it was perhaps still possible to believe that enough of this instant wealth would trickle down to maintain the post-war trend of improved living standards for the majority of American workers.

The detailed statistics presented in this report contest the trickle-down proposition in numerous ways. The negative findings make it hard for even the committed supply-side ideologue to claim that the Reagan years worked for most American workers. Had the slowdown and worsening distribution of incomes been the price for increased investment in the future, one might have been able to make a case that it was worth it. But in the 1980s, resources were squandered that should have been used to initiate and support an economic revival in the 1990s.

In the 1980s, resources were squandered that should have been used to initiate and support an economic revival in the 1990s.

It is a sorry record. One can only hope that this expensive failure has taught us the importance of policies designed to promote income growth for *all* Americans.

Jeff Faux
President,
Economic Policy Institute

The
State of
Working
America

EXECUTIVE SUMMARY

*T*he State of Working America: 1990-91 Edition paints a comprehensive picture of the changing living standards of American workers and their families by bringing together a variety of data on family incomes, taxes, wages, jobs, unemployment, wealth, poverty, and prices.

Our findings confirm that the economic recovery of the 1980s, despite its length, left the typical working American family in many ways worse off than at the peak of the last business cycle. Moreover, the living standards of large segments of the population deteriorated significantly. Specifically, we find:

Family Incomes

The income of the typical (median) American family grew more slowly in the 1980s than in any prior business cycle in the post-war period. The growth that did occur came not from higher wages but from more hours and weeks worked in the year. Working wives made up the bulk of increases in family incomes.

Not all income groups experienced sluggish growth. Upper income groups, particularly the richest 1%, saw their incomes grow substantially in the 1980s. This growth was fueled in part by high real interest rates and the stock market boom. Inequality among wage-earners also increased as real wages among high income groups rose and real wages among the broad middle class and lower income groups fell. In particular, declining wages led to lower incomes for the bottom 40% of families.

Taxes

Changes in federal, state, and local taxes since 1977 have worsened the distribution of after-tax income by taxing the middle class and the poor more heavily and giving large tax cuts to the richest 1%. A less progressive personal income tax, higher payroll taxes, and lower corporate taxes resulted in an average federal tax break of $45,565 in 1990 for the richest families.

Wages

In inflation-adjusted terms, average hourly wages fell more than 9% between 1980 and 1989. Hourly benefits, such as pensions, health insurance, and paid time off, fell by

The income of the typical American family grew slowly in the 1980s . . . and came not from higher wages but from more hours and weeks worked.

1

13.8%. Compensation fell the most among blue-collar and service workers, young workers, and workers without a college education. The erosion was also greater among men than among women. Reflecting these trends, the wages of young male high school graduates in 1987 were 18% lower than in 1979. These workers actually earned less in 1987 than 24 years earlier in 1963.

Two-thirds of the roughly 10% drop in hourly compensation between 1980 and 1989 was due to a shift towards jobs in lower paying industries. Other causes of falling wages include growing international competition, the shrinkage of union membership, and the erosion of the real value of the minimum wage. There is no reason to expect a reversal of the shift towards lower paying jobs.

At the other end of the workforce, the pay of chief executive officers of major corporations grew far faster than the pay of CEOs in competitor nations such as Japan and West Germany.

... young male high school graduates ... actually earned less in 1987 than 24 years earlier in 1963.

Employment and Underemployment

The 1989 unemployment rate of 5.3% was low compared to 1979 and the early 1980s; it was high relative to the unemployment rates of the post-war period through 1973. Today many more people work in part-time or temporary jobs because they cannot find full-time or permanent work. There was also an expansion of low-paying self-employment in the 1980s, together with an increase in the number of people who hold more than one job because of economic hardship. Together with unemployment, these developments put at least a fifth of the workforce in situations of labor market distress.

Wealth

The distribution of wealth is even more concentrated at the top than the distribution of income. Financial asset values in the 1980s grew more rapidly than the values of housing and other tangible assets. Because ownership of financial assets is concentrated among the rich, the result was even greater inequality in the distribution of wealth. The average net worth of the top 0.5% of families rose 6.7% between 1979 and 1989, while the average net worth of families in the bottom 90% fell by 8.8%.

2

Poverty

The poverty rate increased in the 1980s, and more of the poor now have incomes below half of the poverty level. Poverty rates have increased most among children and persons in female-headed families. Decreased governmental aid and lower wages are the primary reasons. Among female-headed families, cuts in government benefits raised the poverty rate by 8.6 percentage points between 1979 and 1988.

Young Families

The economic position of the typical young family deteriorated during the 1980s. Because young families depend almost entirely on labor income, the fall in real wages during the 1980s affected them more than older families. Young noncollege educated workers were hit particularly hard. Since they have less seniority than older workers, these workers had difficulty finding or keeping jobs in the better paying, unionized industries that shrunk in the 1980s. As a result, these workers are now much more likely to be employed in low-paying industries and much less likely to be covered by a union contract than in 1979. The income deterioration among young families has been most acute for the 55% of young families headed by workers without college degrees and for young black families.

Housing, Health Care, and Education

Housing, health care, and education are crucial to family well-being and, in the case of education, to creating equal opportunity for new generations.

- As a result of high interest rates and home prices in the 1980s, the percentage of households owning their own homes dropped, particularly among the young. In addition, the burden of housing costs for renters rose. Families with children have been squeezed particularly hard by rising housing costs.
- Like housing expenses, the cost of health care has risen substantially. Insurance coverage deteriorated also because of employer cutbacks and the growth of the service sector, which provides few fringe benefits to its workers.
- Opportunities among American students are very unequal. Spending on public schools is low and uneven. Moreover, the growing gap between public and private

The economic position of the typical young family deteriorated during the 1980s.

3

college fees has transformed higher education into a two-tiered system. And while the education of minority students has improved, many still lack access to higher education and advanced degrees.

International Comparisons

Compared with other countries, U.S. per capita income growth has been relatively sluggish and driven by a greater proportion of the population working rather than by higher productivity. Despite slower growth, U.S. per capita income still leads the industrial world when measured in terms of what incomes buy in each country. However, income is much more concentrated among the rich in the U.S. than in other industrial countries, and the U.S. also has substantially higher levels of poverty.

Wages in the U.S. have been virtually stagnant since 1979, while wages in other countries have grown strongly.

Wages in the U.S. have been virtually stagnant since 1979, while wages in other countries have grown strongly. By some measures, the wages in other countries are already considerably higher than ours. Correcting for population growth, job growth in the U.S. has not been much greater than that of most other countries. Finally, U.S. public spending on job training and placement programs is among the lowest in the industrial West. Such neglect is likely to have a negative effect on future productivity, resulting in continued wage stagnation.

INTRODUCTION:
THE ECONOMIC CONTEXT

*I*n the last half of the 1980s questions began to be raised concerning the trend of income and wages in the U.S. economy. Who was benefitting from Reaganomics? Was the economy producing a disproportionate number of low wage jobs? Was the middle class shrinking? This is an appropriate time to reexamine these issues based on the accumulated evidence. Our analysis builds on the prior work of the Institute and the authors (Economic Policy Institute, 1986; Mishel, 1986; Mishel and Simon, 1988; Rose and Fasenfest, 1988).

What Happened?

Slow Income Growth: By any measure the growth of income and wealth in the 1980s was minimal, and far less than the growth of the 1970s, 1960s or 1950s. For instance, median family income grew by just 0.4% per year between 1979 and 1989, a rate half that of the 1973 to 1979 period. In fact, the $1,369 income growth over the *10 years* after 1979 equalled the amount that incomes rose every *20 months* in the 1967-1973 period.

Rising Inequality: Of course, some people did benefit greatly from recent economic policy. The richest 1%, for instance, did exceedingly well, as reflected in their 74% income growth in the 1980s. Meanwhile, the bottom 40% of the population suffered either reduced incomes or had no income growth. This dramatic disparity in income trends has restored income inequality to its highest level of the post-war period, reversing several decades of progress, and left us with a poverty rate in 1989 that surpasses that of any year in the 1970s.

Jobs and Wages: The unemployment rate in 1989 was roughly the same as in the prior business cycle peak. All the other indicators of labor market performance, however, showed drastic deterioration over the decade of the eighties. By the end of the decade, underemployment had grown, as millions of people who wanted full-time or permanent work were working in part-time or temporary jobs.

5

Millions more were working at two or more jobs because their first one paid so poorly. Real hourly wages dropped by 9.3%. Fringe benefits fell even more, by 13.8%. A third of the workforce were earning poverty level wages. The biggest losers were the 75% of the workforce without a college degree, particularly men (especially black men), and young workers. For instance, the wage of a young male high school graduate in 1987 was 18% lower than a comparable worker in 1979 and less than a comparable worker in 1963, 24 years earlier.

The Future: There is no reason to expect a reversal of these trends. Real wages have fallen in each of the last four years. Moreover, BLS job predictions suggest that the skill and education requirements of jobs are expected to grow more slowly in the 1990s than in the 1970s and 1980s.

Why?

It is now clear what has and what has not caused these disappointing income and wage developments.

The Importance of Wages: Since wages provide the bulk of most families' income (the exceptions being the rich who receive substantial interest, dividend and capital gains income and the poor who receive government transfer payments), the recent fall in real wages has placed severe economic pressure on most families. "Working harder for less" has been the necessary requirement for families to improve or hold on to their standard of living. Among married couple families with children, for instance, the bottom four-fifths of families would have had lower income in 1987 than in 1979 if the women in these families had not increased their earnings.

Productivity and Wage Growth: Slow productivity growth can only partly explain the slow wage growth of the 1980s. After all, compared to the 1970s, productivity grew slightly faster but real wages *fell* faster in the 1980s. The reason is that there has been a shift of income from wages to capital income (see below) and there has been an erosion of worker bargaining power, both union and nonunion, including an erosion of the minimum wage.

Capital Income: A major factor fueling the tremendous income growth among the rich has been the fast growth of capital income such as interest, dividends and capital gains. In fact, capital incomes grew three times as fast as labor incomes in the 1980s. As a result, the 1980s were the first decade in the post-war period where labor's share of income fell while capital's share of income rose.

Distribution of Wages: The dramatic fall in the wages of young and noncollege educated workers is primarily the result of a change in the distribution of wages. Simply put, it has become increasingly hard for workers without a college degree to earn a middle class standard of living. This is problematic since three-fourths of today's workforce (even those 25 to 34 years old) have not completed college and even by the year 2000 at least 70% of the workforce will not be college graduates.

Trade and Deindustrialization: It is precisely those groups of workers who have been adversely affected by increased import competition and the decline of manufacturing that have experienced the greatest deterioration in wages. The pressures on manufacturing wages and jobs have lowered the wages of all noncollege educated workers, particularly men. The shift of employment from high-paying to low-paying industries reduced average hourly compensation by 0.5% each year in the 1980s.

Taxes: The shifting of the tax burden from the very rich to everyone else compounded the problems stemming from more unequal market incomes. The redistribution of the tax burden provided $25,000 to each family in the upper 1% each year while adding to everybody else's taxes. Changes in the structure, however, have not been the major reason for rising inequality: only about one-fourth of the increase in the income share of the upper 1% can be ascribed to tax changes. The remainder is due to a growing inequality of wage and capital income.

Poverty and Race: A new mythology about poverty equates the growth in poverty to growth in an underclass which is primarily black and in female-headed households. The increase in poverty is then said to be due to the growth of this part of the population, not to economic factors. But the higher poverty in the 1980s has occurred *primarily among whites*—the black poverty rate was about the same in 1979 and 1989—and among *male-headed* families. Even among poor female-headed families, whites comprise more than half of the population and have been the fastest growing component of this type of poverty. Moreover, only one out of five female family

7

heads is a "never married" mother: most are widowed or divorced. The major question raised by poverty among female-headed families is "why does a woman have to have access to a man's income to avoid poverty?" The truly powerful explanations of the growth in poverty in the 1980s are centered in the sizeable reductions in government assistance and the growth of poverty wage jobs.

The Implications

There are several important implications of our analysis of wage and income developments and their causes.

1. By the fundamental measure of real incomes, Reaganomics (upward redistribution of income, deregulation, unregulated import competition, lowering of the economic safety net) was not a success: people are working more at lower wages. New policies will be needed if the erosion of living standards is to be reversed in the 1990s.

2. Reversing these income trends will require halting the erosion of competitiveness and the shrinkage of our industrial base. The job opportunities in manufacturing and related industries comprise about a third of all private sector jobs and are key to the ability of a broad segment of our population—the noncollege educated workforce—to earn a middle class income. We are unlikely to be able to offer good-paying jobs requiring a college degree to more than a small minority of the workforce for the foreseeable future.

3. To raise the standard of living of American workers also requires raising the wage level of our service economy, where the majority works. Service sector wages in the United States are far less than the average wage, a situation not true in most competitor countries. Raising minimum wages, eliminating government hostility to unionization and extending fringe benefits to part-time and temporary workers are some of the policy options available to raise service sector wages and thus provide incentives for new investment and productivity.

4. Policies are needed to enhance a family's ability to cope with the need to have more family members working while also raising children. Obtaining quality, affordable childcare and parental leave rights is an important starting point.

5. To generate greater economic growth we will have to close the "third deficit"—the deficit in public investment in infrastructure and in our workforce's training and education.

METHODS OF ANALYSIS

Time Periods

Economic indicators fluctuate considerably with short-term swings in the business cycle. For example, incomes tend to fall in recessions and rise during expansions. Therefore, economists usually compare business cycle peaks with peaks and troughs with troughs, so as not to mix apples and oranges. In this book, we examine changes between business cycle peaks. The initial year for most tables is 1947 or, if necessary, 1948 or 1949. The intermediate years in the analysis are 1967, 1973, and 1979, all of which were business cycle peaks. *The latest year for which data are available is used as the peak of the current business cycle.*

Some information was available only for other years. If this information was important enough, we included it.

Growth Rates

Since business cycles differ in length, we usually present the annual growth rates in each period rather than the total growth. In addition, we always use compound (log) annual growth rates rather than simple annual rates. Compound annual growth rates are just like compound interest on a bank loan: the rate is compounded continuously rather than yearly.

While annual growth rates may seem small, over time they can amount to a large change. For example, the median incomes of families headed by persons aged under 25 fell 2.5% per year between 1979 and 1989 (Table 1.3). Over the full period, incomes declined by a considerable 21.8%.

Adjusting for Inflation

In most popular discussions, the Consumer Price Index for All Urban Consumers (CPI-U), often called simply "the Consumer Price Index," is used to adjust dollar values for inflation. However, some hold that the CPI-U overstated inflation in the 1970s by measuring housing costs inappropriately. In 1982, the CPI-U was revised to address these objections. Not all agree that it should have been revised.

We chose not to use the CPI-U so as to avoid any impression that this report overstates the decline in wages and understates the growth in family incomes. Instead, we adjusted dollar values for inflation using the fixed-weight Personal Consumption Expenditures index (1982 quantity weights). The PCE index is a broad-based measure of the prices of everything on which households spend money. It measures overall price changes more conservatively than the CPI-U. One advantage is that it is based on all households, rather than just urban households. In addition, there is a consistent series for the PCE that begins in 1929. An alternative would have been to use the experimental CPI-U-X1 index, which approximates what the CPI-U would be if it had started to use the revised measure of housing costs in 1967. We chose not to use the CPI-U-X1 because it starts in 1967, is based on a small sample in its experimental phase, and is computed differently for different periods. Results using the PCE and CPI-U-X1 are similar.

The original data on which we draw were calculated with a variety of price indices. Whenever possible, we readjusted the figures using the PCE. In Chapter 6 (*Poverty*), however, we used the CPI-U rather than the PCE. This is because Chapter 6 is based almost entirely on publications of the Census Bureau that use the CPI-U. The Census Bureau recently started to publish a parallel series of statistics that use the CPI-U-X1. However, the Bureau has not reissued its earlier reports using the CPI-U-X1. Moreover, the net effect of all of the criticisms of the measurement of poverty is that current methods *understate* it. Simply switching to the CPI-U-X1 without incorporating other revisions would lead to an even greater understatement. A fuller discussion of these issues appears in Chapter 6.

Household Heads

We often categorize familes by the age or the race/ethnic group of the "household head." This is the person in whose name the home is owned or rented. If the home is owned jointly by a married couple, either spouse may be designated the household head. Every family has a single household head.

Sources

The statements in the text are supported throughout by data in the tables. For each table, there is a table note at the end of the book which gives sources and methods (pages 281–312).

ACKNOWLEDGMENTS

T he preparation of this publication required the assistance of most of the EPI staff. Amanda Barlow and Stephanie Scott diligently created and edited the text and tables. Jeff Faux read each chapter carefully and provided his usual high quality comments. Edith Rasell carefully reviewed several chapters and assisted us in our analysis of education and health issues. Lory Camba helped with data gathering and computations. Kevin Quinn advised us on the subject of housing. The efforts of the communications staff of Roger Hickey, Christin Driscoll, Danielle Currier, Lisa Beavers, and Caleb Marshall are also very much appreciated.

Many outside of EPI also contributed. We drew heavily on the work of the following: Chris Tilly and Randy Albelda; Roberton Williams; Frank Sammartino and Richard Kasten; Wendell Primus; Lynn Karoly; Larry Katz and Kevin Murphy; David Ellwood; Michael Stone; Bob Costrell; Lucy Gorham and Ben Harrison; Richard Freeman, McKinley Blackburn, and David Bloom; Barry Bluestone; Sheldon Danziger and Tom Donley; Scott Barancik; Timothy Smeeding, Barbara Boyle Torrey, and Martin Rein; and Denise DiPasquale.

Others provided useful data or helpful advice: Tom Karier, Juliet Schor and Laura Leete-Guy, Robert Blecker, Ruy Teixeira, Ginny duRivage, Joel Popkin, Iris Lav, Chris Kask, Arthur Neef, Jennifer Davis, and John Stinson, Jr.

We are also grateful for the assistance of the Census Bureau staff, especially Mark Littman, Charles Nelson, and Ed Welniak.

CHAPTER 1

TABLE 1.1

Median Family Income, 1947–1989*

(1989 dollars)

Year	Median Family Income
1947	$14,741
1967	26,470
1973	31,144
1979	32,844
1989	34,213
Total Increases:	
1947–67	$11,729
1967–73	4,673
1973–79	1,701
1979–89	1,369

* Income includes all wage and salary, self-employment, pension, interest, rent, government cash assistance, and other money incomes.

TABLE 1.2

Annual Growth of Median Family Income, 1947–1989

(1989 Dollars)

Period	Median Family Income Growth		Median Family Income, Size-Adjusted*
	Percent	Dollars	Percent
1947–67	2.9	$586	N/A
1967–73	2.7	779	N/A
1973–79	0.9	283	1.4
1979–88	0.3	95	0.4
1979–89	0.4	137	N/A

*Family income adjusted for changes in the size of families.

FAMILY INCOME: SLOWER GROWTH, INCREASING INEQUALITY

A person's economic well-being depends upon his/her access to economic resources. Since most Americans live in families in which income is shared, family income is the best single measure of how Americans are doing economically.

Over the last 10 years family income has grown more slowly than it did in the 1970s and far more slowly than it did in the period between the end of World War II and 1973. This income growth slowdown has not affected all families equally. Upper income groups, particularly the upper 1%, experienced significant income growth in the 1980s. The bottom 40% of families actually experienced a decline in income. This resulted in a dramatic rise in the gap between high and low income families, reversing the entire post-war progress in lessening inequality. Families in the middle achieved only modest income growth, primarily attained by the increased earnings and presence of working wives. In fact, all of the income growth in the 1980s among married-couple families with children was due to the increased earnings of wives.

A major factor fueling the growing inequality was the acceleration of capital income growth in the 1980s due to high real interest rates and the stock market boom, both of which primarily benefitted the richest families. In contrast, hourly wages and fringe benefits, which provide support for most families, grew slower than inflation. Inequality among wage-earners also rose as real wages among high income groups rose and wages among the broad middle class and lower income groups fell.

Over the last 10 years family income has grown more slowly than . . . in the 1970s and . . . between . . . World War II and 1973

Sluggish Income Growth

Tables 1.1 and **1.2** show changes in family income, adjusted for changes in consumer prices, in various cyclical peak (or low unemployment) years since World War II. As explained in the introductory section on methodology, examining income changes from business cycle peak to business cycle peak eliminates the distortion caused by the fact that incomes fall drastically in a recession and then recover in the upswing (**Figure 1A**).

There was a substantial increase in family income in the two decades (1947–1967) immediately following World War II, when the median family income increased by $11,729 for an annual rate of growth of 2.9% (Table 1.2). Family in-

FIGURE 1A

Median Family Income, 1967–1989

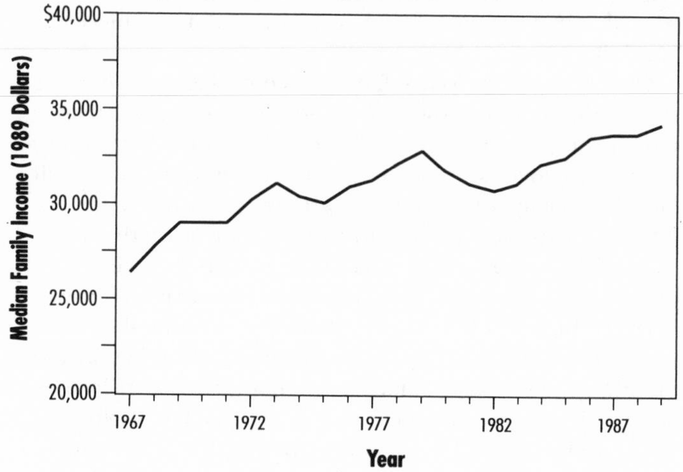

Median Family Income (1989 Dollars)

$40,000				
35,000				
30,000				
25,000				
20,000				

1967   1972   1977   1982   1987

Year

FIGURE 1B

Annual Increase in Median Family Income, 1947-1989

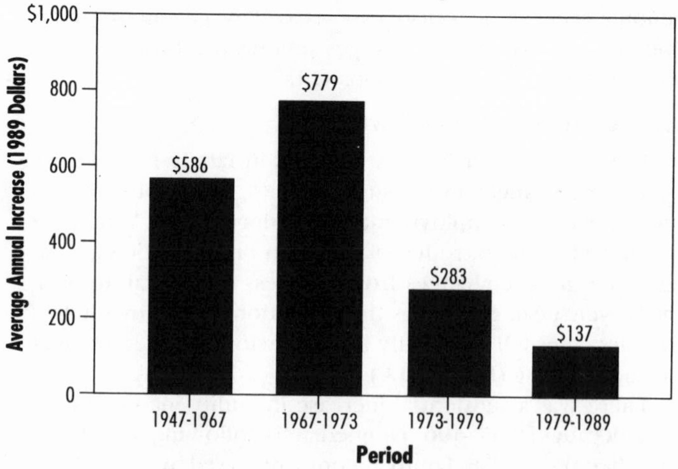

Average Annual Increase (1989 Dollars)

Period	Average Annual Increase
1947-1967	$586
1967-1973	$779
1973-1979	$283
1979-1989	$137

Period

comes continued to grow into the early 1970s, but since 1973 have risen very slowly and especially since the last business cycle peak in 1979 (**Figure 1B**). In 1989, median family income was only $1,369 greater than it was in 1979. This translates into a growth of just $137, or 0.4%, per year in the last 10 years, which is equivalent to a rate of growth less than half the 0.9% annual growth of the 1973–79 period and only one-seventh the rate of income growth of the post-war years prior to 1973. In fact, the $1,369 income growth over the *10 years* since 1979 equals the amount that incomes rose every *year and three-quarters* in the 1967–1973 period.

A cyclical peak-to-peak comparison especially overstates incomes in the 1980s because of the severity of the 1982 recession. For instance, taking account of all of the years over the business cycle shows that family incomes in the 1979–89 cycle averaged just $32,564, which is $280 less than the $32,844 median family income in 1979. Also, the average family income over the recent business cycle of $32,564 was $1,529 greater than the $31,035 family income prevailing in the 1973–78 cycle. This $1,529 gain, which takes account of the income losses during recessions, is about half of the $2,831 gain between cyclical peaks in years 1973 and 1989.

We can also examine measures of family income growth, which adjust for changes in family size, on the theory that if the same total family income is shared by fewer family members then the economic well-being of each family member has improved. Such measures can be misleading, however, since the recent decline in the average family's size is partially due to lower incomes, i.e., some families feel they can not afford as many children as they could have, had incomes continued to rise at post-war rates. Yet a family deciding to have fewer children because its income is lower appears "better off" in size-adjusted family income measures. Nevertheless, even when income growth is adjusted for the shift towards smaller families (as in Table 1.2), the income growth from 1979 to 1988 (for which comparable measures are available) is only slightly more than an "unadjusted" measure (0.4% versus 0.3%). Moreover, a size-adjusted family income measure also shows far slower growth in recent years than during the 1973–79 period (0.4% versus 1.4%).

. . . the income growth over the 10 years since 1979 equals the amount that incomes rose every year and three-quarters in the 1967–73 period.

TABLE 1.3

Growth of Median Family Income
By Age of Household Head, 1967–1989

(1989 Dollars)

	Median Family Income By Age of Household Head					
Year	Under 25	25–34	35–44	45–54	55–64	Over 65
1967	19,500	27,011	30,828	32,286	26,834	13,107
1973	20,711	31,544	36,974	39,341	33,030	16,607
1979	21,826	32,457	38,499	42,510	36,859	18,965
1989	17,064	30,873	40,202	46,101	37,643	23,083

	Annual Growth Rate of Median Family Income By Age of Household Head					
Period	Under 25	25–34	35–44	45–54	55–64	Over 65
1967–73	1.0%	2.6%	3.0%	3.3%	3.5%	3.9%
1973–79	0.9	0.5	0.7	1.3	1.8	2.2
1979–89	-2.5	-0.5	0.4	0.8	0.2	2.0

TABLE 1.4

Growth of Median Family Income By Race/Ethnic Group,
1947–1989

(1989 Dollars)

	Median Family Incomes By Race and Hispanic Origin of Household Head			Ratio to White Family Income of:	
Year	White	Black	Hispanic*	Black	Hispanic*
1947	$15,354	N/A	N/A	N/A	N/A
1967	27,474	$16,266	N/A	59.2	N/A
1973	32,549	18,785	$22,522	57.7	69.2
1979	34,273	19,408	23,759	56.6	69.3
1989	35,975	20,209	23,446	56.2	65.2

	Annual Growth Rates		
Period	White	Black	Hispanic
1947–67	2.9%	N/A	N/A
1967–73	2.8	2.4%	N/A
1973–79	0.9	0.5	0.9%
1979–89	0.5	0.4	-0.1

* Persons of Hispanic origin may be of any race.

16

Young Families Hurt Most

Table 1.3 shows that the largest drop in incomes has occurred among the youngest families. The average income of families headed by someone under age 25 has declined at an annual rate of 2.5% since 1979. Theirs is also the only age group for which median family income is lower today than it was in 1967; such young families have $2,436 less income to spend in real dollars than their 1967 counterparts had when they were starting out.

Families headed by someone between the ages of 25 and 34 have also fared poorly relative to earlier years. These families saw their incomes erode 0.5% per year from 1979 to 1988. This is in stark contrast to the 6 years between 1967 and 1973, when income for this group increased at a 2.6% annual rate, or even to the 6 years between 1973 and 1979 when income grew at an 0.5% pace. Many families in this age group are likely to be bringing up young children and trying to buy a home of their own. The income problems of these young families thus represent income problems for the nation's children. Families with household heads aged 25 to 34 in 1989 had incomes $1,584 less than their counterparts did 9 years earlier in 1979. The deterioration of incomes for these young families is one of the most significant income developments of the last 10 years and will be explored further in Chapter 7.

The incomes of the 35 to 44 and 45 to 54 age groups have grown modestly—from 0.4% to 0.8% per year—since 1979. In contrast, family income for these age groups grew by more than 3.0% per year between 1967 and 1973, rising by more than $6,000 by the end of the period. Elderly family incomes for those headed by someone over 65 have increased throughout the last 10 years, although at a pace only half that of the 1967–1973 period. However, median incomes for families headed by someone aged 55 to 64 have barely grown since 1979.

Slow Income Growth Affects All Racial Groups

Sluggish income growth has affected all racial groups, as **Table 1.4** illustrates. White families, who fared the best from 1967 to 1973, have on average experienced very modest 0.5% annual growth in real income since 1979, less than half the 0.9% annual income growth of the 6 years from

. . . the largest drop in incomes has occurred among the youngest families.

17

TABLE 1.5

Income Growth By Type of Family

Family Type	Percent of Population 1987	Family Income Growth* 1973–79	Family Income Growth* 1979–88
		(Annual Growth Rates)	
All Families	100.0%	1.3%	0.4%
Families with Children	55.7	1.1	0.1
Married Couples	41.5	1.5	0.5
Single Mothers	8.8	2.5	-1.5
Childless Families	44.3	N/A	N/A
Nonelderly	30.9	1.3	0.4
Elderly	13.4	2.1	1.4

*Growth in mean family income, adjusted for family size, of the middle quintile.

TABLE 1.6

Average Income of the Top 5% Compared to the Bottom 80%, 1947–1989

(1989 dollars)

Year	Average Family Income for Families in the: Top 5%	Average Family Income for Families in the: Bottom 80%	Ratio of Average Income of Top 5% to Average Income of Bottom 80%
1947	$ 60,701	$12,357	4.9
1967	89,274	21,915	4.1
1973	109,131	25,919	4.2
1979	118,249	27,317	4.3
1989	148,591	28,743	5.2
Change, 1979–89			
Level	$ 30,343	$ 1,426	21.3
Percent	25.7%	5.2%	4.9

1973 to 1979. Black families, with a median income more than 40% lower than that of whites, experienced slower income growth in the 1973–79 period than whites (0.5% versus 0.9%) and then maintained slow 0.4% annual growth through the 1980s. The median income of families of Hispanic origin actually declined 0.1% per year between 1979 and 1989.

The ratio between white and black median family income fell from 1967 to 1973 but has remained fairly constant since 1973, reflecting recent slow income growth among both groups. The decline in Hispanic family incomes, however, has led to a *larger* gap between white and Hispanic families. The ratio of Hispanic to white median income fell from 69.3% in 1979 to just 65.2% in 1989.

. . . And All Types of Families

The slowdown in income growth in the 1980s occurred among all types of families, those with and without children as well as elderly and nonelderly childless families (**Table 1.5**). Families with children were affected the most; their incomes grew 1.1% annually from 1973 to 1979 but were essentially stagnant after 1979. Income stagnation among these families reflects a slowdown of income growth among married couples, falling from 1.5% to 0.5% per year, and a drastic turnaround among single mothers whose incomes grew 2.5% per year from 1973 to 1979 but *fell* 1.5% per year from 1979 through 1988. A majority of the population, 55.7%, live in families with children.

Childless families also experienced slower income growth in the 1980s. Recent income growth among elderly families was greater than that of other types of families, but at two-thirds the rate of the 1973 to 1979 period.

Growing Inequality

Over the last 10 years, the vast majority of American families have experienced either very modest income growth or an actual erosion in their standard of living. The small minority of upper-income families, however, has had substantial income growth. The result has been an increase in inequality. The rich have gotten richer; the poor are more numerous and are poorer than they have been in decades.

Table 1.6 shows the post–World War II history of the U.S. income distribution. In 1947, the richest 5% of the

The rich have gotten richer; the poor are more numerous and are poorer than they have been in decades.

19

TABLE 1.7

Shares of Family Income Going to Various Fifths, and to Top 5%

	Lowest Fifth	Second Fifth	Middle Fifth	Fourth Fifth	Top Fifth	TOTAL	Breakdown of Top Fifth	
							Top 5%	Next 15%
1947	5.0	11.9	17.0	23.1	43.0	100	17.5	25.5
1967	5.5	12.4	17.9	23.9	40.4	100	15.2	25.2
1973	5.5	11.9	17.5	24.0	41.1	100	15.5	25.6
1979	5.2	11.6	17.5	24.1	41.7	100	15.8	25.9
1989	4.6	10.6	16.5	23.7	44.6	100	17.9	26.7
Point Change:								
1979-89	-0.6	-1.0	-0.1	-0.4	2.9	0	2.1	0.8

Share Going to:

TABLE 1.8

The Effects of Shifts in Family Income Inequality, 1979-1989

(1989 Dollars)

A. Real Family Income Growth By Fifth, 1979-89

Lowest Fifth	Second Fifth	Middle Fifth	Fourth Fifth	Top Fifth	Top 5%
$-183	$294	$1,500	$4,093	$14,537	$30,343
-1.9%	1.4%	4.6%	9.1%	18.6%	25.7%

B. Real Family Income Growth if Inequality Had Not Increased Since 1979

Lowest Fifth	Second Fifth	Middle Fifth	Fourth Fifth	Top Fifth	Top 5%
$1,062	$2,370	$3,575	$4,923	$8,518	$12,910

C. Changes in Incomes Due to Increased Inequality*

Lowest Fifth	Second Fifth	Middle Fifth	Fourth Fifth	Top Fifth	Top 5%
$-1,245	$-2,075	$-2,075	$-830	$6,018	$17,433
-12.8%	-9.6%	-6.3%	-1.8%	7.7%	14.7%

*Measured as difference between income growth presented in Panels A and B above.

population had $4.90 of income for every $1 received by the bottom 80%. By 1967 inequality had lessened—so that the ratio improved to $4.10 to $1. Since 1979 this ratio has increased, so much that inequality in 1989 exceeded the level in 1947.

This growing inequality reflects the fact that the incomes of the best-off 5% of families grew 25.7% from 1979 to 1989, some 5 times faster than the income growth of the bottom 80% of families. In dollar terms, the upper 5% saw their incomes grow $21 for every dollar of income growth received by families in the lower-income four-fifths.

Table 1.7 presents the percentage distribution of income among the various fifths (or "quintiles") of the population, and the top 5%. The upper 20% received 44.6% of all income in 1989. The upper 5% received more of total income, 17.9%, than the families in the bottom 40%, who received just 15.2% in 1989. As we will see in a later chapter providing international comparisons, income in the U.S. is distributed far more unequally than in comparable industrialized countries.

Income distribution has grown even more unequal since 1979. In 1989, the share of total income in each of the three lowest income fifths (i.e., the bottom 60% of families) was even smaller than their share was in 1947. Since 1979, the bottom 80% has lost income share, and only the top 20% gained. Moreover, the 1989 income share of the upper fifth, 44.6%, was far greater than they received during the entire post-war period and even higher than the 43% received in 1947. Even among the rich, the growth in benefits was skewed to the very top, as the highest 5% saw their income share rise by 2.1 percentage points, which makes up the bulk of the 2.9 percentage point total rise in the income share of the upper fifth.

The implications for individual family incomes of these seemingly small changes in income shares are considerable. The three panels of **Table 1.8** illustrate the effect of the recent growth of income inequality on families in each income fifth and for families in the upper 5%. Panel A shows "negative growth," or income shrinkage, of 1.9% for families in the bottom two-fifths and small growth for the second fifth. The only substantial income growth was among the top 20%. Again, the top 5% is shown to have by

. . . inequality in 1989 exceeded the level in 1947.

21

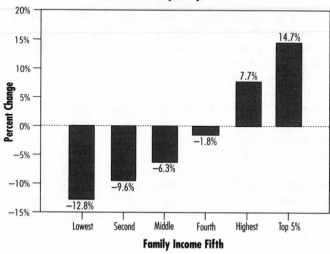

FIGURE 1C

Changes in Family Incomes Due to Increased Inequality, 1979-1988

Percent Change

Family Income Fifth

- Lowest: −12.8%
- Second: −9.6%
- Middle: −6.3%
- Fourth: −1.8%
- Highest: 7.7%
- Top 5%: 14.7%

TABLE 1.9

Income Growth By Fifth and Family Type, 1979–1988*

Income Fifth	All Families	Families With Children			Childless Families	
		All	Married Couples	Single Mothers	Non-elderly	Elderly
Highest	16.6%	15.4%	17.3%	6.3%	14.0%	18.0%
Fourth	9.5	6.9	9.1	− 4.1	9.4	15.4
Middle	5.0	1.5	5.7	−11.3	5.1	14.3
Second	− 0.5	− 5.0	0.6	−19.8	1.5	13.7
Lowest	− 7.6	−15.0	− 4.7	−23.4	− 4.6	13.5

* Size-adjusted family income.

22

far the largest income growth (in percentage and dollar terms).

Panel B presents the growth of real family income which would have occurred if each of the income groups had maintained its 1979 share of income. Panel C and **Figure 1C** draw on this information in order to show the difference between actual income growth (Panel A), and that which would have occurred without a shift in the income distribution (Panel B). It shows only the richest 20% have benefitted from recent changes in income inequality, which raised their incomes by $6,018 per family. The shift to greater inequality meant $17,433 more in family income for the upper 5%, but a $2,075 *loss* per family in the second and middle fifths. The incomes of families in the bottom 60% declined by between 6.3% and 12.8% due to the shift in income distribution. On the other hand, widening income inequality allowed the incomes of families in the upper 5% to grow by 14.7% and was responsible for more than half the income growth of this group.

Inequality has widened among each type of family in much the same pattern as has occurred overall—income declines for families at the very bottom and rapid income growth for the best-off families (**Table 1.9**). For instance, the incomes of the bottom fifth declined for each family type, except elderly families. The greatest income decline was among the bottom 40% of single-mother families, a group whose income fell at least 20% from 1979 to 1988. In fact, the incomes of the bottom four-fifths of single-mother families have all fallen in recent years. On the other end, elderly families in each income fifth obtained significant and comparable income growth, so income inequality did not grow appreciably for the elderly. This pattern of income growth among the elderly reflects growing social security benefits at all income levels.

. . . only the richest 20% have benefitted from recent changes in income inequality . . .

TABLE 1.10

Income Growth Among Top Fifth and By Fifth, 1977–1990

(1990 Dollars)

Income Group	Average Family Income in:			Percent Change	
	1977	1980	1990*	1977–90	1980–90
All	$ 36,247	$ 36,138	$ 41,369	14.1%	14.5%
Top Fifth:	78,965	81,589	105,209	33.2	28.9
Top 1%	281,383	315,648	548,970	95.1	73.9
Next 4%	97,739	100,534	125,800	28.7	25.1
Next 5%	69,335	69,439	82,154	18.5	18.3
Next 10%	54,407	55,505	63,663	17.0	14.7
Bottom Four Fifths:					
Fourth	42,148	41,957	44,908	6.5	7.0
Middle	31,311	30,268	30,964	– 1.1	2.3
Second	20,205	19,237	19,348	– 4.2	0.6
Lowest	8,531	8,082	7,725	– 9.5	– 4.4

*Estimate.

FIGURE 1D

Family Income Growth, 1980-1990

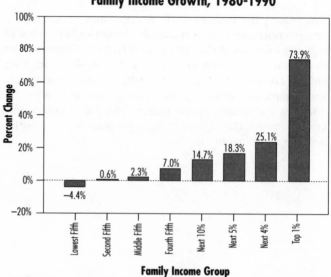

24

Table 1.10 and Figure 1D examine changes among various income groups using a more comprehensive measure of income (it includes capital gains and distributes corporate profits among families). The data provide finer detail on upper income groups, but unfortunately are only available for 1977 and 1980—not for the last business cycle peak in 1979. Estimates have been made for 1990. Table 1.10 shows the bottom 20% losing income over the 1980s, coupled with sluggish income growth for the second and middle fifths. These trends began prior to 1980, as shown by the income declines of the bottom 60% of families from 1977 to 1980.

At the other end of the income scale, however, there was considerable income growth. The highest income fifth of families saw their incomes rise by 28.9% in the 1980s, which was more than 4 times the 7% income growth of the next richest fifth. In fact, the income *gain* of the average family in the upper 20% over the 1980s, $23,620, is more than the average income *level* of families in the bottom two fifths.

The most spectacular income growth was among the upper 1%, whose incomes grew by 74% over the 1980s. The $233,322 average income *gain* of the richest 1% of families in the 1980s is nearly double the average income level of the next best-off 4% of the population and is more than 5 times the average family income in 1990.

Income growth within the upper fifth was very unequal over the 1980s. Families with income in the 80th to 90th percentile range (the "next 10%" group, Table 1.10) experienced nearly 15% income growth, far better than any group in the bottom 80% but only one-fifth of the income growth of the upper 1%.

The highest income fifth of families saw their incomes rise by 28.9% in the 1980s . . .

TABLE 1.11

Changes in Family Income Shares, 1977–1990

Income Group	Family Income Shares in:			Share Change	
	1977	1980	1990	1977–90	1980–90
All	100.0%	100.0%	100.0%	0.0%	0.0%
Top Fifth:	46.5	47.4	51.8	5.3	4.4
Top 1%	8.7	9.4	13.3	4.6	3.9
Next 4%	11.8	12.0	13.0	1.2	1.0
Next 5%	10.1	10.3	10.2	0.1	-0.1
Next 10%	15.8	15.7	15.3	-0.5	-0.4
Bottom Four Fifths:	53.8	52.9	48.8	-5.0	-4.1
Fourth	22.6	22.5	21.5	-1.1	-1.0
Middle	15.7	15.5	14.4	-1.3	-1.1
Second	10.6	10.4	9.2	-1.4	-1.2
Lowest	4.9	4.5	3.7	-1.2	-0.8

TABLE 1.12

Distribution of Aggregate Income Gains, 1977–1990

Income Group	Aggregate Gains in Real Family Income* (1990 $ billions)		Share of Income Gains (Percent)	
	1977–90	1980–90	1977–90	1980–90
All	$1,331	$1,072	100.0%	100.0%
Top Fifth:	844	695	63.4	64.8
Top 1%	311	266	23.4	24.9
Next 4%	208	171	15.6	16.0
Next 5%	139	106	10.4	9.9
Next 10%	189	151	14.2	14.1
Bottom Four Fifths:	503	393	37.8	36.7
Fourth	254	199	19.1	18.5
Middle	154	119	11.5	11.1
Second	82	61	6.1	5.6
Lowest	14	14	1.1	1.3

*Growth in income based on changes in income per family and growth in number of families due to population growth.

The rapid income growth of the top fifth relative to the bottom four-fifths of the population led to a substantial increase in the share of total income accruing to the rich (**Table 1.11**). By 1990, the upper 20% of families received more than half (51.8%) of all income, increasing their share of income by 4.4 percentage points since 1980. However, within the upper fifth, the top 5% gained a greater share of income while the remaining 15% saw their share of total income decline. The unbalanced income growth of the 1980s thus caused the bottom 95% of the population to lose income share to the upper 5%. Reflecting their spectacular income growth, the upper 1% of families increased their share of income from 9.4% in 1980 to 13.3% in 1990. As a result, the income share of the upper 1% (13.3%) is now greater than that of the bottom 40% (12.9%).

. . . the income share of the upper 1% is now greater than that of the bottom 40%.

Table 1.12 and **Figure 1E** provide an even more pointed characterization of the unbalanced income growth of the 1980s by showing the share of all income growth accruing

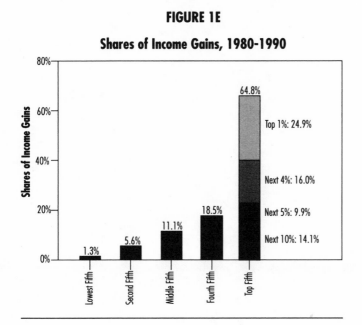

FIGURE 1E

Shares of Income Gains, 1980-1990

TABLE 1.13

Sources of Family Income for Each Fifth of Families, 1988

| Income Group | Sources of Income | | | | |
	Labor	Capital	Government Transfer	Other	Total
All	72.3%	16.6%	6.8%	4.4%	100.0%
Top Fifth:	71.9	23.0	1.8	3.2	100.0
Top 1%	50.5	47.8	0.4	1.2	100.0
Next 4%	70.8	23.3	1.8	4.2	100.0
Next 5%	80.9	13.3	2.1	3.7	100.0
Next 10%	83.4	10.0	2.8	3.8	100.0
Bottom Four Fifths:	73.2	9.4	11.9	5.5	100.0
Fourth	80.7	9.8	5.0	4.4	100.0
Middle	74.8	9.8	9.5	6.0	100.0
Second	64.4	8.8	19.7	7.2	100.0
Lowest	35.3	6.4	51.5	6.9	100.0

to the various income groups. Between 1980 and 1990, the nation's total family income grew by $1.07 trillion because of a modest rise in the average family income and a growing population. Fully 65% of this total income growth was received by the richest fifth of families. The upper 1% received one-fourth of the total income growth in the 1980s, which was more than that received by the bottom 60% of the population. The upper 10% of families gained as much income in the 1980s, $543 billion, as did the remaining 90% of the population, who received income gains of $544 billion.

Labor Income Shrinking

In the 1980s, the fortunes of individual families depended on the *sources* of their incomes: labor income, capital income, or government assistance. A major reason for the unequal growth in family incomes is that, in recent years, a greater share of our national income has been in the form of capital incomes (such as rent, dividends, interest payments, capital gains) and a smaller share has been earned as wages and salaries. Since most families receive little or no capital income, this shift has had a substantial impact on income distribution.

Table 1.13 presents data that show the sources of income for families in each income group. The top fifth gets a far larger percentage of its income from financial assets compared to the other 80% of the population. The top 1% receives nearly half its income from financial assets. Those without access to capital income depend either on wages (the broad middle) or on government transfers (the bottom) as their primary source of income. As a result, the cutback in government cash assistance primarily affects the income prospects of the lowest 40% of the population, but particularly the bottom fifth. The income prospects of families in the 20th to 99th percentile, on the other hand, depend primarily on the level and distribution of wages and salaries.

A major reason for the unequal growth in family incomes is that . . . a greater share of our national income has been in the form of capital incomes . . .

29

TABLE 1.14

Real Income Growth By Type of Income, 1979–1989

Income Type	Total Growth, 1979–89
1) Total Capital Income	66.2%
a) Rent	-12.5
b) Dividends	42.1
c) Interest	73.4
2) Total Labor Income	22.3
a) Wages and Salaries	22.8
b) Other Labor Income	17.8
3) Proprietors' Income*	18.1
Total Market-Based Income**	28.4

*Business and farm owners' income.

**Personal income less transfers.

FIGURE 1F

Growth of Income by Type, 1979-1989

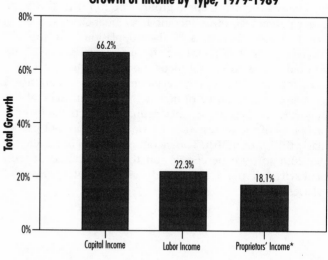

*Business and farm owners' income.

Table 1.14 and **Figure 1F** show that income accruing to owners of capital has been growing far faster than labor income. In the 10 years between 1979 and 1989, those who owned income-producing property such as real estate, corporate stock, bonds, and other interest-bearing assets saw their incomes from these sources increase by 66.2%. The fast growth in capital income is primarily due to strong growth in interest payments of 73.4% which was caused by the high real (inflation-adjusted) interest rates of the 1980s. Dividend income grew by less, but by a still substantial 42.1%. The growth in capital, or property-based, income is actually somewhat understated in Table 1.14 since the data do not include capital gains realized in the stock market boom.

The fast growth in capital income is primarily due to strong growth in interest payments. . . caused by high real interest rates . . .

During the same period, total labor income, which includes the pay of executives and professionals as well as hourly workers, grew only one-third as fast as capital income—22.3%. (This rise in labor income primarily reflects a larger employed population working longer hours and is consistent with declining real hourly wages.) Farmer and small business owners' incomes rose 18.1%.

The post-1979 shift away from labor income and toward capital income is unique in the post-war period (**Table 1.15**) and is partly responsible for the recent surge in inequality.

TABLE 1.15

Shares of Market-Based Income By Type, 1948–1989

Income Type	1948	1967	1973	1979	1989
1) Total Capital Income	10.7%	14.4%	13.6%	14.9%	19.3%
a) Rent	3.2	3.2	1.8	0.3	0.2
b) Dividends	3.5	3.3	2.6	2.6	2.9
c) Interest	4.0	7.9	9.2	12.0	16.2
2) Total Labor Income	69.1	73.9	74.7	74.6	71.1
a) Wages and Salaries	67.8	70.4	69.8	68.0	65.0
b) Fringe Benefits	1.4	3.6	4.8	6.7	6.1
3) Proprietors' Income*	20.2	11.7	11.7	10.4	9.6
Total Market-Based Income**	100.0	100.0	100.0	100.0	100.0

*Business and farm owners' income.

**Personal income less transfers.

TABLE 1.16

Change in Adjusted Family Income By Source of Income, 1979–1987*

	Family Earnings	Capital Income	Government Transfers**	Total
By Fifths:				
Highest	12.2%	16.9%	6.4%	17.4%
Fourth	4.4	19.4	17.1	8.6
Middle	0.6	8.5	11.0	4.5
Second	- 4.6	- 8.7	2.9	- 1.0
Lowest	-11.4	-16.7	-10.7	- 9.5
Total	5.4	14.4	3.4	9.6
By Family Type:				
Families with Children	5.5	13.1	-11.5	4.7
Married Couples	7.8	20.0	-12.1	7.5
Single Mothers	4.6	-17.6	-19.9	- 3.6
Childless Families				
Nonelderly	4.2	2.7	-13.8	4.2
Elderly	2.1	11.0	9.9	11.9

*Size-adjusted family income.

**Includes cash and noncash transfers.

Since the rich are the owners of income-producing property, the fact that the assets they own have commanded an increasing share of the nation's income automatically leads to income growth that is concentrated at the top.

Capital income was 19.3% of total income in 1989, nearly double the 10.7% share in 1948. Half of the increase in capital income's share of total income between 1948 and 1989 occurred after 1979, driven by the high real interest rates of the 1980s. Labor income's share of total income declined from 1979 to 1989, reversing the pre-1979 trend in which labor income's share rose or held its own over the prior three decades. The share of wage and salary income in 1989 was the lowest in the post-war period. There was also a shrinkage of the share of fringe benefits in the 1980s, the first shrinkage over the last four decades.

Table 1.16 relates changes in the growth of capital income, labor earnings, and government cash transfers to the

The share of wage and salary income in 1989 was the lowest in the post-war period.

changing economic fortunes of families by income group and family type. Overall capital income per family grew by 14.4% from 1979 to 1987, far faster than the 5.4% and 3.4% growth, respectively, in family earnings and government transfers. This large growth in capital income primarily benefitted the upper 40% of the population. In fact, the bottom 40% had less capital income in 1987 than in 1979 (when it had very little anyway).

The slow growth in government transfers was also distributed unevenly. The bottom fifth, which relies on transfers for half of its income, actually received 10.7% less in 1987 than in 1979. As we will see in Chapter 6, this cutback in transfer payments was a major cause in the rise in poverty over the 1980s.

Total family earnings grow because of changes in wage rates together with changes in the number of people working in each family and the average annual hours they work. Despite growth in workers per family and in annual hours worked, family earnings grew just 5.4% between 1979 and 1987. For the bottom 60%, there was essentially no growth or an absolute decline in family earnings. Only the upper fifth experienced a sizeable growth in family earnings. These data show that the income shrinkage of the bottom two-fifths has been driven by reduced labor earnings and less or very little government assistance. On the other end, the rapid income growth of the richest 20% was fueled by both increased labor earnings and greater capital income.

The data in Table 1.16 on income growth by family type show that the cutback in government assistance has reduced incomes for each type of nonelderly family. Since social security benefits went relatively unscathed in the 1980s, the elderly were able to continue to receive increased government assistance. The fastest earnings growth was among married couples. As we will show, this growth is entirely due to the increased earnings of the women in these families.

A finer breakdown of the spectacular income growth of the upper income groups is provided in **Table 1.17**. For the upper 1%, the greatest gain has come from cashing in on the stock market boom. In 1990, these "capital gain realizations" will be roughly $175,536 per family, some $91,842 more than received by these families in 1980. Capital gains were responsible for 40% of the income growth of the

Capital gains were responsible for 40% of the income growth of the upper 1%.

33

TABLE 1.17

Sources of Income of High-Income Families, 1980–1990

(1990 Dollars)

	Average Family Income From:				
Income Group	Wages and Salary	Self-Employment	Capital Gains Realizations	Other Capital Income	Total*
Top 1%					
1980	$110,427	$ 36,546	$ 83,694	$ 78,953	$316,032
1990	198,452	60,601	175,536	102,901	548,970
Dollar Change	88,025	24,055	91,842	23,948	232,938
Percent Change	79.7%	65.8%	109.7%	30.3%	73.7%
Next 4%					
1980	$ 61,695	$ 10,067	$ 6,763	$ 16,430	$100,656
1990	72,191	12,372	12,184	20,582	125,800
Dollar Change	10,496	2,305	5,421	4,152	25,144
Percent Change	17.0%	22.9%	80.1%	25.3%	25.0%
Next 5%					
1980	$ 52,354	$ 3,737	$ 2,187	$ 7,131	$ 69,523
1990	61,257	4,051	2,815	8,318	82,154
Dollar Change	8,903	314	628	1,187	12,631
Percent Change	17.0%	8.4%	28.7%	16.6%	18.2%
Bottom 90%					
1980	$ 21,106	$ 720	$ 290	$ 1,655	$ 27,699
1990	21,742	749	299	2,117	29,334
Dollar Change	636	29	9	462	1,635
Percent Change	3.0%	4.0%	3.2%	27.9%	5.9%

*Transfer and "other incomes" are not shown in table but are included in total income.

For families in the bottom 95% . . . income from capital gains was negligible.

upper 1%. For families in the bottom 95%, but particularly those in the bottom 90%, income from capital gains was negligible.

The upper 1% also experienced tremendous wage growth in the 1980s (79.7%), greater than that of other upper income families (up 17%) and far greater than that of the bottom 90% (3%). The *increase* in earnings of the very rich in the 1980s, $88,025, is more than four times as much as the $21,742 *total* earnings of an average family in the lower 90% in 1990.

34

The Upper Income Consumption Binge

There is a widely held impression that "we" Americans were on a consumption binge in the 1980s. It is true that there was a drop in the personal saving rate out of current income (although not relative to wealth). But it is definitely not true that consumption growth accelerated in the 1980s (**Table 1.18** and **Figure 1G**). In the 10 years since 1979 per

TABLE 1.18

Growth Rates of Real Per Capita Income and Consumption, 1948–1989

	Growth Rates of Real Per Capita:		
Period	Personal Income	Disposal Personal Income*	Personal Consumption Expenditures
1948–67	2.64%	2.48%	2.29%
1967–73	3.61	3.41	3.14
1973–79	2.01	1.77	2.23
1979–89	1.52	1.52	1.74

*After-tax personal income.

FIGURE 1G

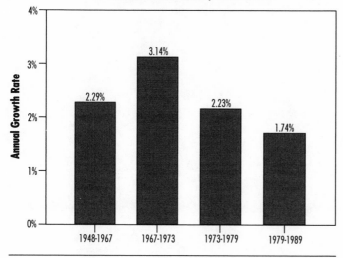

Personal Consumption Expenditures Per Capita Annual Growth Rates, 1948-1989

TABLE 1.19

Consumption Growth By Income Fifth, 1972–73 to 1988

	Consumption Expenditures
All	1.61%
By Income Fifth	
Top	2.18
Fourth	1.61
Middle	1.11
Second	1.09
Lowest	1.35

capita consumption rose by 1.74 per year, or at a pace 22% less than the 2.23% growth per year in the 1973–79 period. And, as with most every economic indicator, consumption growth in the last decade has been far slower than that in the prior three decades. This slower consumption growth reflects the slower growth in personal income both before and after-tax. There appears to have been no "binge" on the part of the average American.

It is also possible to examine consumption growth by income class. Unfortunately, the only time periods for which there are comparable surveys are 1972–73 and 1984–88 (**Table 1.19**). These data limitations prevent an analysis of the acceleration or deceleration of consumption growth in the 1980s by income quintiles. The available data, however, suggest that consumption growth since 1972–73 has been most rapid among the best-off households, especially the richest 20%.

. . . consumption growth in the last decade has been far slower than that in the prior three decades.

More Women Working

Family earnings growth has not only been slow and unequal, it has also increasingly come from greater work effort—from a rise in the number of earners per family and in the average weeks and weekly hours worked per earner. The primary source of the increased work effort has been women, including many with children. As detailed in Chapter 3, this increased work effort has occurred simultaneously with a fall in real wages for men and for many women in the 1980s. The result has been increases in annual earnings through more work rather than through higher wages.

This is troublesome for several reasons. This type of earnings growth is "self-limiting," meaning it can only go on until all adult (or even teen) family members are full-time, full-year workers. Moreover, there are significant costs and problems associated with this type of growth, one of the most significant being the lack of affordable, adequate child care. The problem is not that more women or mothers are going to work, but that so many are doing so because it is the only way to maintain family income in the face of lower real wages. It is a sign of the poor performance of the economy when increased work is elicited through falling real wages of family members.

37

TABLE 1.20

Growth in Number of Earners Per Family, 1979–1987

	Male Earners	Female Earners	Total Earners
A. All Families			
Earners Per Family			
1979	0.75	0.59	1.34
1987	0.89	0.75	1.64
Change			
Level	0.14	0.16	0.29
Percent	19%	27%	22%
Percent Change in Earners Per Family By Fifth			
Top	10%	23%	15%
Fourth	11	22	16
Middle	20	25	21
Second	23	30	26
Lowest	32	32	32
B. Married Couples With Children			
Earners Per Family			
1979	1.19	0.79	1.98
1987	1.15	0.87	2.02
Change			
Level	−0.04	0.08	0.04
Percent	−3%	10%	2%
Percent Change in Earners Per Family By Fifth			
Top	−6%	10%	0%
Fourth	−4	10	2
Middle	−1	14	6
Second	−3	16	−4
Lowest	−3	4	−1

Table 1.20 gives one measure of work effort, the number of earners per family. Between 1979 and 1987 there was a 22% rise in average earners per family to 1.64. By 1987, there were as many female earners per family, 0.75, as there were male earners per family in 1979. Broken down by income fifth, one sees that the greatest increase in earners per family has been in the lower income groups. The number of earners per family grew by 26% to 32% among the bottom 40%. In contrast, the number of earners per family grew by 15% to 16% among the top 40%.

Married couples have essentially been adding more women workers at the same time that there has been a partial decline in male workers. Between 1979 and 1987 there was a 16% rise in female earners per family. There was only a slight 2% rise in total earners per family, however, because in 1987 there were somewhat fewer male earners per married-couple family. In 1987, as well as in 1979, married-couple families with children had, on average, two members working in the labor market at some time during the year.

The growth of male, female, and total family earnings in married-couple families with children is detailed in **Table 1.21**. In each income fifth there was a substantial increase in the annual earnings of the highest paid adult female, presumably the mother in the family. The overall rise in

. . . increased work is elicited through falling real wages of family members.

TABLE 1.21

Earnings Growth in Married-Couple Families By Member and Fifth,* 1979–1987

Fifth	Highest Adult Male	Highest Adult Female	Total Family Earnings
Top	12.0%	51.9%	16.9%
Fourth	0.8	44.1	7.3
Middle	- 2.5	39.5	3.5
Second	- 7.6	37.9	- 1.4
Lowest	-15.4	18.4	-10.8
Total	1.9	44.4	7.8

*Size-adjusted changes for married couples with children.

TABLE 1.22

Effect of Adult Female Earnings Growth on Married-Couple Family Income,* 1979–1987

Fifth	Change in Family Income		Difference: Effect of Increased Adult Female Earnings on Family Income
	Actual	Not Including Increased Adult Female Earnings	
Top	16.7%	7.6%	9.1%
Fourth	6.7	– 1.0	7.7
Middle	3.3	– 3.0	6.3
Second	– 1.4	– 6.7	5.3
Lowest	– 9.2	–11.6	2.4
Total	7.5	0.2	7.3

* Married couples with children.

FIGURE 1H

Effect of Increased Female Earnings on Income of Married Couples with Children, 1979–1987

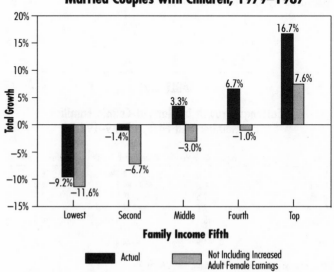

mothers' annual earnings was 44.4% between 1979 and 1987, a growth of 4.6% annually. Earnings growth for these women was greater within the upper income groups.

Despite the rise in women's earnings in these families, overall earnings growth was only 7.8% overall and actually negative for the bottom 40%. This results from the fall in annual earnings among adult men in these families.

Women's Work Keeps Family Income From Falling

Table 1.22 and **Figure 1H** show the role of the increased earnings of mothers on total family *incomes* by presenting what the change in family incomes would have been if the mothers in married-couple families had not increased their earnings level since 1979, other things being equal. In fact, the total family income rise of 7.5% is nearly all due to increased mothers' earnings. Without the increased earnings of the mothers in married-couple families there would have been no increase in family incomes between 1979 and 1987. The increased earnings of mothers raised family incomes more in the better-off families. More than half of the substantial family income gain among the top fifth of 16.7% was due to the increased earnings of the wives.

These increased earnings can come from higher wages, or from greater work effort due to more wives working or more hours or weeks worked per working wife. **Table 1.23**

> *The total family income rise of 7.5% is nearly all due to increased mothers' earnings.*

TABLE 1.23

Factors Explaining Wives' Increased Earnings,* 1979–1987

	Weekly Wages**	Average Weeks Worked		Percent With Earnings
		All Wives	Working Wives	
1979	.0246	23.0 wks	39.2 wks	58.9%
1987	.0302	28.2	42.8	66.1
Change:				
Level	.056	5.2 wks	3.6 wks	7.2 pct pts
Percent	22.8%	22.5%	9.1%	12.2%

*In married-couple families with children. Data have been rounded.

**Weekly wages are divided by annual poverty threshold because of family size adjustment and therefore reflect earnings per week as a fraction of the *annual* poverty level.

TABLE 1.24

Relative Importance of Factors Explaining
Wives' Increased Earnings, 1979–1987*

Higher Wages**	50.1
Work Effort: Increased Annual Hours Worked per Wife***	49.9
Total Change in Earnings	100.0%

*Based on log decomposition of annual earnings growth into growth in average weeks worked and real weekly wages per wife in married couples with children.

**Measured by change in real weekly wage, so reflects higher hourly wages but also more hours per week.

***The effect of greater labor force participation of wives and more weeks worked per year by the average working wife.

shows the factors driving higher earnings among mothers in married-couple families with children. There has been an increase in both real wages and work effort. Weekly wages of the wives in these families rose by 22.8%. Unfortunately, there are no available data on the changes in the hours worked per week by these women. But if overall trends among women apply (weekly hours to 2.5%), the bulk of the rise in weekly wages is due to increased real hourly wages.

There has, however, been a substantial rise of 22.5% in the annual weeks worked by the average mother in a married-couple family. This is a result of more wives working, up to 66.1% in 1987 from 58.9% in 1979, as well as to 9% more weeks worked per year by working wives.

Table 1.24 measures the degree to which the increased annual earnings of wives are due to greater weekly wages versus more weeks spent in the labor market. The rise in annual earnings is equally due to more weeks worked and higher weekly wages. Taking into account the rise in weekly hours (a work effort factor embedded in the weekly wage data), which among all employed women measured 2.5% in this period, it is clear that more work effort, as measured by more annual hours worked, explains slightly more than half the rise in wives' annual earnings.

. . . more work effort . . . explains slightly more than half the rise in wives' annual earnings.

More Work, Less Time Off

As we have shown, the increased earnings of wives in married-couple families with children have been responsible for nearly all of the income growth in these families, especially for middle income families. More than half of the increase in earnings by wives is due to more wives working and to more weekly hours and weeks per year worked by employed wives. The earnings from this increased work effort are a positive financial gain but, as we have discussed, they come with associated costs: increased work-related spending, child-care costs and problems, the loss of leisure time, and added stress. The downside of the increased work effort is delineated in the next few tables.

A two-earner family has considerably more expenses than a one-earner family with a comparable income. Each earner in a family requires transportation to work and frequently needs appropriate clothes. With two earners there are many household tasks that must be completed for the family

TABLE 1.25

Effect of Second Earner on Household Expenditures*

(1990 Dollars)

	Average Income and Expenditures		Difference Between Two-Earner and One-Earner Families	
	1-Earner Families	2-Earner Families	Dollars	Percent
Low-Income Families				
Income				
Income	$ 12,952	$ 21,990	$ 9,038	70%
Annual Wage	10,576	18,996	8,420	80
Expenditures				
Work-Related	4,802	7,128	2,326	48
Transportation	3,795	5,225	1,450	38
Child Care	63	525	462	733
Food Away From Home	574	825	251	44
Other Expenditures	13,136	15,494	2,358	18
Middle Income Families				
Income				
Income	$ 27,876	$ 38,475	$ 10,598	38%
Annual Wage	26,192	36,399	10,207	39
Expenditures				
Work-Related	5,933	9,139	3,206	54
Transportation	4,503	6,435	1,932	43
Child Care	81	677	596	736
Food Away From Home	817	1,210	392	48
Other Expenditures	7,227	9,165	1,939	27

*Married Couples with Children.

The work-related expenses of two-earner families are 48% more than those of one-earner families.

by purchasing services previously performed by a family member. A major example is the cost of child care. Other examples would be home repair and some meal preparation.

Table 1.25 shows the differences in expenditures between one- and two-earner families. Among low-income families, the work-related expenses of two-earner families are 48% more than those of one-earner families. In contrast, non-work related expenditures, "other expenditures," were only 18% greater in two-earner families. The major additional expenses for two-earner families are transportation and child care. Among middle income families, two-earner families spend 54% more on work-related items than one-earner families. One interpretation of these higher expenditures is that the average two-earner family has more income than the average one-earner family. This explanation fails, however, because the growth of non work-related expenditures only rose by half as much, 27%.

These added financial costs to two-earner families are large enough so as to significantly reduce the net gain from increased earners. Among middle income families, for instance, the added financial costs of $3,206 absorb 31% of the added $10,207 of annual wages associated with the second earner.

These expenses are averages among families that do and those that do not have to purchase child care. Many families do not have to pay for child care because their children are in school or because they can rely on unpaid relatives for assistance. For instance, only 32% of families with employed mothers pay for child care (**Table 1.26**). A much higher percentage (from 54.7% to 61.3%) of families

Added financial costs to two-earner families . . . significantly reduce the net gain from increased earners.

TABLE 1.26

Child Care Expenditures and Family Income for Employed Women With Children

(1990 Dollars)

	Number of Women (000)	Number Paying for Child Care (000)	Percent Paying for Child Care	Average Week-ly Child Care Expenses*	Average Monthly Family Income*	Percent of In-come Spent on Child Care Per Month**
Total	18,244	5,831	32.0%	$53.18	$3,586	6.4%
Age of Youngest Child:						
Less Than 1 Year	1,473	806	54.7	62.00	4,218	6.4
1 and 2 Years	3,451	2,114	61.3	61.29	3,584	7.4
3 and 4 Years	2,602	1,509	58.0	51.76	3,375	6.6
5 Years and Older	10,718	1,401	13.1	37.18	3,454	4.7
Number of Children Less Than 5 Years Old:						
1 Child	6,030	3,510	58.2	54.00	3,526	6.6
2 or More Children	1,496	919	61.4	74.12	4,019	8.0

*Refers only to women making child care payments.

**Average weekly child care expenditures were converted to a monthly average.

TABLE 1.27

Trends in Paid and Unpaid Work, 1969–1987

Persons By Number of Children	Average Hours of Market Work			Average Hours of Non-Market Work*			Average Total Hours of Work		
	1969	1987	Change 1969–87	1969	1987	Change 1969–87	1969	1987	Change 1969–87
None									
Men	1,393	1,365	– 28	668	841	173	2,061	2,206	145
Women	794	925	131	1,422	1,319	–103	2,216	2,244	28
One									
Men	2,153	2,136	– 17	683	845	162	2,836	2,981	145
Women	819	1,248	429	1,776	1,479	–297	2,595	2,727	132
Two									
Men	2,260	2,233	– 27	708	867	159	2,968	3,100	132
Women	623	1,060	437	2,042	1,718	–324	2,665	2,778	113

*Work such as child care, household management tasks, and so on.

TABLE 1.28

Per Capita and Per Adult Income Growth

	Income Growth		Adult/Population*
	Per Capita	Per Adult	
		(Annual Growth Rates)	
1948–67	2.58%	2.90%	–0.32%
1967–73	3.16	2.42	0.74
1973–79	1.72	0.86	0.86
1979–88	1.45	1.18	0.27

*Annual change in the adult proportion of the population.

with young children (ages 0 to 4) must pay for child care. For these families, the financial cost of child care absorbs from 6.4% to 7.4% of their incomes.

Another cost of having family members spend more time in the paid labor force is that there is an erosion of leisure time. The trends in annual hours of work, broken down into paid labor market work and unpaid household work, from 1969 to 1987, are presented in **Table 1.27**. The total amount of work has increased in this time period, suggesting that people have less leisure time.

Consider the situation of men and women with two children. The average woman with two children worked 437 more paid hours in 1987 than in 1969, a 70% increase. However, some time was saved by the fact that women with two children performed 324 fewer hours of unpaid household labor. The reduction in household labor was probably due to increased purchases of needed services but was also due to increased household work performed by men in these families, up 159 hours from 1969 to 1987. The net effect of these changes is to have added 132 and 113 more annual work hours, respectively, for men and women with two children. This amounts to an addition of roughly three weeks of full-time work for each parent in families with two children.

Incomes Weak by Any Measure

The same pattern of income growth that we have described with family income data can also be demonstrated with another measure of economic well-being, per capita income. For instance, sluggish income growth is also evident in a measure of per capita income, which grew just 1.45% annually from 1979 to 1988, or about half as fast as in the 1948 to 1973 period (**Table 1.28**). Further insight can be gained by disaggregating this per capita income growth into its demographic component—the ratio of adults to children—and the underlying income growth per adult. This is necessary since per capita income will grow simply if an increased proportion of the population are adults (who receive most of the income) and a decreased proportion are children (who receive hardly any direct income). Disaggregating in this manner shows that recent adult income growth has been at a rate (1.18%) just 40% of that achieved in the early post-war period.

. . . per capita income grew just 1.4% annually from 1979 to 1988.

CHAPTER 2

TABLE 2.1

Total U.S. Tax Burden, 1947–1989

	Government Revenue as Percent of GNP
1947	24.6%
1957	25.9
1967	28.3
1973	30.9
1979	31.1
1989	32.0

TABLE 2.2

Tax Revenues in OECD Countries As Percent of GDP 1967–1987

Country	Tax Revenues as Percent of GDP*			Point Change 1967–87
	1967	1979	1987	
Sweden	37.1%	49.5%	56.7%	19.6
Denmark	33.1	44.5	52.0	18.9
Norway	36.6	45.7	48.3	11.7
Netherlands	35.7	45.0	48.0	12.3
Belgium	33.5	44.5	46.1	12.6
France	34.7	40.2	44.8	10.1
Luxembourg	30.8	40.2	43.8	13.0
Austria	35.3	41.0	42.3	7.0
Ireland	28.7	31.2	39.9	11.2
New Zealand	25.4	32.9	38.6	13.2
West Germany	32.2	37.7	37.6	5.4
United Kingdom	32.9	32.8	37.5	4.6
Greece	23.3	30.1	37.4	14.1
Italy	26.2	26.6	36.2	10.0
Finland	31.6	33.3	35.9	4.2
Canada	28.2	30.6	34.5	6.3
Spain	16.8	23.4	33.0	16.2
Switzerland	21.6	31.1	32.0	10.4
Portugal	19.7	26.0	31.4	11.7
Australia	23.4	27.9	31.3	7.9
Japan	18.3	24.4	30.2	11.9
United States	**27.3**	**29.0**	**30.0**	**2.7**
Turkey	16.2	20.8	24.1	7.9

*Social insurance included. United States numbers differ from those in Table 9.1 because the tables come from different sources and because taxes are given relative to gross domestic product (GDP).

TAXES: LOWER FOR THE WEALTHY, HIGHER FOR EVERYONE ELSE

I n Chapter 1, we showed that family incomes before taxes have stagnated and grown much more unequal over the past decade. This chapter broadens our analysis by examining changes in the amount and distribution of taxes. Changes in federal, state, and local taxes in the 1980s have worsened the distribution of after-tax income by taxing the middle class and the poor more heavily and giving large tax cuts to the richest 1%. Federal tax changes since 1977 alone will amount to an average tax break of $45,565 in 1990 for the richest families. The causes of this shift include a less progressive personal income tax, higher payroll taxes, and lower corporate taxes. There has also been a steadily increasing reliance on state and local taxes, which tend to be regressive.

Changes in federal, state, and local taxes in the 1980s . . . taxed the middle class and the poor more heavily and gave large tax cuts to the richest 1%.

The Tax Burden: Still Light Overall

In comparative terms, taxes have increased little and the overall tax burden remains one of the lightest among the Western, industrialized countries. **Table 2.1** shows the total tax burden in the U.S. as a percent of GNP, from 1947 to 1989. The overall burden has gradually edged up during the post-war period, but went up by only 1.1% of GNP between ·1973 and 1989. **Table 2.2** gives government revenues as a percent of GNP over time for all OECD countries. Every other country has had a greater increase than the U.S. since 1967. As a result, the U.S. tax burden in 1987 was lower than in any other OECD country save Turkey.

Federal Tax Changes Have Favored the Very Rich

On the other hand, there have been significant changes in the *distribution* of taxes. These changes have combined with changes in pre-tax income to enrich the highest income families—primarily the top 1%—at the expense of literally everyone else.

Family income inequality has increased *after* federal taxes just as it has before federal taxes (**Table 2.3**). The top fifth of families received nearly half (49.9%) of after-tax family income in 1990, up from 43.9% in 1977 and 44.8% in 1980. The share received by the top 1% of families shot up the most, from 7.3% in 1977 to 12.6% in 1990. On the other hand, the shares received by each of the bottom four

49

TABLE 2.3

Shares of After-Tax Income for All Families*

Income Group	Shares			
	1977	1980	1985	1990
All	100.0%	100.0%	100.0%	100.0%
Top Fifth:	43.9	44.8	49.1	49.9
Top 1%	7.3	8.3	11.2	12.6
Next 4%	11.2	11.3	12.3	12.4
Next 5%	9.8	9.9	10.2	9.9
Next 10%	15.6	15.3	15.4	15.0
Bottom Four Fifths:				
Fourth	22.8	22.6	22.0	21.7
Middle	16.3	16.2	15.3	14.9
Second	11.6	11.4	10.2	9.9
Lowest	5.7	5.4	4.3	4.3

*Only federal taxes are taken into account

TABLE 2.4

Effects of Federal Tax Changes on Shares of After-Tax Income

Income Group	1990 After-Tax Income Shares at:		Difference: Change in Shares Due to Federal Taxes
	1977 Rates	1990 Rates	
All	100.0%	100.0%	0.0
Top Fifth:	48.6	49.4	0.8
Top 1%	10.9	12.2	1.3
Next 4%	12.4	12.4	0.0
Next 5%	10.0	9.9	-0.1
Next 10%	15.2	14.9	-0.3
Bottom Four Fifths:			
Fourth	21.9	21.5	-0.4
Middle	15.1	14.8	-0.3
Second	10.1	9.9	-0.2
Lowest	4.4	4.3	-0.1

fifths and the second-richest tenth of families declined steadily over the 1977–1990 period.

Changes in federal taxes since 1977 have contributed to the increased inequality of after-tax family incomes. Column 1 of **Table 2.4** shows what the distribution of after-tax income would be in 1990 if each income group still paid the same percent of its income in taxes as in 1977. Column 2 shows the actual distribution of after-tax income in 1990. (These numbers differ slightly from those in Table 2.3; see endnotes.) Column 3 is the change in after-tax income shares caused by federal tax changes since 1977. Such changes added 1.3 percentage points to the share of the top 1% and reduced the shares of every income group in the bottom 95%.

Federal tax changes have increased income inequality because federal taxes have become much less progressive since 1977, as shown by the changes in federal tax rates between 1977 and 1990 (**Table 2.5** and **Figure 2A**). Federal tax rates for income groups in the bottom 95% each increased by 0.2 to 1.0 percentage points, while the percent of income paid in taxes by the top 1% of families fell by 8.3 percentage points.

. . . federal taxes have become much less progressive since 1977.

TABLE 2.5

Effective Federal Tax Rates in 1977 and 1990

Income Group	Effective Federal Tax Rates		Change in Tax Rates, 1977–90
	1977	1990	
All	22.8%	23.0%	0.2
Top Fifth:	27.1	25.7	-1.4
Top 1%	35.4	27.1	-8.3
Next 4%	26.9	26.2	-0.7
Next 5%	25.0	25.5	0.5
Next 10%	23.9	24.6	0.7
Bottom Four Fifths:			
Fourth	21.9	22.5	0.6
Middle	19.6	20.2	0.6
Second	15.6	16.6	1.0
Lowest	9.4	9.6	0.2

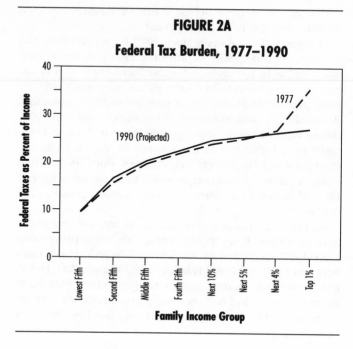

FIGURE 2A

Federal Tax Burden, 1977–1990

Federal Taxes as Percent of Income

1977

1990 (Projected)

Family Income Group

(x-axis labels: Lowest Fifth, Second Fifth, Middle Fifth, Fourth Fifth, Next 10%, Next 5%, Next 4%, Top 1%)

TABLE 2.6

Changes in Federal Taxes in Selected Periods, 1977–1990

Income Group	Change in Effective Federal Tax Rates			
	1977–80	1980–85	1985–90	Total 1977–90
All	0.5	−1.5	1.2	0.2
Top Fifth:	0.2	−3.2	1.6	−1.4
Top 1%	−3.6	−6.9	2.2	−8.3
Next 4%	0.9	−3.7	2.1	−0.7
Next 5%	1.3	−2.2	1.4	0.5
Next 10%	1.2	−1.8	1.3	0.7
Bottom Four Fifths:				
Fourth	1.1	−1.4	0.9	0.6
Middle	0.5	−0.8	0.9	0.6
Second	0.0	0.5	0.5	1.0
Lowest	−1.0	2.3	−1.1	0.2

The shift in the federal tax burden took place in stages (**Table 2.6**). The top 1% received their generous tax cuts between 1977 and 1985. The tax reform of 1986 restored some progressivity to the system, though not enough to make up for previous tax giveaways. The net effect of changes since 1985 has been to take back whatever small cuts the middle class had received between 1977 and 1985—and then some—while leaving the top 1% with the vast bulk of their prior tax cuts intact.

What Federal Tax Changes Mean in Dollars

When we translate these tax rate changes into dollars per family, the results are stunning. **Table 2.7** gives the details. Column 1 shows the average after-tax family income in 1990 for each income group. Columns 2 through 4 show the changes in 1990 taxes paid due to federal tax changes that were enacted in different periods between 1977 and 1990. The final column shows the total difference in 1990 taxes due to all of these changes combined.

The tax reform of 1986 restored some progressivity to the system, though not enough to make up for previous tax giveaways.

TABLE 2.7

Effect of Federal Tax Changes on Family After-Tax Income, 1977–1990

Income Group	Average Pre-Tax Family Income (1990)	The Effect on 1990 After-Tax Family Incomes of Federal Tax Changes in Selected Periods			
		1977–80	1980–85	1986–90	Total 1977–90
All	$ 41,369	$ −207	$ 621	$ −496	$ −83
Top Fifth:	105,209	−210	3,367	−1,683	1,473
Top 1%	548,970	19,763	37,879	−12,077	45,565
Next 4%	125,800	−1,132	4,655	−2,642	881
Next 5%	82,154	−1,068	1,807	−1,150	−411
Next 10%	63,663	−764	1,146	−828	−446
Bottom Four Fifths:					
Fourth	44,908	−494	629	−404	−269
Middle	30,964	−155	248	−279	−186
Second	19,348	0	−97	−97	−193
Lowest	7,725	77	−178	85	−15

TABLE 2.8

Effective Tax Rates for Specific Federal Taxes, 1977–1990

| | Effective Tax Rates | | | | | | | |
| | Personal Income Tax | | Social Insurance Taxes | | Corporate Income Tax | | Excise Taxes | |
Income Group	1977	1990	1977	1990	1977	1990	1977	1990
All	11.1%	11.3%	6.5%	8.6%	3.9%	2.3%	1.3%	0.8%
Top Fifth:	16.0	15.6	5.2	6.8	5.0	2.8	0.9	0.5
Top 1%	25.1	21.5	1.2	1.6	8.8	3.7	0.3	0.3
Next 4%	16.5	16.3	4.3	6.5	5.3	2.9	0.8	0.5
Next 5%	13.8	13.2	6.4	9.2	3.8	2.5	1.0	0.6
Next 10%	12.1	11.6	7.3	10.1	3.4	2.2	1.1	0.7
Bottom Four Fifths:								
Fourth	9.6	9.0	7.8	10.6	3.2	2.0	1.3	0.9
Middle	7.0	6.7	8.1	10.7	3.0	1.8	1.5	1.0
Second	3.5	3.5	7.6	10.1	2.7	1.6	1.8	1.4
Lowest	-0.6	-1.5	5.3	7.6	1.8	1.1	2.9	2.4

FIGURE 2B

Personal Income Tax Burden, 1977–1990

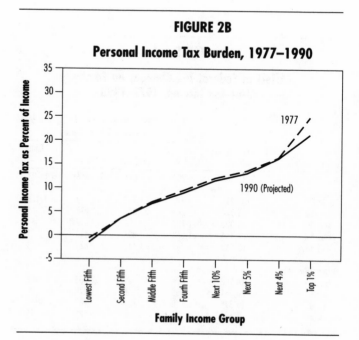

Because of federal tax changes since 1977, the top 1% of families will each receive a tax cut of $45,565 in 1990, courtesy of the bottom 95%. This cut came mainly from steps taken between 1980 and 1985, although changes in the late 1970s also contributed. Tax changes since 1985, including the tax reform of 1986, reduced the tax cut somewhat. The next richest 4% of families received tax cuts that averaged $881 per family in 1990—considerably smaller than the gains of the richest 1%. The rest of the population had sizeable tax increases. The lowest fifth of families had a small tax hike of $15 in 1990; the second fifth, however, had a higher tax increase of $193; and the middle and fourth fifths paid $186 and $269 more per family in 1990. Even the bottom half of the top fifth paid $446 more per family, and the next 5% paid $411.

The Causes of Changes in the Federal Tax Burden

Changes in each of the three main federal taxes—the personal income tax, social insurance (FICA) taxes, and the corporate income tax—have all helped shift the tax burden from the richest 1% of families to the bottom 95%. The personal income tax, which is progressive, has become less so; social insurance (FICA) taxes, which are regressive, have gone up; and corporate income taxes, which are progressive, have declined considerably.

Although the personal income tax is still the most progressive federal tax, it has become less so (**Table 2.8** and **Figure 2B**). Since 1977, the average personal income tax for the top 1% has fallen by 3.6 points. In contrast, reductions in personal income taxes for groups in the bottom 99% have been much smaller.

Since 1977, the overall social insurance tax rate has risen from 6.5% to 8.6% (Table 2.8). The bottom 99% have borne the brunt of increased social insurance taxes; the top 1% has been virtually unaffected (**Table 2.9** and **Figure 2C**). This is partly because the rich earn much of their income from their investments (Chapter 1), which are not subject to social insurance taxes. Another reason is that social insurance taxes applied only to the first $51,300 of earnings in 1990.

The final important change has been that corporate income taxes have decreased since 1977. Since corporations

The personal income tax, which is progressive, has become less so; social insurance (FICA) taxes, which are regressive, have gone up; and corporate income taxes, which are progressive, have declined considerably.

TABLE 2.9

Changes in Specific Federal Taxes, 1977–1990

Income Group	Change in Effective Tax Rates, 1977–1990				
	Personal Income Tax	Social Insurance Taxes	Corporate Income Tax	Excise Taxes	Total
All	0.2	2.1	−1.6	−0.5	0.2
Top Fifth:	−0.4	1.6	−2.2	−0.4	−1.4
Top 1%	−3.6	0.4	−5.1	0.0	−8.3
Next 4%	−0.2	2.2	−2.4	−0.3	0.7
Next 5%	−0.6	2.8	−1.3	−0.4	0.5
Next 10%	−0.5	2.8	−1.2	−0.4	0.7
Bottom Four Fifths:					
Fourth	−0.6	2.8	−1.2	−0.4	0.6
Middle	−0.3	2.6	−1.2	−0.5	0.6
Second	0.0	2.5	−1.1	−0.4	1.0
Lowest	−0.9	2.3	−0.7	−0.5	0.2

Figure 2C

Social Insurance Tax Burden, 1977–1990

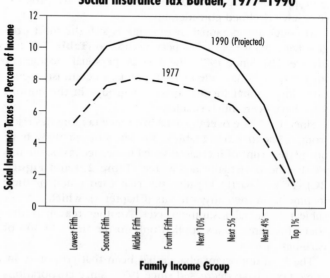

56

are owned by households through shares of stock, households also bear the burden of corporate taxes. The burden can be transferred to households in a variety of ways. In this analysis, it is assumed that half of corporate taxes are borne by stockholders in the form of lower dividends and slower stock appreciation, and half are paid by consumers in the form of higher prices.

Between 1977 and 1990, federal corporate taxes declined from 3.9% to 2.3% of overall family income (Table 2.8). According to our burden assumptions, corporate taxes are progressive; thus, lower corporate taxes have benefitted the rich much more than other groups. In particular, the top 1% of families saw their corporate tax burdens reduced by 5.1 percentage points, from 8.8% of family income to 3.7% (Table 2.9 and **Figure 2D**). The bottom four fifths, on the other hand, received decreases of from 0.7 to 1.2 percentage points.

The cause of the decline in corporate tax revenues is that more and more of corporate income is *untaxed*. Untaxed corporate profits rose from 0.3% of GNP in 1977 to 2.9% in

The cause of the decline in corporate tax revenues is that more and more of corporate income is untaxed.

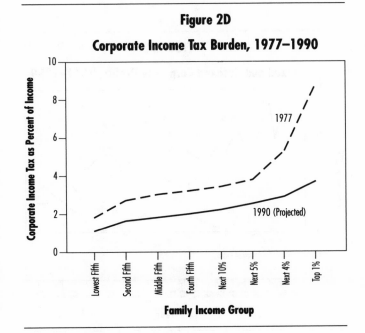

Figure 2D

Corporate Income Tax Burden, 1977–1990

57

TABLE 2.10

Taxed and Untaxed Corporate Profits, 1977–1989
(Nonfinancial Corporations Only)

| | As Percent of GNP in: | | | |
	1977	1980	1985	1989
All Profits, Taxed and Untaxed	8.3%	6.5%	7.6%	7.2%
Taxed Profits	8.1	6.7	4.2	4.2
	0.3	–0.1	3.4	2.9
Untaxed Profits				
Net Interest	1.5	2.0	2.0	2.8
Depreciation Allowances	–0.5	–0.6	1.4	0.5
Other Deductions	–0.8	–1.6	–0.0	–0.4
Corporate Profits Taxes*	3.0	2.5	1.7	1.9
Profits After Taxes				
Taxable Profits Only	5.1	4.2	2.5	2.3
All Profits	5.3	4.1	5.9	5.3

*Federal, state, and local combined.

FIGURE 2E

Taxed and Untaxed Corporate Profits, 1947–1989

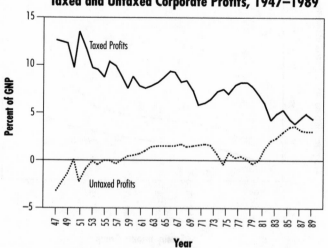

58

1989 (**Table 2.10**). Thus, while total corporate profits, taxed and untaxed, have declined just a bit since 1977 as a share of GNP, taxed profits have been cut virtually in half: from 8.1% of GNP to 4.2% (Table 2.10; see also **Figure 2E**).

There are two main reasons for the shift from taxed to untaxed profits: increased indebtedness and a more favorable tax treatment of depreciation. Since 1977, corporations have increasingly raised money by selling bonds (i.e., they have borrowed) rather than stocks to raise money. As a result, corporations have been paying out more and more of their gross profits as interest payments (on bonds) rather than as dividend payments (on stocks). This is reflected in Table 2.10 in the steady increase in net interest payments, from 1.5% of GNP in 1977 to 2.8% of GNP today. Since corporations have to pay taxes on dividend payments but not on interest payments, their tax liabilities have shrunk.

The second reason for lower corporate taxes is a more favorable tax treatment of capital depreciation. Corporations are now able to take tax deductions on purchases of new equipment and other investments sooner. Since this allows them to defer some of their taxes for several years, accelerated depreciation amounts to an interest-free loan. The main tax break of this type came between 1980 and 1985, when untaxed profits due to depreciation allowances went from –0.6% of GNP to 1.4% (Table 2.10). Since 1985, Congress has taken back part of this tax cut, reducing untaxed profits in this category to 0.5% of GNP.

There are two main reasons for the shift from taxed to untaxed profits: increased indebtedness and a more favorable tax treatment of depreciation.

TABLE 2.11

Corporate Profits Tax Rates, 1947–1989
(Nonfinancial Corporations Only)

| | Corporate Taxes* as Percent of: | |
	Taxable Profits	Actual Profits
1947	37.1%	50.9%
1957	48.0	48.6
1967	41.8	35.1
1977	37.3	36.2
1980	36.9	37.5
1985	41.1	22.8
1989	45.0	26.5

*Federal, state, and local combined.

FIGURE 2F

Corporate Profits Taxes, 1947–1989

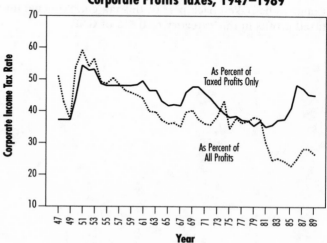

Federal, state, and local taxes combined.

Table 2.11 shows the results of these changes. Since 1977, corporate taxes have declined from 36.2% of actual profits to 26.5%, while *increasing* as a percent of taxed profits. Moreover, the current effective tax rate, 26.5%, is barely over half of what corporate taxes were in 1947 and 1957 (Table 2.11 and **Figure 2F**). This long-term decline has amounted to an even larger tax cut for rich families.

There is a small exception to the decreased progressivity of federal taxes: excise taxes have declined since 1977. Excise taxes—sales taxes levied on alcohol, gasoline, cigarettes, and so on—are the most regressive federal taxes (Table 2.8 and **Figure 2G**). This is because families with higher incomes spend smaller proportions of their incomes on gasoline, cigarettes, alcohol, and other goods subject to excise taxes (**Table 2.12**). The decline in federal excise taxes, from 1.3% of family incomes in 1977 to 0.8% in 1990, has reduced the tax burden somewhat on the bottom 99% of families, with slightly greater tax cuts going to low income families (Table 2.9 and Figure 2E).

Excise taxes—sales taxes levied on alcohol, gasoline, cigarettes, and so on—are the most regressive federal taxes.

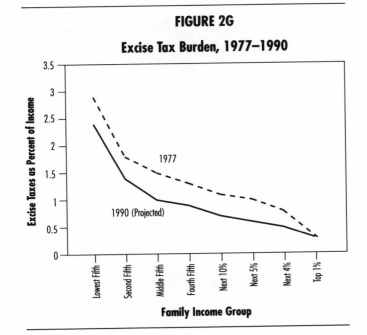

FIGURE 2G

Excise Tax Burden, 1977–1990

1977

1990 (Projected)

Excise Taxes as Percent of Income

Family Income Group

61

TABLE 2.12

Expenditures On Tobacco, Alcoholic Beverages, and Motor Fuels as Percentages of After-Tax Family Income, 1990

Income Group	Percentage of After-Tax Income Spent on:		
	Tobacco	Alcoholic Beverages	Motor Fuels
All Families	1.1%	2.0%	2.7%
Top Fifth	0.5	1.6	1.5
Fourth Fifth	1.1	2.2	2.9
Middle Fifth	1.6	2.2	3.5
Second Fifth	2.1	2.3	4.2
Bottom Fifth	4.0	3.7	6.9

TABLE 2.13

Federal vs. State and Local Tax Burdens, 1947–1989

	Revenue as Percent of GNP	
	Federal	State/Local
1947	18.8%	5.8%
1957	18.3	7.6
1967	18.7	9.6
1973	19.4	11.5
1979	20.1	11.0
1989	20.0	12.0

The Shift to State and Local Taxes

It has been primarily state and local tax increases that have pushed up the tax burden during the post-war period (**Table 2.13**). Since state and local taxes are less progressive than federal taxes, the distribution of the overall tax burden is considerably less progressive than the distribution of federal taxes alone.

State and local governments rely predominantly on regressive sources of funds: sales taxes, property taxes, and nontax revenues such as fines, fees, royalties, and so on. **Table 2.14** gives the percent of family income that families in each income class contributed to each of these revenue sources in 1987. The bottom row gives a rough index of the progressivity of each revenue source: the ratio of the percent paid by the top income class to the percent paid by the bottom class. A value over 1 indicates a progressive source, 1 means a proportional source, and less than 1 indicates a

It has been primarily state and local tax increases that have pushed up the tax burden during the post-war period.

TABLE 2.14

Regressive State and Local Taxes and Nontax Revenues, 1987

| Family Income Class ($000) | Effective Tax Rate | | |
	Sales/Excise/Other*	Property Taxes	Nontax Revenues**
<$10	10.7%	5.5%	5.1%
10–15	6.1	3.6	2.8
15–20	5.2	3.6	2.4
20–30	4.5	2.8	2.1
30–40	3.9	2.5	1.9
40–50	3.8	2.5	1.9
50–60	3.5	2.5	1.8
60–70	3.4	3.2	1.7
70–90	3.1	2.8	1.5
90+	3.3	3.7	1.2
All	4.4	3.1	2.1
Progressivity Index***	0.31	0.68	0.23

*Other taxes include vehicle licenses, severance taxes, etc.

**Fines, certain fees, rents, royalties, tuition, hospital charges, etc.

***Ratio of rate on top income class to rate on bottom.

63

TABLE 2.15

Federal vs. State and Local Taxes, 1989
as Percent of Revenue at Each Level

Type of Tax	Federal	State and Local
Progressive	53.9%	19.4%
Personal Income Tax	42.9	15.5
Corporate Income Tax	10.1	3.9
Estate/Gift Taxes	0.9	0.0
Regressive	45.4	68.7
Excise/Customs/Sales/Other*	5.0	37.3
Contributions for Social Insurance	40.3	9.0
Property	0.0	22.4
Nontax Revenues**	0.8	11.9
TOTAL	100.0	100.0

*Other taxes include vehicle licenses, severance taxes, etc.

**Fines, certain fees, rents, royalties, tuition, hospital fees, etc.

FIGURE 2H

Federal Revenue Sources, 1989

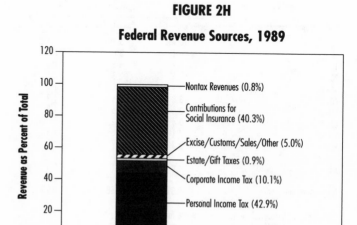

64

regressive source. As Table 2.14 indicates, these state and local revenue sources are all regressive. Sales and excise taxes are regressive because families with higher incomes usually spend a lower proportion of their incomes (they save more). Property taxes are regressive because the rich both keep a smaller proportion of their wealth in real estate and have lower rent and mortgage payments as a proportion of their incomes. Nontax revenues are also regressive, but are probably less burdensome overall than sales and property taxes because some of them are fees for lower-cost services such as public universities and hospitals, which benefit low and middle income families.

State and local governments rely far more on regressive taxes than does the federal government. In spite of increases in social insurance taxes, 53.9% of federal revenues still come from progressive sources, but only 19.4% of state/ local revenues are raised progressively (**Table 2.15**, **Figure 2H**, **Figure 2I**).

State and local governments rely far more on regressive taxes than does the federal government.

FIGURE 2I

State and Local Revenue Sources, 1989

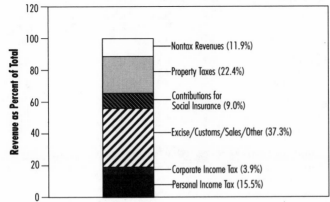

Nontax Revenues (11.9%)
Property Taxes (22.4%)
Contributions for Social Insurance (9.0%)
Excise/Customs/Sales/Other (37.3%)
Corporate Income Tax (3.9%)
Personal Income Tax (15.5%)

TABLE 2.16

Federal vs. State and Local Personal Income Taxes, 1987

Family Income Class ($000)	Effective Tax Rate	
	Federal	State and Local*
<$10	2.4%	0.8%
10–15	4.7	1.2
15–20	6.5	1.6
20–30	7.4	2.0
30–40	8.4	2.4
40–50	9.5	2.5
50–60	8.9	2.5
60–70	12.4	2.4
70–90	10.1	2.5
90+	26.4	2.3
All	9.8	2.1
Progressivity Index**	10.87	2.81

*Weighted average.

**Ratio of rate on top income class to rate on bottom.

TABLE 2.17

The Composition of Taxes, 1947–1989
As Percent of GNP

Type of Tax	1947	1967	1973	1979	1989
Progressive*	13.4%	13.0%	13.4%	14.2%	13.1%
Federal	12.9	11.9	11.6	12.2	10.8
State and Local	0.5	1.1	1.8	2.1	2.3
Regressive**	10.9	14.5	16.4	15.6	17.3
Federal	5.8	6.6	7.7	7.8	9.1
State and Local	5.1	7.9	8.7	7.8	8.2
Nontax Revenue***	0.3	0.8	1.0	1.2	1.6
Federal	0.0	0.1	0.1	0.1	0.2
State and Local	0.3	0.7	0.9	1.1	1.4

*Personal and corporate income taxes; estate and gift taxes.

**Customs, excise, sales, and other taxes; property taxes; contributions for social insurance. Other taxes include vehicle licenses, severance taxes, etc.

***Fines, certain fees, rents, royalties, tuition, hospital fees, etc.

In fact, even the personal income tax is less progressive at the state and local levels. **Table 2.16** compares effective personal income tax rates in 1987 for the federal tax and for a weighted average of state/local taxes. The progressivity index is a high 10.87 for the federal income tax, but only 2.81 for the average state income tax. As the table indicates, state and local income taxes are progressive only at low incomes; families earning amounts over $30,000 all pay about the same tax rate.

Table 2.17 traces the percent of GNP taxed by progressive and regressive taxes, together with nontax revenues, at peaks of business cycles since 1947. While progressive taxes have fallen slightly since 1947, regressive taxes have increased their share of GNP substantially—from 10.9% to 17.3%. This has resulted from increases at both the federal and state/local levels. Nontax revenues have risen but remain low, at only 1.6% of GNP in 1989.

While progressive taxes have fallen slightly since 1947, regressive taxes have increased their share of GNP substantially.

CHAPTER 3

WAGES: WORKING LONGER FOR LESS

Introduction

Hourly wages, in inflation-adjusted terms, fell more than 9% between 1980 and 1989. Hourly benefits, such as pensions and health insurance, fell even more, by 13.8%. However, because of increases in annual hours worked by the average worker, *annual* wages in the late 1980s were the same as in 1979, despite the drop in hourly wages. Thus, underlying the modest family income growth in recent years has been a population working longer hours at lower wages.

The erosion of real wages and benefits has been uneven. It has been greater among blue collar and service workers than white collar workers, greater among younger than older workers, greater among those with less than a college education than the college educated, and greater among men than women. Reflecting these trends, the wage of a young male high school graduate in 1987 was 18% lower than in 1979. These workers actually earned less in 1987 than did their counterparts 24 years earlier in 1963.

The expansion of low-wage jobs has led to a rising fraction of the workforce earning poverty level wages, increasing from 25.7% in 1979 to 31.5% in 1987. This shift towards low-wage employment has occurred among both men and women, and within each racial/ethnic group, especially Hispanics.

The decline in fringe benefits meant that in 1989, compared with 1980, fewer workers received health insurance coverage or were enrolled in pension plans. They also received less paid leave, such as vacations and holidays.

The decline in wages and benefits cannot be explained by productivity trends, since real wages fell faster in the 1980s than in the 1970s while productivity growth rose somewhat faster in the 1980s than in the 1970s. A significant part of the last decade's pay erosion has been a structural shift toward lower paying jobs, which accounted for two-thirds of the roughly 10% drop in hourly compensation between 1980 and 1989. The major force behind the changing employment structure was growing international competition, reflected in the large trade deficit, and the overall shift of employment from high-paying to low-paying industries. The shrinkage of union membership and the erosion of the real value of the minimum wage also led to lower overall pay levels. One group fared well in the 1980s: chief execu-

Underlying the modest family income growth in recent years has been a population working longer hours at lower wages.

69

TABLE 3.1

Trends in Average Wages and Average Hours, 1967–1987

Year	Productivity Per Hour (1982=100)	Real Wage Indices (1982=100)			Hours Worked Trends		
		Annual Wages	Weekly Wages	Hourly Wages	Annual Hours	Weeks Per Year	Hours Per Week
1967	86.6	93.7	92.1	87.8	1,738	45.4	38.3
1973	96.7	106.2	104.5	101.2	1,657	44.7	37.1
1979	100.3	102.5	102.4	101.0	1,619	44.5	36.3
1982	100.0	100.0	100.0	100.0	1,579	44.2	35.7
1987	109.9	102.1	101.6	97.7	1,714	45.8	37.4
Change		(Annual Growth Rates)					
1967–73	1.7%	2.1%	2.1%	2.4%	−0.8%	−0.3%	−0.5%
1973–79	0.5	−0.6	−0.3	0.0	−0.4	−0.1	−0.4
1982–87	1.9	0.4	0.3	−0.5	1.6	0.7	0.9
1979–87	1.1	0.0	−0.1	−0.4	0.7	0.4	0.4

tive officers of major corporations, whose take-home pay grew far faster than the pay of CEOs in our successful competitors, Japan and Germany. There is a much wider gap between the pay of executives and average workers in the U.S. than in other industrialized countries.

In the 1990s, there will not be an explosive growth of jobs that have higher educational and skill requirements nor a shift towards higher paying jobs. In fact, skill requirements are expected to increase in the 1990s at a rate far slower than in recent decades. Consequently, there is no reason to expect a reversal of the shift towards lower paying jobs that occurred in the 1980s.

More Hours at Lower Wages

The annual wage and salary of the average worker in inflation-adjusted terms was slightly less in 1987 than in 1979 (**Table 3.1**). In order to prevent a large drop in annual earnings, the average worker had to work 1,714 hours in 1987, or 95 more than the 1,619 hours worked in 1979. This increase is equivalent to each worker working nearly 2.5 full-time weeks more in 1987 than in 1979. The end result was that the average worker in 1987 was working 5.9% *more* hours at an hourly wage 3.3% *less* than in 1979.

Real hourly wages fell 0.5% per year during the economic recovery from 1982 to 1987. This is the only recovery since World War II during which real hourly wages fell. In fact, the yearly growth of 0.4% in *annual wages* since the bottom of the recession in 1982 was solely due to the 1.6% yearly growth in *annual hours* worked.

These wage and hour trends in the 1980s represent a shift from earlier trends. For instance, the recent increase in annual hours worked reverses the trend from 1967 to 1979 in which reductions in weekly hours and weeks worked led to fewer annual hours of work. Real hourly wages rose 2.4% between 1967 and 1973 and were stable between 1973 and 1979, but fell by 0.4% per year between 1979 and 1987.

Productivity growth between recent cyclical peaks has been lower than that of the pre-1973 economy (Table 3.1). However, lower productivity growth is not sufficient to explain the drop in real wages. Hourly productivity actually *increased* by 1.1% annually after 1979 while real hourly wages *fell*. Moreover, while wage trends worsened after 1979, with a switch from no growth to negative growth,

Lower productivity growth is not sufficient to explain the drop in real wages. Hourly productivity actually increased by 1.1% annually after 1979 while real hourly wages fell.

TABLE 3.2
Change in Hourly Compensation, Wages, and Benefits, 1980–89

(1989 Dollars)

Year**	Hourly Wage	Hourly Benefits*	Payroll Taxes	Total Compensation	
				Excluding Taxes	Including Taxes
1980	$12.93	$ 1.50	$ 1.21	$14.42	$15.64
1989	11.72	1.29	1.27	13.01	14.28
Change, 1980–89					
Dollar	$–1.21	$–0.21	$ 0.06	$–1.41	$–1.36
Percent					
Total	–9.3%	–13.8%	4.6%	–9.8%	–9.7%
Annual	–1.1%	– 1.7%	0.5%	–1.1%	–1.0%

*Benefits are exclusive of payroll taxes and are primarily pension and insurance costs.

**Data refer to private sector workers in March of each year. The earliest year for which data are available is 1980.

FIGURE 3A
Average Hourly Compensation, Wages, and Benefits
All Private Sector Workers, 1980–89

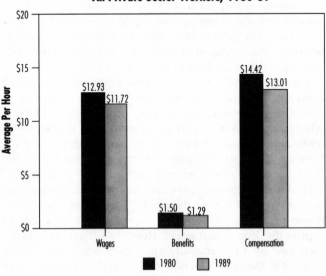

72

annual productivity growth accelerated from 0.5% between 1973 and 1979 to 1.1% between 1979 and 1987. The drop in real wages cannot be ascribed to a compensating growth in fringe benefits such as pensions and health insurance either. This is evident by tracing benefit growth from the earliest to the most recent time for which detailed fringe benefit data are available, March 1980 to March 1989. Between 1980 and 1989 the real value of hourly fringe benefits fell by 13.8%, even faster than the 9.3% fall in hourly wages (**Table 3.2**). It should be noted that the data in Table 3.2 show an even larger drop in real hourly wages than the data in Table 3.1, a 1.1% annual drop versus an 0.4% annual drop. Since the data in Table 3.2 are drawn from a survey of employers rather than one of households, they are probably more accurate. Unfortunately, the employer survey data are not available for earlier years.

The post-1980 drop in hourly wages amounted to a cut of $1.21 per hour which, when coupled with the $0.21 per hour fall in benefits, lowered overall compensation (exclusive of payroll tax changes) by $1.41 per hour (**Figure 3A**). Payroll taxes paid by employers rose 4.6% over this period.

Low-Paid Occupations Fare Worst

We now turn our attention to how the various segments of the workforce fared during the 1980s. In general, the workers who experienced the greatest fall in real wages were those who initially had lower wages, were without a college degree, were in blue collar or service occupations, or were in the younger age brackets.

The post-1980 drop in hourly wages amounted to a cut of $1.21 per hour which, when coupled with the $0.21 per hour fall in benefits, lowered overall compensation by $1.41 per hour.

TABLE 3.3

Hourly and Weekly Earnings of Production and Nonsupervisory Workers, 1947-1989*

(1989 Dollars)

Year	Average Hourly Earnings	Average Weekly Earnings
1947	$ 5.50	$221.68
1967	8.94	339.81
1973	10.18	375.73
1979	10.33	368.75
1982	10.12	352.25
1989	9.66	335.20
Annual Growth Rates		
1947–67	2.4%	2.1%
1967–73	2.2	1.7
1973–79	0.2	-0.3
1979–89	-0.7	-1.0
1982–89	-0.7	-0.7

*Production and nonsupervisory workers comprise more than 80% of wage and salary employment.

FIGURE 3B

Earnings Growth for Production Workers, 1947-1989

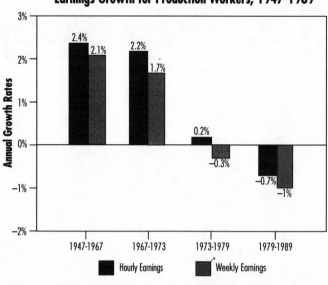

74

The data in **Table 3.3** and **Figure 3B** show wage trends for the 80% of the workforce who are "production and nonsupervisory workers." This category includes factory workers, construction workers, and a wide variety of service sector workers, ranging from restaurant and clerical workers to nurses and teachers. For all these workers, average hourly earnings have fallen $0.67 over the last ten years, a decline of 0.7% each year. In contrast, hourly earnings rose 0.2% annually in the 1973–79 period and grew 2.2% to 2.4% per year from 1967 to 1973. Because of reductions in weekly hours since 1979 as well as hourly earnings, weekly earnings fell at a rate of 1.0% each year. The earnings of production and nonsupervisory workers in 1989 were $335.20 per week (in 1989 dollars), less than what they were in 1967!

Table 3.4 presents wage and benefit trends between 1980 and 1989 for major occupational groups. The lower the pay, the more wages and compensation fell in the 1980s. White collar pay fell the least, with wages down 2.3% since 1980 and overall compensation down 3.1%. The most dramatic reductions were for service workers, whose wages fell 18.2%, a drop of $1.32 per hour from $7.26 to just $5.94. In 1980, service workers received far fewer benefits than those in other occupations—$0.58 per hour—yet still saw their benefits reduced by 26.1%.

The earnings of production and nonsupervisory workers in 1989 were $335.20 per week less than what they were in 1967!

TABLE 3.4

Hourly Wages and Benefits By Occupational Groups, 1980–1989*

Year	White Collar			Blue Collar			Services		
	Wages	Benefits	Compensation	Wages	Benefits	Compensation	Wages	Benefits	Compensation
1980	$14.20	$ 1.59	$15.79	$12.86	$ 1.63	$14.49	$ 7.26	$ 0.58	$ 7.84
1989	13.88	1.42	15.30	11.31	1.50	12.81	5.94	0.43	6.37
Change, 1980–89									
Dollars	$-0.32	$-0.17	$-0.49	$-1.55	$-0.13	$-1.68	$-1.32	$-0.15	$-1.47
Percent									
Total	-2.3%	-10.4%	-3.1%	-12.0%	-7.8%	-11.6%	-18.2%	-26.1%	-18.8%
Annual	-0.3	-1.2	-0.3	-1.4	-0.9	-1.4	-2.2	-3.4	-2.3

*See definitions in Table 3.2. Compensation and benefits exclude payroll taxes.

TABLE 3.5

Wages for All Workers By Wage Percentile, 1967–1988

(1989 Dollars)

Year	Wage Percentile*				
	10	25	Median	75	90
Weekly Wage					
1967	$71.40	$176.60	$329.90	$501.40	$692.70
1973	79.80	186.40	358.20	562.90	793.10
1979	92.40	194.60	338.70	564.40	796.80
1988	86.40	184.70	348.90	574.60	820.80
Hourly Wage					
1979	$ 3.91	$ 5.65	$ 8.55	$ 13.30	$ 18.72
1988	3.49	5.25	8.65	13.58	19.32
Changes					
Weekly Wage					
1967–73	$ 8.46	$ 9.76	$ 28.32	$ 61.47	$100.39
1973–79	12.58	8.24	–19.53	1.56	3.72
1979–88	–5.99	–9.95	10.19	10.14	23.98
Hourly Wage					
1979–88	–0.42	–0.40	0.10	0.28	0.60
Annual Growth Rates					
Weekly Wage					
1967–73	1.9%	0.9%	1.4%	1.9%	2.3%
1973–79	2.4	0.7	–0.9	0.0	0.1
1979–88	–0.7	–0.6	0.3	0.2	0.3
Hourly Wage					
1979–88	–1.3	–0.8	0.1	0.2	0.4

*The worker at the 25th percentile earns less than 75% but more than 25% of the workforce.

76

Blue collar workers also experienced substantial reductions in pay. The hourly wage of blue collar workers fell 12%, or $1.55 an hour from $12.86 to $11.31. Hourly benefits fell 7.8%. By 1989, blue collar hourly compensation was down 11.6%, or $1.68 less an hour than in 1980.

Low-Wage Workers Lose, High-Wage Workers Gain

Low-wage workers have seen the purchasing power of their wages fall dramatically while higher wage workers have experienced modest improvements in real wages. This has led to a dramatic increase in wage inequality. For instance, the bottom 75% of male workers and the bottom 25% of female workers saw their wages decline between 1979 and 1988. The best paid workers, those in the upper 10%, had annual wage increases of 0.4% for males and 1.5% for females.

Wage trend data for all wage and salary workers are presented in **Table 3.5**. Both the wage levels and the wage changes for workers at different percentiles such as the median (the 50th percentile) and the 10th, 25th, 75th, and 90th percentiles, are presented. As a result, we can trace wage trends for the worker at the 50th percentile (the median worker), who earns more than 50% of the workforce, as well as for the worker at the 75th percentile, who earns more than 75% of the workforce.

As Table 3.5 shows, the median worker in 1988 earned a weekly wage of $348.90, $10.19 higher than the $338.70 weekly wage earned in 1979, implying a rise of just 0.3% per year. Most of even this minimal increase, however, is due to more hours worked per week, since median hourly wages increased by just 0.1% per year. Unfortunately, the data do not allow comparisons to hourly wage trends before 1979. The weekly wage data show that weekly wages for the median worker fell considerably between 1973 and 1979, at an 0.9% annual rate of decline. However, the trends in hours worked per week from Table 3.1 suggest that roughly half of the decline in weekly wages in the 1973–79 period was due to fewer hours worked per week and half was due to lower hourly wages. By 1988, weekly wages for the median worker were $10 lower than in 1973. Productivity, on the other hand, rose by at least 13.7% in this period (Table 3.1).

Low-wage workers have seen the purchasing power of their wages fall dramatically while higher wage workers have experienced modest improvements in real wages.

77

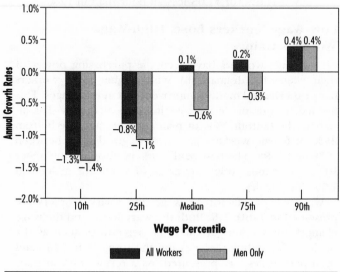

FIGURE 3C

Growth of Hourly Wages by Wage Percentile
All Workers and Men Only, 1979-1987

Wage Percentile

■ All Workers   ▨ Men Only

During the 1980s, the hourly wage of the worker at the 25th percentile fell $0.40, from $5.65 in 1979 to $5.20 in 1988, a drop of 0.8% per year (see **Figure 3C**). The wages of workers at the 10th percentile fell even faster, by 1.3% annually. In contrast, high-wage workers (at the 75th or 90th percentile) saw their hourly wages grow by 0.2% to 0.4% annually.

The most dramatic changes in the level and structure of wages have occurred among men (**Table 3.6** and Figure 3C). The weekly wage of the median male worker fell 0.5% annually between 1973 and 1988. As a result, the median male weekly wage fell from $486.10 in 1973 to $451.50 in 1988. Wages for low-wage male workers have fallen so much since 1979 that weekly wages in 1988 were lower than they were in 1967. For instance, the 1988 weekly wage of a worker at the 25th percentile, $246.20, was $26.30 less than that of an equivalent worker in 1967, 21 years earlier. A generation of economic growth has failed to produce higher wages for these workers.

The median male weekly wage fell from $486.10 in 1973 to $451.50 in 1988.

78

The recent wage deterioration among men was widespread, as the entire bottom 75% of the male workforce experienced wage reductions. However, weekly wages among high-wage male earners, those in the upper 10%, have grown modestly since 1973, including a 0.4% annual growth since 1979.

In contrast to male workers, wage growth for the median female worker has been positive since 1967, although women still make only roughly two-thirds of what men do. However, wage growth has slowed in each period, falling

The entire bottom 75% of the male workforce experienced wage reductions.

TABLE 3.6

Wages for Male Workers By Wage Percentile, 1967–1988

(1989 Dollars)

| Year | Wage Percentile* | | | | |
	10	25	Median	75	90
Weekly Wage					
1967	$122.80	$272.50	$428.80	$593.80	$791.70
1973	128.90	290.80	486.10	678.00	921.00
1979	132.80	276.50	470.80	690.60	929.60
1988	115.20	246.20	451.50	697.70	964.50
Hourly Wage					
1979	$ 4.47	$ 6.91	$ 11.02	$ 16.29	$ 21.17
1988	3.93	6.28	10.47	15.91	21.97
Changes					
Weekly Wage					
1967–73	$ 6.13	$ 18.31	$ 57.28	$ 84.20	$129.35
1973–79	3.89	−14.33	−15.27	12.63	8.60
1979–88	−17.55	−30.27	−19.39	7.11	34.81
Hourly Wage					
1979–88	−0.54	−0.64	−0.55	−0.38	0.81
Annual Growth Rates					
Weekly Wage					
1967–73	0.8%	1.1%	2.1%	2.2%	2.5%
1973–79	0.5	−0.8	−0.5	0.3	0.2
1979–88	−1.6	−1.3	−0.5	0.1	0.4
Hourly Wage					
1979–88	−1.4	−1.1	−0.6	−0.3	0.4

*The worker at the 25th percentile earns less than 75% but more than 25% of the workforce.

TABLE 3.7

Wages for Women Workers By Wage Percentile, 1967–1988

(1989 Dollars)

Year	Wage Percentile*				
	10	25	Median	75	90
Weekly Wage					
1967	$45.20	$106.80	$209.80	$329.90	$450.90
1973	55.90	123.30	234.90	358.20	496.30
1979	67.70	142.80	250.30	366.80	514.60
1988	68.50	143.60	266.80	430.90	615.60
Hourly Wage					
1979	$ 3.38	$ 4.93	$ 6.87	$ 9.77	$ 13.43
1988	3.21	4.75	7.27	11.07	15.33
Changes					
Weekly Wage					
1967–73	$10.73	$ 16.48	$ 25.07	$ 28.32	$ 45.41
1973–79	11.82	19.47	15.48	8.66	18.27
1979–88	0.77	0.88	16.42	64.09	101.00
Hourly Wage					
1979–88	−0.18	−0.17	0.40	1.29	1.90
Annual Growth Rates					
Weekly Wage					
1967–73	3.6%	2.4%	1.9%	1.4%	1.6%
1973–79	3.2	2.4	1.1	0.4	0.6
1979–88	0.1	0.1	0.7	1.8	2.0
Hourly Wage					
1979–88	−0.6	−0.4	0.6	1.4	1.5

*The worker at the 25th percentile earns less than 75% but more than 25% of the workforce.

from 1.9% to 1.1% and then to 0.7% in the three periods shown in **Table 3.7**. Hourly wages among low-wage women at the 10th and 25th percentiles, as among low-wage men, have fallen since 1979. But since low-wage women have been increasing the hours they work per week, their weekly wages have been stable. The most significant wage growth has occurred among high-wage women at the 75th and 90th percentiles, whose hourly wages rose by 1.4% to 1.5% per year between 1979 and 1988.

The Male/Female Wage Gap

From 1979 to 1988, the median hourly wage for men fell 5% while the median hourly wage for women rose 5.8% (Tables 3.6 and 3.7). This has led to a reduction in the hourly wage gap between men and women by 7.1 percentage points, from 62.3% in 1979 to 69.4% (**Table 3.8**).

This narrowing of the male/female wage gap is the result of both improvements in real hourly wages for women and real wage reductions for men. Table 3.8 provides an assessment of how much the narrowing of the male/female wage differential is due to rising real wages for women, and how much is due to the real wage loss of men. If real wages among men had not fallen but had remained at their 1979

Hourly wages among low-wage women . . . have fallen since 1979. But since low-wage women have been increasing the hours they work per week, their weekly wages have been stable.

TABLE 3.8

Changes in the Gender Wage Differential, 1979–1988

(1989 Dollars)

| Year | Median Hourly Wage | | |
	Male	Female	Ratio
1979	$11.02	$6.87	62.3%
1988	10.47	7.27	69.4
1988*	11.02	7.27	66.0
Change, 1979–1988	$-0.55	$0.40	7.1% pts.
Contribution to Narrower Gap**	48%	52%	100.0%

*Wages assuming no decline in the real male median hourly wage between 1979 and 1988.

**Male contribution to narrower differential is the difference between the actual differential and the differential with no decline in male wages.

81

TABLE 3.9

Shares of Workers By Wage Level and Gender, 1979–1987

Share of Workers Earning:*

	Less Than the Poverty Line	Poverty to Two Times Poverty	Two Times to Three Times Poverty	Three Times Poverty and Above	Total
All Workers					
1979	25.7%	39.7%	20.4%	14.2%	100.0%
1987	31.5	37.9	17.9	12.7	100.0
Change, 1979–87	5.8	–1.8	–2.5	–1.5	
Men					
1979	17.8%	33.2%	26.9%	22.1%	100.0%
1987	24.4	34.5	22.1	19.0	100.0
Change, 1979–87	6.6	1.3	–4.8	–3.1	
Women					
1979	35.2%	47.6%	12.6%	4.5%	100.0%
1987	39.5	41.7	13.2	5.5	100.0
Change, 1979–87	4.3	–5.9	0.6	1.0	

*Defined according to whether someone working full-time, year-round at a particular hourly wage can maintain a family of four at once, twice, or three times the poverty threshold.

> **48% of the increased equality between men's and women's wages achieved since 1979 was due to falling real wages among men and 52% was due to rising women's real wages. Even after this progress women still earned one-third less than men.**

level, the wage gap would have closed by 3.7 rather than the actual 7.1 percentage points. Thus, 48% of the increased equality between men's and women's wages achieved since 1979 was due to falling real wages among men and 52% was due to rising women's real wages (3.7% divided by 7.1%). Even after this progress, of course, women still earned one-third less than men.

The Expansion of Low-Wage Jobs

Another useful way of characterizing changes in the wage structure is to examine the trend in the proportion of workers earning low, middle, and high wages. These trends are presented in **Table 3.9** for all workers and for men and women. The workforce is divided into four wage groups based on multiples of the "poverty wage level," or the hourly wage a full-time, year-round worker must earn to sustain a family of four at the poverty threshold. Thus, workers are assigned to a wage group according to whether they earned less than the poverty wage level, more than the poverty wage but less than twice the poverty wage, two to three times the poverty wage, and three times the poverty wage and above.

The data in Table 3.9 and **Figure 3D** show that there was a significant expansion of workers earning poverty wages between 1979 and 1987. In 1979, 25.7% of the workforce earned poverty level wages. By 1987, 31.5% of the workforce earned poverty level wages. Thus, an additional 5.8% of the workforce earned poverty level wages in 1987 than in 1979. There was a downward shift in the entire wage structure as there were proportionately fewer workers in each of the middle- and high-wage groups in 1987 than in 1979.

Women are much more likely to earn low wages than men. In 1979, 35.2% of women earned poverty level wages, nearly double the 17.8% of men earning such low wages. Women are also much less likely to earn very high wages. In 1979, only 4.5% of women but 22.1% of men

In 1979, 25.7% of the workforce earned poverty level wages. By 1987, 31.5% of the workforce earned poverty level wages.

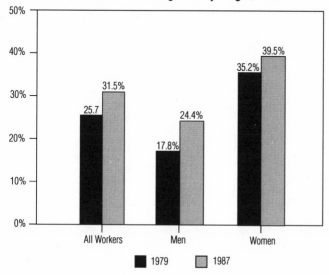

FIGURE 3D

Percent of Workers Earning Poverty Wages, 1979-1987

TABLE 3.10

Shares of Workers By Wage Level and Race/Ethnic Group, 1979–1987

Share of Workers Earning:*

	Less Than the Poverty Line	Poverty to Two Times Poverty	Two Times to Three Times Poverty	Three Times Poverty and Above	Total
Whites					
1979	24.3%	39.2%	21.0%	15.4%	100.0%
1987	29.3	37.7	18.9	14.0	100.0
Change,					
1979–87	5.0	–1.5	–2.1	–1.4	
Blacks					
1979	33.9%	41.2%	17.7%	7.2%	100.0%
1987	40.6	39.5	14.3	5.6	100.0
Change,					
1979–87	6.7	–1.7	–3.4	–1.6	
Hispanics					
1979	31.7%	43.9%	16.4%	8.0%	100.0%
1987	42.1	39.2	12.3	6.5	100.0
Change,					
1979–87	10.4	–4.7	–4.1	–1.5	

*Defined according to whether someone working full-time, year-round at a particular hourly wage can maintain a family of four at once, twice, or three times the poverty threshold.

earned at least three times the poverty wage level.

There has been an expansion of low-wage employment among *both* men and women, but the larger shift downward has been among men—whose low-wage share of employment rose 6.6 percentage points from 17.8% in 1979 to 24.4% in 1987. Since 1979, the share of women earning low wages grew by 4.3 percentage points, so that by 1987 nearly 40% of women workers earned no more than a poverty level wage.

Among men, the overall changes in the wage structure have meant proportionately fewer high-wage and more low-wage male workers. For instance, there was an increased proportion of men earning from one to two times the poverty level wage but a shrinking proportion of men in the two highest wage groups.

The picture among women is mixed. There was job growth at the high end among women, as the shares of women earning at least two or three times the poverty wage increased. But most of the shifting of the structure of women's wages was downward as low-wage jobs for women expanded far more (a rise of 4.3 percentage points) than high-wage jobs (a rise of 1.6 percentage points).

Table 3.10 shows that this expansion of low-wage jobs has occurred among white, black, and Hispanic workers. The downward shift in wages was greatest among minorities, especially Hispanics. Even before this downward shift in the wage structure, minorities were far more likely to earn low wages; in 1979, 33.9% of blacks, 31.7% of Hispanics, and 24.3% of whites earned poverty level wages. By 1987, an *additional* 10.4%, 6.7%, and 5% of, respectively, the Hispanic, black, and white workforces were low-wage earners.

At the other end, proportionately fewer workers of every race/ethnic group in 1987 earned relatively high wages of at least twice the poverty level. For instance, the share of white workers with wages more than twice the poverty level fell 3.5 percentage points from 1979 to 1987. There was an even greater loss of high-wage jobs among minorities, even though minority workers were already far less likely to be high-wage workers in 1979 (and even more so in 1987).

Benefit Reduction

This section examines the trends in the provision of fringe benefits. As we saw earlier in Table 3.2, the real value

> *[The] expansion of low-wage jobs has occurred among white, black, and Hispanic workers. The downward shift in wages was greatest among minorities, especially Hispanics.*

TABLE 3.11

Hourly Benefit Costs, By Type, 1980–89

(1989 Dollars)

| Year | Total Fringes** | Pension and Savings | Health Insurance Adjusted for Inflation in: | | Others |
			All Goods and Services*	Health Insurance*	
1980***	$ 1.50	$ 0.74	$ 0.72	$ 1.63	$ 0.04
1989	1.29	0.42	0.85	0.85	0.02
Change,					
1980–89					
Dollars	$-0.21	$-0.32	$ 0.13	$-0.78	$-0.02
Total Percent	–13.8%	–43.5%	18.8%	–47.9%	–46.2%

*The value of life insurance, and sickness and accident insurance is included but comprises only 10% of the total. The two 1980 inflation-adjusted measures of real insurance costs per hour worked differ because health insurance prices rose about two times faster than average prices.

**Exclusive of payroll taxes.

***Earliest data available.

FIGURE 3E

Hourly Benefits by Type, 1980-1989

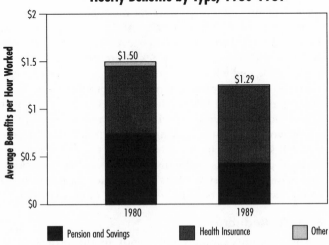

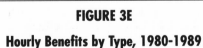

of both wages and fringe benefits has fallen in recent years. In the 1980s, employers reduced pension and health coverage and provided fewer days off with pay. These benefit reductions have affected workers across the wage scale, but again, low-wage workers have experienced the greatest fall-off in health and pension coverage.

Table 3.11 and **Figure 3E** examine the trend in employers' provision of the major benefit plans, pensions, and health insurance between 1980 (the earliest available data) and 1989. The average employer contribution for pension and savings plans was 43.5% less in 1989 than in 1980, a drop of $0.32 per hour.

Measured by average inflation, employer-provided health insurance benefits rose 18.8%, or by $0.13 per hour worked. However, the far faster inflation in health insurance *costs* means that the real health insurance coverage provided per hour worked actually declined by 47.9% from 1980 to 1989. That is, employers did not increase their spending on health insurance as fast as health insurance prices were rising, so the quantity and quality of health insurance provided by employers has fallen drastically since 1980.

Along with a widening inequality of wages, there has also been a widening inequality in the receipt and value of the major fringe benefits. The share of workers covered by their employer's health insurance plan fell 5 percentage points, from 61.9% in 1979 to 56.9% in 1987 (**Table 3.12** and

Employers did not increase their spending on health insurance as fast as health insurance prices were rising, so the quantity and quality of health insurance provided by employers has fallen drastically since 1980.

TABLE 3.12

Health Insurance Coverage By Wage Fourth

Year	All Workers	Wage Fourth*:			
		Bottom Fourth	Second Fourth	Third Fourth	Top Fourth
Has Employer Health Insurance Plan (%)					
1979	61.9%	27.9%	56.4%	76.6%	86.3%
1987	56.9	20.6	51.8	72.5	82.6
Change, 1979–1987	–5.0	–7.3	–4.6	–4.1	–3.7

*Based on distribution of hourly wages.

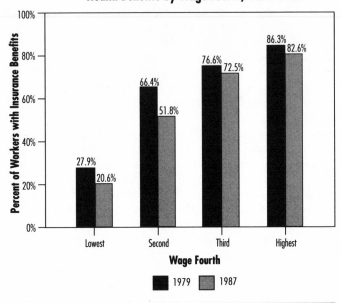

FIGURE 3F

Health Benefits by Wage Fourth, 1979-1987

Percent of Workers with Insurance Benefits

Lowest: 27.9% (1979), 20.6% (1987)
Second: 66.4% (1979), 51.8% (1987)
Third: 76.6% (1979), 72.5% (1987)
Highest: 86.3% (1979), 82.6% (1987)

Wage Fourth

■ 1979 ▨ 1987

TABLE 3.13

Pension Coverage By Wage Fourth

Year	All Workers	Wage Fourth*:			
		Bottom Fourth	Second Fourth	Third Fourth	Top Fourth
Employer Pension Plan Available (%)					
1979	53.6%	22.5%	46.1%	66.5%	79.1%
1987	53.0	24.2	45.4	64.6	78.0
Change, 1979–1987	–0.6	1.7	–0.7	–1.9	–1.1
Included In Pension Plan (%)					
1979	85.1%	59.5%	76.4%	88.2%	94.4%
1987	78.3	40.7	68.5	83.5	90.6
Change, 1979–1987	–6.8	–18.8	–7.9	–4.7	–3.8

*Based on distribution of hourly wages.

Figure 3F). Among the lowest paid fourth of the workforce, however, the proportion of workers offered an employer health insurance plan fell 7.3 percentage points, so that by 1987 only 20.6% had any coverage. The higher the wage the more likely one is to have employer-provided health coverage. Nevertheless, proportionately fewer workers in each segment of the wage scale had employer provided health coverage in 1987 than in 1979.

There was only a slight erosion of the *availability* of pension plans between 1979 and 1987 (**Table 3.13** and Figure 3F). In fact, by 1987, low-wage workers were slightly more, and high-wage workers were slightly less likely to have an employer with a pension plan. However, vesting and other requirements frequently exclude some workers from participating in plans that employers can make available to others. Between 1979 and 1987 there was a sizeable 6.8% drop in the proportion of workers actually *included* in their employers' pension plans. This was especially true for workers in the bottom fourth of the wage ladder. In 1987, only 40.7% of these low-wage workers were allowed into their employers' pension plans, down from 59.5% in 1979. On the other end of the wage scale, 90.6% of the workers in the highest fourth were included in their employers' pensions plans.

Workers are also receiving less time off for vacations and holidays (**Table 3.14**). The longest historical comparison

Between 1979 and 1987 there was a sizeable 6.8% drop in the proportion of workers included in their employers' pension plans.

TABLE 3.14

Trends in Days Off With Pay, 1947–1988

Year	Number of Days Off With Pay Per Year*	
	Nonfarm Business	Manufacturing
1947	N/A	15.9 days
1967	N/A	17.9
1973	N/A	20.5
1979	N/A	23.1
1981	19.8 days	22.9
1988	17.9	21.8

*Assuming 2,080 hours paid per year. Days off would include, for instance, holiday, vacation, sick, and funeral leave. Earliest data for nonfarm sector are for 1981.

TABLE 3.15

Change in Days Off With Pay, 1980-89

	Total	White Collar	Blue Collar	Service Workers
Pay For Time Off*				
1980	$ 1.16	$ 1.38	$ 1.06	$ 0.50
1989	1.00	1.30	0.87	0.34
Change, 1980-89				
Dollars	$-0.16	$-0.08	$-0.19	$-0.16
Percent	-13.6%	-5.8%	-18.0%	-32.0%
Days Off With Pay**				
1980	26.5	28.8	24.6	19.9
1989	25.0	27.5	22.8	16.1
Change, 1980-89				
Days	-1.5	-1.3	-1.7	-3.8
Percent	-5.6%	-4.5%	-7.1%	-19.1%

*The cost per hour worked of all pay for time off. For instance, one week's vacation pay at $10 an hour for 40 hours is $400. Spread over 2,000 hours of work, the cost of this vacation pay is $0.20 an hour.

**Holidays, vacation, and so on.

TABLE 3.16

International Comparison of Manufacturing Workers' Hours, 1987

	Total Annual Hours Worked	Paid Time Off (Days)		
		National Holidays	Paid Leave	Other Absence
Japan	2,168	19	9	3
United States	1,949	11	19	6
United Kingdom	1,947	8	23	N/A
France	1,645	8	26	16
West Germany	1,642	12	29	16

available is for manufacturing workers. For these employees, the number of paid days off rose from 15.9 per year in 1947 to 23.1 days in 1979. But this trend towards increased time off with pay was reversed in the 1980s. In 1988, the average manufacturing worker enjoyed 21.8 days off with pay, 1.1 days less than in 1979. For the nonfarm business workforce as a whole, there was a loss of 1.9 days off with pay, with a drop from 19.8 days in 1979 to 17.9 days in 1988.

A different data source provides confirmation of an erosion of paid time off since 1980 (**Table 3.15**). From 1980 to 1989, employer costs for paid days off fell by 13.6% for all workers and by 18% and 32%, respectively, for blue collar and service workers. These lower employer costs imply a reduction of 1.5 days off with pay for the average worker since 1980 and a whopping 3.8-day reduction for service workers.

Workers in other industrialized countries are provided more paid time off than are U.S. workers (**Table 3.16**). The only workers to have less paid time off each year than U.S. workers are Japanese workers, who also work substantially more hours per year.

. . . a reduction of 1.5 days off with pay for the average worker . . . and a whopping 3.8- day reduction for service workers.

91

TABLE 3.17

Real Wage Trends By Education Level, 1963–1987

| | Educational Attainment | | | | |
Year	Grades 8–11	High School	Some College	College or More	Change in College/High School Wage Differential
Change in Weekly Wage*					
1963–71	18.6%	18.2%	17.8%	29.0%	14.2% pts.
1971–79	0.3	1.4	–3.4	–9.6	–18.3
1979–87	– 6.3	–4.0	1.5	8.0	18.7
Change in Relative Supply**					
1963–71	–35.2%	7.6%	20.3%	17.8%	
1971–79	–48.6	–4.8	23.3	24.1	
1979–87	–41.9	–4.8	6.7	15.6	

*Weekly wage changes based on indices which hold fixed the composition of employment by gender and experience.

**Change in log share of aggregate hours worked. A group's relative size in the labor market is growing (shrinking) in importance to the extent the number is positive (negative) and large.

FIGURE 3G

Changes in Wages by Education, 1979-1987

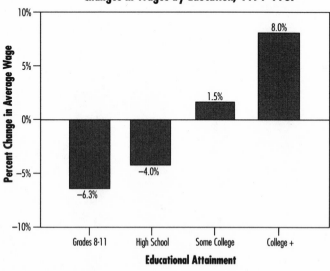

92

The Growing Education Wage Gap

This section reviews how the overall deterioration of real wages has affected workers with various levels of education and experience and begins our analysis of the underlying causes of the growing wage inequality.

Table 3.17 and **Figure 3G** present the changes in real weekly wages for workers at various education levels, along with a measure of the changes in the relative supply of workers at each education level for the period 1963 to 1987. The study from which these data are drawn only provides data for 1963, 1971, 1979, and 1987. Over the entire period, 1963–1987, the wages of educated workers rose faster than those of workers with less education. However, although the wages of college graduates grew much more rapidly than those of other workers in the 1960s and 1980s, they fell by 9.6% in the 1970s.

These trends have led to large fluctuations in the wage gap between college and high school graduates (Table 3.17). For instance, the wage gap between college and high school graduates grew strongly from 1963 to 1971, up 14.2 percentage points, fell 18.3 percentage points from 1971 to 1979, and then rose by 18.7 percentage points between 1979 and 1987. As a result, by 1987 the wages of college graduates relative to high school graduates were higher than at any time since 1963.

This trend of increased economic returns to the college educated does not reflect rapid wage growth for college graduates. From 1979 to 1987, their wages grew by 8%, only about one-fourth as fast as college graduate wages rose in the 1960s (Table 3.17). In fact, the average college graduate earned less in 1987 than in 1971. Underlying the rising return to education is an absolute fall in the real wages of less educated workers. An average high school graduate in 1987 earned 4% less than in 1979, and less than in 1971. Thus, the increase in the returns to education since 1979 does not mean, as some analyses have implied, that there has been an overall improvement in labor market performance or that there has been a large increase in better paying higher skilled jobs. Since average real wages for less educated and low-wage workers have deteriorated, it is unlikely that the skills demanded of these average workers rose in the 1980s. Rather, the increase in the college/high school wage gap reflects a modest increase in the demand for college educated workers,

Underlying the rising return to education is an absolute fall in the real wages of less educated workers.

93

TABLE 3.18

Real Wage Trends By Education Level and Gender, 1963–1987

	Educational Attainment				
Period	Grades 8–11	High School	Some College	College or More	Change in College/High School Wage Differential
Change in Weekly Wages*					
Men					
1963–71	19.4%	18.7%	17.1%	30.0%	13.9% pts.
1971–79	–0.3	1.5	–4.2	–10.4	–18.7
1979–87	–7.3	–7.4	–1.3	7.0	22.0
Change in Weekly Wages*					
Women					
1963–71	15.8%	16.9%	20.1%	25.3%	10.9% pts.
1971–79	3.2	1.2	–1.0	–6.5	–12.3
1979–87	–2.6	5.1	9.8	12.0	9.8

*Weekly wage changes based on indices that hold fixed the composition of employment by experience.

TABLE 3.19

Distribution of Earners, By Age and Education Level, 1987

	All Earners Ages 25–64			Earners Ages 25–34		
Education Level	Men	Women	Total	Men	Women	Total
Less Than 4 Years High School	16.4%	12.6%	14.7%	13.5%	8.4%	11.2%
4 Years High School	37.2	43.4	40.0	40.6	42.3	41.3
1 to 3 Years College	18.7	21.2	19.8	20.3	23.9	21.9
4 Years or More College	27.6	22.8	25.5	25.6	25.5	25.5
All Persons with Earnings	100.0	100.0	100.0	100.0	100.0	100.0

not an across-the-board, economy-wide trend toward higher skilled and higher wage jobs.

Supply and demand analysis suggests that if demand relations are stable, then the group whose supply is growing fastest should have the smallest growth in wages. In fact, the large relative increase in educated workers in the 1970s helps explain the falling real wages of college educated workers in that period (Table 3.17). However, changes in the number of college educated workers cannot explain the fast growth in the wages of these workers since they had the fastest growth of both wages *and* numbers. This means that the rise in the college/high school wage gap can only be explained by changes in the jobs available to these different groups of workers, i.e., changes in demand. Factors that affect the demand for workers are technological change, shifts in employment by occupation and industry, and international trade.

Likewise, since the number of noncollege educated workers grew relatively slowly in the 1980s, one would have expected, other things being equal, that their wages would have risen relatively *quickly*: in fact, their wages have fallen. Thus, the deterioration of wages among less educated workers must be related to changes in the job structure—the type and number of jobs available to them.

There have been more dramatic changes in educational differentials among men than among women (**Table 3.18**). For instance, the college/high school wage differential rose twice as much in the 1980s for men as for women, after having fallen 50% more for men than for women in the 1970s. This differing pattern of changes in the college/high school wage gap for men and women suggests that changes in the types of jobs available to men are the primary force driving the overall growth in these education wage differentials.

A wage pattern providing wage growth for college educated workers and wage stagnation or erosion for those without a college degree means that the vast majority of workers have not improved their wage position in the 1980s. The proportion of the workforce on the losing end of the higher education wage differential is far greater than that reaping the benefits. In 1987, only 25.5% of the workforce aged 25 to 64 had completed college (**Table 3.19**

> *The rise in the college/high school wage gap can only be explained by changes in the jobs available to these different groups of workers.*

95

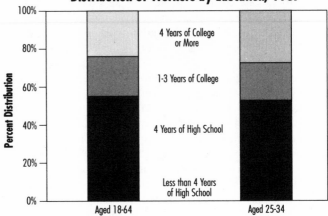

FIGURE 3H

Distribution of Workers by Education, 1987

Percent Distribution

- 4 Years of College or More
- 1-3 Years of College
- 4 Years of High School
- Less than 4 Years of High School

Aged 18-64   Aged 25-34

TABLE 3.20

Real Wage Trends By Work Experience, 1963–1987

	Years of Work Experience							
Years	1–5	6–10	11–15	16–20	21–25	26–30	31–35	36–40
Change in Weekly Wage*								
1963–71	18.6%	24.6%	22.4%	24.5%	20.7%	22.9%	20.0%	17.7%
1971–79	–3.5	–7.6	–5.2	–4.0	–4.2	–2.5	1.5	2.0
1979–87	–6.5	–2.8	–5.3	–2.9	0.0	1.7	–1.7	–1.5

*Weekly wage changes based on indices that hold fixed the composition of employment by gender and education.

and **Figure 3H**). The educational groups experiencing falling wages since 1979 (those with a high school degree or less) comprised 54.7% of the workforce. Another 21.9% of the workforce, those with from 1 to 3 years of college, had a minimal 1.5% growth in wages from 1979 to 1987.

Young Workers Have Been Hurt Most

The wages of younger workers have been falling since 1971 whereas the wages of older workers have either fallen at a slower pace or have risen modestly (**Table 3.20**). As a result, there have been significant changes in the wage differentials between younger and older workers. The real weekly wages of workers with from 1 to 15 years experience fell roughly 10% since 1971. In contrast, the wages of workers with from 26 to 30 years experience were about the same in 1987 as in 1979.

The wages of younger workers have been falling since 1971 whereas the wages of older workers have either fallen at a slower pace or have risen modestly.

TABLE 3.21

Weekly Wage Trends By Education Level and Work Experience, 1963–1987

	Men		Women	
	1–5 Years Experience	26–30 Years Experience	1–5 Years Experience	26–30 Years Experience
High School Graduates				
Weekly Wage (1987 Dollars)				
1963	$248.91	$406.78	$185.37	$213.85
1971	296.29	480.55	220.75	259.86
1979	298.61	487.99	206.60	266.51
1987	244.94	477.99	199.36	296.51
Dollar Change				
1963–71	$ 47.38	$ 73.77	$ 35.38	$ 46.01
1971–79	2.32	7.44	−14.15	6.65
1979–87	−53.67	−10.00	−7.24	30.00
Percent Change				
1963–71	19.0%	18.1%	19.1%	21.5%
1971–79	0.8	1.5	−6.4	2.6
1979–87	−18.0	−2.0	−3.5	11.3
College Graduates or More				
Weekly Wage (1987 Dollars)				
1963	$382.89	$596.72	$286.57	$358.78
1971	462.67	792.54	341.10	433.44
1979	413.17	745.31	313.03	419.88
1987	460.42	794.14	348.16	446.74
Dollar Change				
1963–71	$ 79.78	$195.82	$ 54.53	$ 74.66
1971–79	−49.50	−47.23	−28.07	−13.56
1979–87	47.25	48.83	35.13	26.86
Percent Change				
1963–71	20.8%	32.8%	19.0%	20.8%
1971–79	−10.7	−6.0	−8.2	−3.1
1979–87	11.4	6.6	11.2	6.4

Since the wages of both younger and noncollege educated workers have fallen most rapidly, it follows that the wages of workers who are both young and noncollege educated have dramatically fallen (**Table 3.21** and **Figure 3I**). The weekly wage of a young male high school graduate in 1987 was 18% less than that for the equivalent worker in 1979, a drop of $53.67 in weekly pay to $244.94. This dramatic 2.1% annual drop in wages reversed all of the wage growth among young male high school graduates from 1963 to 1979. As a result, the wage of a young male high school graduate was lower in 1987 than in 1963, nearly 25 years earlier. The wages earned by young noncollege educated women have been falling since 1971, so that weekly wages in 1987 were just $14 more per week than in 1963.

This deterioration of wages among young noncollege educated workers affects the majority of young workers, since only a small portion of the workforce has college degrees. As Table 3.19 shows, 54.1% of men and 50.7% of women earners aged 25 to 34 (an age range where most persons have completed their education) attained no more

The weekly wage of a young male high school graduate in 1987 was 18% less than that for the equivalent worker in 1979 . . .

FIGURE 3I

Wages of Workers with 1-5 Years of Experience By Sex and Education, 1963-1987

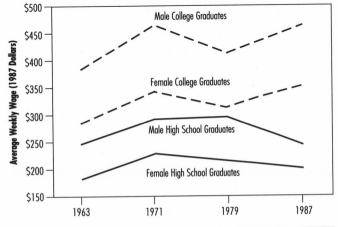

TABLE 3.22

Effect of Structural Employment Shifts on Pay Levels, 1980–89

Occupation Group	1989 Pay Levels With Employment Composition of:		Effect of 1980–89 Employment Composition Shift		Actual Change, 1980–89
	1980*	1989**	Dollars	Percent	
All Workers					
Wages	$12.45	$11.72	$-0.73	-5.8%	-9.3%
Benefits	1.45	1.29	-0.16	-11.2	-13.8
Compensation	13.90	13.01	-0.89	-6.4	-9.8
White Collar					
Wages	$14.16	$13.88	$-0.28	-2.0%	-2.3%
Benefits	1.50	1.42	-0.08	-5.1	-10.4
Compensation	15.66	15.30	-0.36	-2.3	-3.1
Blue Collar					
Wages	$12.04	$11.31	$-0.73	-6.1%	-12.0%
Benefits	1.68	1.50	-0.18	-10.4	-7.8
Compensation	13.72	12.81	-0.91	-6.6	-11.6
Service Workers					
Wages	$ 6.43	$ 5.94	$-0.49	-7.7%	-18.2%
Benefits	.57	.43	-0.14	-24.4	-26.1
Compensation	7.00	6.37	-0.63	-9.0	-18.8

*March 1989 pay levels using 1980 Census weights for sizes of industries and occupations.
**March 1989 pay levels using current 1989 weights for sizes of industries and occupations.

than a high school degree. 21.9% of this age group had completed some college and only about one in four of them had graduated from college. The wages of those completing some college are more comparable to those of high school than of college graduates.

The overall situation of young workers and families is explored further in Chapter 7.

Trade and Structural Changes in the Labor Market

The 1980s was a decade of rapid structural change. Increased international competition and large trade deficits were major forces influencing labor market developments. Technological and occupational changes, the shift towards smaller workplaces and firms, deunionization, deindustrialization, and the restructuring of employment towards two-tier wage systems and contingent work (considered in Chapter 4) all have affected the types of available jobs.

Many of these changes affect pay levels by changing the distribution of jobs across occupations and industries. Their effect on pay levels over the 1980–89 period is presented in **Table 3.22**. Columns one and two show the level of pay for several occupational groupings in 1989, and the level of pay that would have prevailed in 1989 if the 1980 distribution of employment had been maintained. The net effect of changes in the distribution of jobs was to lower the average hourly compensation of all workers by $0.89, or by 6.4%. These structural shifts led to larger percentage reductions in benefits (–13.8%) than in wages (–9.3%). Overall, structural shifts account for 6.4%, or two-thirds, of the total 9.8% reduction in hourly compensation between 1980 and 1989.

The largest dollar loss due to structural changes in employment was among blue collar workers, whose hourly compensation fell $0.91, or 6.6%. Service workers, however, lost the most in percentage terms, a cut of 9% in hourly compensation.

The effect of changes in the distribution of jobs was to lower the average hourly compensation of all workers by $0.89, or by 6.4%.

101

TABLE 3.23

Demand Shifts From Changes in Trade Deficit and Domestic Industry and Occupation Shifts, 1973–1985

| | Change in Relative Demand* Due to: | | | |
| | Trade Deficit** | | Domestic Shifts | |
Group	1973–79	1979–85	1973–79	1979–85
Men				
Drop outs (8–11 years)	−0.2%	−1.5%	−6.0%	−5.2%
High School Graduates (12 years)	−0.1	−0.7	−3.7	−2.9
Some College (13–15 years)	0.2	0.4	−0.3	1.2
College Graduates (16+ years)	0.4	1.5	5.0	3.1
Women				
Drop outs (8–11 years)	−0.8%	−3.8%	−6.7%	1.2%
High School Graduates (12 years)	−0.2	−0.3	2.3	1.8
Some College (13–15 years)	−0.1	1.1	7.5	3.6
College Graduates (16+ years)	−0.1	1.5	5.5	1.1

*Change in log relative demand. A negative (positive) number means a reduced (increased) relative demand for a type of worker.

**Demand shifts from trade deficit refer to demand shifts from trade deficit in manufactured goods.

The growth of a large national trade deficit accompanied the growing global competition in the 1980s and was responsible for the loss of millions of jobs and pressure for wage moderation, if not wage cuts, in many American industries. As shown in **Table 3.23**, it was precisely the workers most adversely affected by trade developments who experienced the greatest wage deterioration in the 1980s. These data show the change in the relative demand for each group of workers due to both trade and domestic factors between 1973 and 1985. For instance, the growth in the trade deficit between 1979 and 1985 led to a reduced demand for male high school graduates (down 0.7% in relative demand) and an increased demand for male college graduates (up 1.5% in relative demand).

Trade developments shifted the availability of work (the relative demand for labor) towards more educated workers and away from noncollege educated workers in manufacturing and related industries, particularly for men. Unemployment and lower wages for noncollege educated males employed in manufacturing spilled over to adversely affect similar workers employed in other sectors, as workers displaced from manufacturing jobs were forced to compete for work in other sectors of the economy.

Domestic factors alone resulted in less need for noncollege educated men after 1973. However, these domestic factors caused a *slower* erosion of the demand for noncollege educated men in 1979–1985 than in 1973–79. Consequently, domestic factors cannot explain the accelerated erosion of wages that occurred for these workers after 1979. However, the growth of the trade deficit after 1979 caused the overall demand shifts against noncollege educated men to continue at the same 1973–79 pace. The trade deficit also led to a lower demand shift for some women, particularly those without a high school degree.

The flip side of this decrease in demand for noncollege educated workers has been the growing relative demand for college educated workers. Domestic factors alone would have led to a slower growth in demand for college educated workers in the 1979–1985 period. The employment shifts associated with the trade deficit, however, raised demand for college educated workers in the 1980s. The combination of the lower growth in college educated workers and the growth in demand for them induced by the trade deficit

> *It was precisely the workers most adversely affected by trade developments who experienced the greatest wage deterioration in the 1980s.*

103

TABLE 3.24
Employment Growth By Sector, 1979–1989
(In Thousands)

Industry Sector	Employment			Industry Share of Job Growth	Median Weekly Earnings, 1989
	1979	1989	Job Growth		
Goods Producing	26,461	25,634	– 827	– 4.4%	
Mining	958	722	– 236	– 1.3	$565
Construction	4,463	5,300	837	4.5	431
Manufacturing	21,040	19,612	–1,428	– 7.6	415
Durable Goods	12,760	11,536	–1,224	– 6.5	445
Nondurable Goods	8,280	8,076	– 204	– 1.1	373
Service Producing	63,363	82,947	19,584	104.4%	
Transportation, Communications, Utilities	5,136	5,705	569	3.0	$502
Wholesale	5,204	6,234	1,030	5.5	412
Retail	14,989	19,575	4,586	24.4	276
Finance, Insurance, Real Estate	4,975	6,814	1,839	9.8	406
Services	17,112	26,892	9,780	52.1	357
Government	15,947	17,728	1,781	9.5	472
Total	89,823	108,581	18,758	100.0	

TABLE 3.25
Changes in Employment Share By Sector, 1979–1989

Industry Sector	Share of Employment		Change in Employment Share, 1979–1989
	1979	1989	
Goods Producing	29.5%	23.6%	–5.9%
Mining	1.1	0.7	–0.4
Construction	5.0	4.9	–0.1
Manufacturing	23.4	18.1	–5.4
Durable Goods	14.2	10.6	–3.6
Nondurable Goods	9.2	7.4	–1.8
Service Producing	70.5%	76.4%	5.8%
Transportation, Communication, Utilities	5.7	5.3	–0.5
Wholesale	5.8	5.7	–0.1
Retail	16.7	18.0	1.3
Finance, Insurance, Real Estate	5.5	6.3	0.7
Services	19.1	24.8	5.7
Government	17.8	16.3	–1.4
Total	100.0	100.0	0.0

caused the relatively fast growth of wages among college educated workers in the 1980s.

The Shift to Low-Paying Industries

The employment shift to low-wage sectors in the 1980s was a consequence of trade deficits and deindustrialization as well as stagnant or falling productivity growth in service sector industries. This section examines the significant erosion of wages and compensation that resulted.

Recent employment growth by major industry sector is presented in **Table 3.24**. The 18.8 million (net) jobs created over the last 10 years involved a loss of roughly 1.7 million manufacturing and mining jobs and an increase of 19.6 million jobs in the service sector. The largest amount of job growth (14.4 million) was in the two lowest paying industries—retail trade and services (business, personal, and health). In fact, these two industries accounted for 76.5% of all the (net) new jobs over the last 10 years.

The extent of the shift to low-wage industries is more evident in an analysis of changes in the *shares* of the workforce in various sectors (**Table 3.25**). Several high-wage sectors such as construction, transportation, wholesale, communications, and government increased employment in the 1980s but still were a smaller share of overall employment in 1989 than in 1979. A lower share of employment in these high-wage sectors led to a lower average wage. Overall, the share of the workforce working in the low-wage services and retail trade industries was 7 percentage points higher in 1989 than in 1979. The parallel trend was the 7.7 percentage point drop in the share of the workforce in high-paying industries such as manufacturing, mining, government, transportation, communications, and utilities.

[There was a] 7.7 percentage point drop in the share of the workforce in high-paying industries such as manufacturing, mining, government, transportation, communications, and utilities.

TABLE 3.26

Industry Pay Differentials, 1989

Pay	Goods-Producing Industries	Service-Producing Industries	Goods-Producing Differential*	
			Dollars	Percent
Hourly Compensation**	$15.60	$11.96	$3.64	30.4%
Wages	13.70	10.92	2.78	25.5
Benefits	1.90	1.04	0.86	82.7
a) Insurance	1.28	0.68	0.60	88.2
b) Pension/Savings	0.57	0.36	0.21	58.3
c) Other Benefits	0.05	0.00	0.05	N/A

*Dollars and percent by which pay in goods-producing industries exceeds that in service-producing industries.

**Excluding payroll taxes.

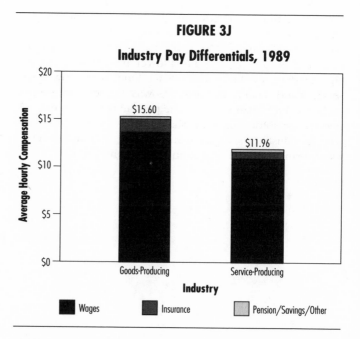

FIGURE 3J

Industry Pay Differentials, 1989

Table 3.26 and Figure 3J illustrate why the shift from goods-producing jobs to service-producing jobs led to lower pay. In 1989, hourly compensation in the goods sector was $15.60, an amount $3.64, or 30.4%, higher than the $11.96 hourly compensation paid in the service sector. The differential was largest in terms of benefits: goods-producing employers spent nearly twice as much on insurance and contributed 58% more to pension plans.

The groups that experienced the most rapid wage deterioration in the 1980s were also the ones most adversely affected by the shift from high-paying to low-paying industries. In **Table 3.27**, each educational level is examined for the proportion of total hours worked by men in each sector. In 1980, 31.4% of the hours of male high school graduates and 45.3% of the hours of males with just 8–11 years of education were worked in manufacturing (Table 3.27). A

The groups that experienced the most rapid wage deterioration in the 1980s were also the ones most adversely affected by the shift from high-paying to low-paying industries.

TABLE 3.27

Distribution of Hours Worked By Men
By Sector and Education, 1980*

Sector	8–11	High School Grad	Some College	College or More
Agriculture/Mining	10.1%	6.7%	4.4%	3.3%
Construction	15.0	11.9	8.4	3.5
Manufacturing	45.3	31.4	25.4	18.7
Low Tech.	11.5	7.0	4.4	2.7
Basic	18.7	20.4	16.5	11.1
High Tech.	2.8	4.0	4.5	4.9
Commun/Transp/Utilities	9.3	10.9	10.1	4.6
Wholesale	4.7	5.3	7.4	5.7
Retail	12.2	13.4	14.1	7.4
Finance/Business/Health Services	4.8	6.8	13.4	28.2
Education/Welfare	2.4	1.8	2.7	18.4
Public Administration	2.4	6.3	9.0	7.6
Other Services	6.2	5.5	5.3	2.5
Total	100.0%	100.0%	100.0%	100.0%
Distribution of Male Earners By Education Level, 1980**				
	22.7%	38.3%	18.6%	20.5%

*Data are averages for 1979–1981.

**Those with less than eight years of education, comprising 9.6% of the total, are included in the 8–11 years category.

107

TABLE 3.28
Distribution of Hours Worked By Women
By Sector and Education, 1980*

Sector	8–11	High School Grad	Some College	College or More
Agriculture/Mining	2.4%	1.7%	1.5%	1.0%
Construction	0.9	1.5	1.2	0.7
Manufacturing	36.2	20.8	12.3	6.5
Low Tech.	18.1	6.5	2.7	1.1
Basic	15.3	11.7	7.1	4.0
High Tech.	2.8	2.6	2.5	1.4
Comm/Transp/Utilities	2.1	5.5	5.5	3.1
Wholesale	1.8	3.3	3.5	2.5
Retail	21.4	19.2	13.9	8.1
Finance/Business/Health Services	15.9	28.8	40.3	28.2
Education/Welfare	6.0	7.5	10.0	43.5
Public Administration	2.1	5.6	7.1	4.5
Other Services	11.4	6.3	4.8	2.0
Total	100.0%	100.0%	100.0%	100.0%

Distribution of Female Earners By Education Level, 1980**

	17.8%	46.4%	19.8%	16.0%

*Data are averages for 1979–1981.

**Those with less than eight years of education, comprising 9.6% of the total, are included in the 8–11 years category.

As with men, a majority of women had education levels not exceeding a high school degree in 1980.

significant portion of the hours worked by noncollege educated males were in other high-paying declining sectors such as government, transportation, and communications. Note that in 1980, 61% of men had a high school degree or less. College educated men were much less vulnerable to the deterioration of manufacturing in the 1980s, as only 18.7% of their hours worked were in manufacturing.

While women were less likely than men to be working in manufacturing, a substantial portion of the hours worked by noncollege educated women in 1980 were in manufacturing (**Table 3.28**). Roughly one-fifth (20.8%) of the hours of women high school graduates and over a third (36.2%) of the hours of women with 8–11 years of schooling were worked in manufacturing. As with men, a majority of women (64.2%) had education levels not exceeding a high school degree in 1980.

108

In contrast, the work of college educated women was concentrated in just two sectors—the finance/business/health services and education/welfare industries.

The degree to which the employment shift from high- to low-paying industries lowers average pay levels depends on two factors. One factor is the amount of shifting that occurs, i.e., the percentage of the workforce that is shifting out of high-paying sectors. The other factor is the size of the pay gap between *expanding and shrinking* industries. Both factors significantly increased in the 1980s (**Table 3.29**). For instance, a measure of the rate of structural shifting in each period shows that there was more rapid shifting in the 1981–87 period than in any other period. The degree of shifting accelerated by 36%, from 0.80 to 1.09 per year, between the 1973–1981 and 1981–87 periods.

A substantial portion of the hours worked by noncollege educated women in 1980 were in manufacturing.

TABLE 3.29

Pay In Expanding and Shrinking Industries, 1948-1987

(1987 Dollars)

	1948–54	1954–62	1962–73	1973–81	1981–87
Annual Rate of Industry Job Shift*	0.91	0.78	0.78	0.80	1.09
Wages and Salaries					
Expanding Industries	$14,938	$13,648	$16,598	$19,144	$19,154
Shrinking Industries	14,204	18,609	16,765	19,058	26,194
Wage Gap**	734	-4,961	-167	86	-7,040
Benefits					
Expanding Industries	817	839	1,603	2,778	2,829
Shrinking Industries	951	2,018	2,091	3,672	6,194
Benefits Gap**	-134	-1,179	-488	-894	-3,365
Compensation					
Expanding Industries	15,753	14,491	18,206	21,921	21,983
Shrinking Industries	15,156	20,623	18,853	22,732	32,387
Compensation Gap**	597	-6,133	-647	-811	-10,404

*The annual percentage points by which employment shares among industries are shifting.

**Dollar gap by which pay of expanding industries is higher or lower than pay in shrinking industries. Expanding (shrinking) industries are those whose share of total employment increased (decreased) over the particular time period.

Note: These are the only time intervals for which data are available.

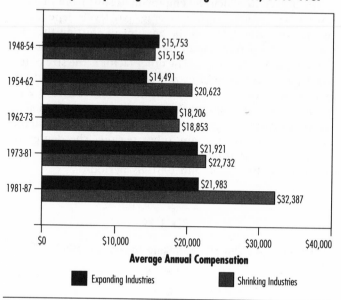

FIGURE 3K

Pay in Expanding and Shrinking Industries, 1949-1987

	Expanding Industries	Shrinking Industries
1948-54	$15,753	$15,156
1954-62	$14,491	$20,623
1962-73	$18,206	$18,853
1973-81	$21,921	$22,732
1981-87	$21,983	$32,387

Average Annual Compensation

■ Expanding Industries   ▨ Shrinking Industries

TABLE 3.30

Effect of Industry Employment Shifts on Pay, 1948–1987

	Effect of Industry Shifts on Annual Pay Growth				
Pay	1948–54	1954–62	1962–73	1973–81	1981–87
Wages	.05%	−.22%	.01%	.00%	−.32%
Benefits	.01	−.05	−.02	−.03	−.15
Compensation	.04	−.28	−.02	−.03	−.48

Note: These are the only time intervals for which data are available.

There was also an increase in the pay gap between the expanding and shrinking industries (**Figure 3K**). In the 1981–87 period, the industries where employment was contracted paid $10,404, or 47%, more in annual compensation than the expanding industries. This was by far the largest compensation gap between expanding and shrinking industries in the post-war era. The biggest differential was in benefits, with shrinking industries offering more than twice as much in annual benefits.

The faster pace of job shifting and the larger pay gap between expanding and shrinking sectors in the 1980s led to a significant reduction in both wages and benefits (**Table 3.30**). Industry employment shifts reduced compensation growth by 0.48% a year from 1981 to 1987, far higher than in any other period. The compensation of the overall workforce was thus reduced by 3% from 1981 to 1987 because of the shift to lower-paying sectors.

The expansion of low-wage industries reduced the wage growth of production and nonsupervisory workers by twice as much as for the average worker. As previously mentioned, production and nonsupervisory workers make up over 80% of all wage and salary employment. In the most recent period for which data are available, 1981–86, the wages paid by expanding industries were $134.69 less per week than those paid by shrinking industries (**Table 3.31**). This pay gap combined with an even faster rate of job shifting to lower wage growth by 0.61% annually. This compares to the 0.32% wage reduction induced by industry shifting overall.

In the 1981–87 period, the industries where employment was contracted paid $10,404, or 47%, more in annual compensation than the expanding industries.

TABLE 3.31

Industry Employment Shifts and Production Worker Weekly Wages, 1972–1986 (1987 Dollars)

| | | Weekly Wages | | | Industry Shift |
	Rate of Industry Job Shift*	Expanding Industries	Shrinking Industries	Gap	Effect on Annual Wage Growth
1972–81	1.23	$295.65	$361.13	$ −65.48	−.24%
1981–86	1.46	287.51	422.20	−134.69	−.61

*The annual percentage points that employment shares among industries are shifting (production workers only).

Note: These are the only time intervals for which data are available.

111

TABLE 3.32

Industry Shift Effect on Annual Wage Growth By Region, 1969–1987

	1969–74	1974–82	1982–87
Nation	.02%	–.05%	–.46%
New England	–.09	–.11	–.21
Mid-Atlantic	–.13	–.15	–.32
South-Atlantic	.33	–.01	–.25
East South Central	.45	.20	–.67
East North Central	–.10	–.27	–.74
West North Central	–.02	.03	–.61
West South Central	.16	.41	–.91
Mountain	–.08	.14	–.68
Pacific	–.01	–.13	–.11

Note: These are the only time intervals for which data are available.

TABLE 3.33

Full-Time Weekly Wages, Union and Nonunion, 1989

Demographic Group	Percent Union	Median Full-Time Weekly Wage		Union Premium*	
		Union	Nonunion	Dollars	Percent
White	17.7%	$503	$384	$119	31.0%
Men	21.2	537	452	85	18.8
Women	13.7	423	317	106	33.4
Black	25.4	423	290	133	45.9
Men	28.0	470	305	165	54.1
Women	22.9	390	276	114	41.3
Hispanic	16.8	417	276	141	51.1
Men	18.5	451	291	160	55.0
Women	14.5	368	255	113	44.3

*The dollar and percent by which the full-time weekly wages of union workers exceed those of nonunion workers.

The middle America regions, both North and South, have been more negatively affected by shifts to low-paying industries than the Eastern and Western coastal regions (**Table 3.32**). Wage growth fell from 0.61% to 0.91% annually in the Northern and Southern Central regions because of a loss of jobs in high-wage sectors. In contrast, job shifting caused wage growth to fall only 0.11% annually in the Pacific region between 1982 and 1987.

The Union Dimension

The percentage of the workforce represented by unions fell more rapidly in the 1980s than in the previous several decades. This falling rate of unionization has lowered wages, not only because some workers no longer receive the higher union wage, but also because there is less pressure on nonunion employers to raise wages. **Table 3.33** shows the union wage premium—the degree to which union wages exceed nonunion wages—for various demographic groups. The difference between union and nonunion wages is greatest for minorities, who earn from 45.9% to 51.1% more in union jobs.

Among both men and women, white workers have the lowest union wage premium. For instance, the union premium for white men was 18.8% in 1989, far less than the 54.1% and 55.0% premiums of black and Hispanic men. The higher union wage premiums of minority workers reflect the lesser wage discrimination faced by minority workers in the union sector.

Table 3.33 also shows that black workers, both male and female, are more heavily unionized than other groups and that black men tend to be represented by unions to a greater degree than black women.

The middle America regions, both North and South, have been more negatively affected by shifts to low-paying industries than the Eastern and Western coastal regions.

TABLE 3.34
Comparison of Union and Nonunion Wages and Benefits, 1989

Occupation or Industry Group	Total Compensation	Wage	Insurance	Pension
All Workers				
Union	$ 16.47	$ 14.13	$ 1.52	$ 0.76
Nonunion	12.31	11.24	0.72	0.35
Union Premium*:				
Dollars	4.16	2.89	0.80	0.41
Percent	33.8%	25.7%	111.1%	117.1%
Blue Collar				
Union	$ 17.46	$ 4.82	$ 1.70	$ 0.87
Nonunion	10.40	9.49	0.66	0.23
Union Premium*:				
Dollars	7.06	5.33	1.04	0.64
Percent	67.9%	56.2%	157.6%	278.3%
Goods-Producing				
Union	$ 17.84	$ 15.00	$ 1.85	$ 0.89
Nonunion	14.6	13.15	1.04	0.44
Union Premium*:				
Dollars	3.18	1.85	0.81	0.45
Percent	21.7%	14.1%	77.9%	102.3%
Service-Producing				
Union	$ 15.11	$ 13.25	$ 1.20	$ 0.64
Nonunion	11.57	10.62	0.62	0.32
Union Premium*:				
Dollars	3.54	2.63	0.58	0.32
Percent	30.6%	24.8%	93.5%	100.0%

*The dollars and percent by which the pay of union workers exceeds that of nonunion workers.

TABLE 3.35
Union Wage Advantage By Race/Ethnic Group and Sex
(1989 Dollars)

	Hourly Wage Benefit of Union Membership*	
	Men	Women
White	$0.50	$0.83
Black	1.61	1.23
Hispanic	2.18	1.53

*The dollar value by which union wages exceed nonunion wages, controlling for worker characteristics, occupation, industry, and other characteristics, in 1984.

The union premium is larger for total compensation, 33.8%, than for wages alone, 25.7% (**Table 3.34**). This reflects the fact that unionized workers are paid insurance and pension benefits that are more than double those of nonunion workers. For blue collar workers, the union premium in insurance and benefits is even larger, with union blue collar workers receiving from 157.6% to 278.3% more than their nonunion counterparts. The union wage differential is also much higher among blue collar workers.

Table 3.35 and **Figure 3L** provide a computation of the union wage premium that controls other factors that might affect wage rates, such as the education, experience, industry, and occupation of the unionized workforce. These data reinforce the earlier findings that all workers gain a wage and benefit premium from unionization, with women and minorities benefitting the most.

The union premium is larger for total compensation, 33.8%, than for wages alone, 25.7%.

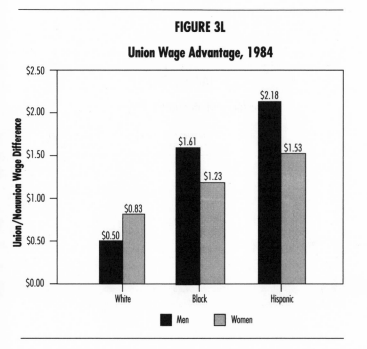

FIGURE 3L

Union Wage Advantage, 1984

FIGURE 3M

Real Value of the Minimum Wage, 1960-1991

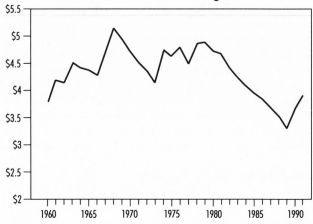

TABLE 3.36

Value of Minimum Wage

Year	Minimum Wage (Current Dollars)	Minimum Wage (1989 Dollars)
1967	$1.40	$4.67
1973	1.60	4.13
1979	2.90	4.86
1989	3.35	3.35
1990	3.80	3.65
1991	4.25	3.92
Period Averages:		
1960s	$1.29	$4.44
1970s	2.07	4.60
1980s	3.33	4.04
1990–91	4.25	3.92

116

An estimate of the effect of deunionization on average wages can be computed from the fall in the unionization rate and the union wage premium. From 1977 to 1987 the percentage of the employed wage and salary in unions fell from 23.8% to 17%. Given a union premium in hourly compensation of 33.8% (Table 3.34), this erosion in union share of 6.8% implies a reduction of overall hourly compensation of roughly 2.3%. If the union premium was only 20% (what studies controlling for worker characteristics tend to find), then deunionization lowered hourly compensation by a still significant 1.4%. Deunionization probably had a larger effect since a shrinking of the union sector has slowed nonunion wage growth (through a weaker threat of unions organizing nonunion employers).

This erosion in union share of 6.8% implies a reduction of overall hourly compensation of roughly 2.3%.

An Eroded Minimum Wage

The real value of the minimum wage has fallen considerably since its high point in the late 1960s (**Figure 3M**). The decline was particularly steep and steady between 1979 and 1989, when inflation whittled the minimum wage (in 1989 dollars) down from $4.86 to $3.35 (**Table 3.36**).

While a full-time, year-round job at the minimum wage kept a family of 3 above the poverty line in 1979, the same job would have placed such a family $2,922 *below* the poverty line in 1989 (**Table 3.37**). Even a two-person family dependent on a minimum wage worker would have been

TABLE 3.37

Amount by Which Earnings of a Full-Time, Full-Year Minimum Wage Worker Are Above (Below) the Poverty Line (1989 Dollars)

Year	Dollar Difference Between Annual Minimum Wage Earnings and Poverty Line, By Family Size		
	2	3	4
1967	$ 2,220	$ 828	($1,675)
1973	882	(551)	(3,128)
1979	1,925	405	(2,329)
1989	(1,373)	(2,922)	(5,707)
1990	(741)	(2,290)	(5,075)
1991	(192)	(1,740)	(4,525)

TABLE 3.38

Hourly Workers Who Earn Minimum Wage or Less,* 1986

	Number of Workers (1,000s)	Percent of Minimum Wage Workforce
Males, over 16	1,744	34.5%
Females, over 16	3,317	65.6
Adults, over 19	3,211	63.5
Teenagers	1,848	36.5
Whites	4,198	83.0
Blacks	714	14.6
Hispanics**	464	9.2
Full-Time	1,737	34.3
Part-Time	3,323	65.7
Total	5,060	100.0

*Excludes 1.7 million salaried workers whose pay per hour is at or below the minimum.

**Hispanics, blacks, and whites add to more than 100% because Hispanics can be of any race.

TABLE 3.39

Distribution of Low Paid Wage and Salary Workers*
By Family Relationship, 1987

	All (Poor and Nonpoor)	
Family Relationship	Workers At or Below Minimum Wage	Workers Above Minimum But Less Than $4.18/hour**
Family heads and spouses	45.1%	50.4%
With children under 18 years	27.4	28.1
Dependents	33.0	28.8
Persons not in families	20.5	20.0
Persons in unrelated subfamilies	1.3	0.9
Total	100.0%	100.0%
Number (thousands)	4,653	4,024

*Restricted to workers in labor force at least 27 weeks.

**Workers paid (in 1987 dollars) between $3.35 and $4.18 per hour, the average value of the minimum wage over the 1960s, 1970s, and 1980s.

118

$1,373 below the poverty line in 1989. After the minimum wage increases of 1990–91, families of two or more persons who rely on a minimum wage worker will still remain well below the poverty line.

It has been argued that the minimum wage is not relevant to poverty, since minimum wage workers tend to be teenagers and others who do not have family responsibilities. In fact, 63.5% of minimum wage workers in 1986 were over 19 (**Table 3.38**). Moreover, of the 4,653,000 workers who earned minimum wage or less in 1987, only 33% were dependents in families (**Table 3.39**). Fully 45.1% of workers at or below the minimum wage were family heads or spouses. Most of these (27.4% out of 45.1%) had children under 18 years old. Another 20.5% did not live in families.

The minimum wage also affects workers who earn more than but close to the minimum. Table 3.39 presents the same information about the 4,024,000 workers who made more than the minimum wage ($3.35) in 1987 but less than $4.18 per hour, the average value of the minimum wage over the 1960s, 1970s and 1980s. Compared to minimum wage workers, they are somewhat more likely to have family responsibilities (50.4%), and less likely to be dependents (28.8%).

Even after the current legislated minimum wage is increased through 1991, it will be worth (in 1989 dollars) only $3.92 in 1991, or $0.94 less than in 1979 and $0.75 less than in 1967. In fact, low-wage workers are starting out the 1990s with a minimum wage whose value in real terms (1989 dollars) of $3.92 is 13% less than the minimum wage of $4.44 that prevailed in the 1960s. Unless new legislation increases the minimum wage after 1991, its real value will drop even further.

Executive Pay Soars

The 1980s was a prosperous decade for top U.S. executives. In stark contrast to the declining real wages of average workers, the pay of the chief executive officers (CEOs) of major U.S. companies grew by 19% from 1979 to 1989

Even after the current legislated minimum wage is increased through 1991, it will be worth (in 1989 dollars) only $3.92 in 1991, or $0.94 less than in 1979 and $0.75 less than in 1967.

TABLE 3.40

Executive Pay Levels, 1979–1989

Country	Annual CEO Pay (Thousands of Dollars)	
	1979	1989
United States		
Pre-Tax Pay	$308.2	$612.8
After-Tax Pay	153.9	429.1
France		
Pre-Tax Pay	119.4	181.7
After-Tax Pay	77.5	111.7
West Germany		
Pre-Tax Pay	136.2	206.7
After-Tax Pay	75.3	112.4
Japan		
Pre-Tax Pay	149.3	371.1
After-Tax Pay	70.9	178.4
United Kingdom		
Pre-Tax Pay	121.2	194.9
After-Tax Pay	35.0	122.2

*Includes the salaries and capital distributions (such as equities and bonds) for CEOs of firms with sales exceeding $790 million.

TABLE 3.41

Real Growth in Executive Pay, 1979–1989

	Percent Change, 1979–1989*	
	Pre-Tax Pay	After-Tax Pay
United States	19%	66%
France	13	7
West Germany	17	15
Japan	22	24
United Kingdom	3	123

*In national currencies adjusted for domestic consumer price increases. Same definitions as in Table 3.40.

(**Tables 3.40** and **3.41**). Given the poor performance of the U.S. economy relative to competitor nations in the 1980s, it may be surprising to find that the pay of the United States' CEOs has far outpaced that of the CEOs in other countries (Table 3.40). The 19% growth in pre-tax pay for U.S. CEOs in the 10 years from 1979 to 1989 was greater than the growth of CEO pre-tax pay of 13%, 17%, and 3%, respectively, in France, Germany, and the United Kingdom. Since tax rates on high income residents have been severely reduced in the U.S. and the United Kingdom over the last 10 years, changes in pre-tax and after-tax pay differ widely. In Britain, for instance, tax rates for the rich have been reduced so much that CEO after-tax pay increased 123% from 1979 to 1989, even though pre-tax pay increased by only 3%. In the United States, after-tax pay of CEOs increased by 66%, more than three times as fast as their pre-tax pay increased. In the 10 years between 1979 and 1989, after-tax CEO pay increased far faster in the U.S. than in Japan, Germany, or France.

CEOs in the U.S. are paid roughly twice as much as the CEOs of our major industrial competitors.

CEOs in the U.S. are paid roughly twice as much as the CEOs of our major industrial competitors (**Table 3.42** and **Figure 3N**). For instance, the average annual compensation of a CEO heading a U.S. firm with at least $100 million of sales was $508,000 in 1988. A comparable executive in Japan makes 62% as much while a CEO in Germany makes 51% as much.

TABLE 3.42

Comparative Pay Levels of Workers and CEOs,* 1988

Country	CEO Total Compensation		Index, Manufacturing Production Worker Hourly Compensation (U.S.=100)**
	Dollars**	Index (U.S.=100)**	
Canada	$267,000	53%	96%
France	255,000	50	99
West Germany	260,000	51	136
Italy	216,000	43	97
Japan	317,000	62	98
United Kingdom	286,000	56	77
United States	**508,000**	**100**	**100**

*CEOs of firms with sales exceeding $100 million.

**Using April 1988 exchange rates.

121

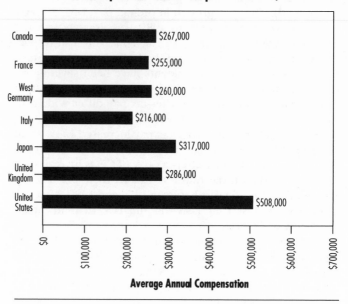

FIGURE 3N

CEO Compensation in the Major 7 Countries, 1988

Country	Average Annual Compensation
Canada	$267,000
France	$255,000
West Germany	$260,000
Italy	$216,000
Japan	$317,000
United Kingdom	$286,000
United States	$508,000

Average Annual Compensation

TABLE 3.43

The Pay Gap Between Executives and Production Workers, 1988

Country	Ratio of CEO Pay to Production Worker Pay*
Canada	9.5
France	8.9
West Germany	6.5
Italy	7.6
Japan	11.6
United Kingdom	12.4
United States	**17.5**

*Assumes CEO works 52 40-hour weeks.

In contrast, the pay of American manufacturing workers was more equal to that of our major competitors in Canada, France, Italy, and Japan in 1988. However, German workers earn 36% *more* than American workers. Only British workers have significantly lower wages than U.S. workers.

The pay gap between CEOs and manufacturing production workers is far larger in the U.S. than in other industrialized countries (**Table 3.43** and **Figure 30**). In 1988, U.S. CEOs were paid 17.5 times as much as manufacturing production workers, a pay gap twice as wide as in Germany, Italy, and France and 50% greater than in Japan (Table 3.43).

Jobs of the Future

The jobs of the future will not be markedly different than the jobs available today. Future jobs will have somewhat greater education and skill requirements, primarily the need for basic literacy and numeracy, but will not necessarily pay more than current jobs. Moreover, the skill and education requirements of jobs are expected to grow more slowly than

The pay gap between CEOs and manufacturing production workers is far larger in the U.S. than in other industrialized countries.

FIGURE 30

Ratio of CEO Pay to Production Worker Pay
Major 7 Countries, 1988

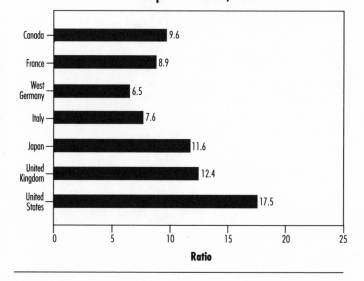

Country	Ratio
Canada	9.6
France	8.9
West Germany	6.5
Italy	7.6
Japan	11.6
United Kingdom	12.4
United States	17.5

Ratio

TABLE 3.44

Effect of Industry and Occupation Employment Shifts on Compensation and Education Requirements, 1973–2000

Pay and Education Requirements	1973–79	1979–86	BLS Projections 1986–2000	BLS Projections 1988–2000
			(Ten Year Rates of Change*)	
			Industry Shift Effects	
Hourly Compensation	−1.65%	−3.20%	−1.42%	−1.17%
Years of Education Required**	0.45	0.55	0.27	0.24
			Occupation Shift Effects	
Hourly Compensation	1.67%	2.18%	0.24%	0.37%
Years of Education Required**	0.85	1.11	0.34	0.38

*To facilitate comparisons of these time periods which are of different length the data have been converted to ten year rates of change—the change if the annual rate of change in these time periods had continued for ten years.

**Percent increase in years of education required over ten year period.

in the 1970s and 1980s. Despite the widely held assumption that higher-paying white collar jobs are the wave of the future, there is little evidence that the deterioration of job quality and wages that took place in the 1980s will be reversed in the 1990s, unless current trends change dramatically. One view of future jobs can be obtained by analyzing labor market trends anticipated by the Bureau of Labor Statistics (BLS) in its two employment projections to the year 2000 (one from 1986–2000, the other 1988–2000).

Key to this analysis is the examination of both the continued expansion of white collar, high-paying *occupations* and the job shift from high-paying to low-paying *industries*. Analyses of future jobs which focus solely on occupational change, as many do, paint too optimistic a picture.

Table 3.44 provides data that allow us to assess the relative importance of industry shifts (e.g., the rising importance of services) and occupation shifts (e.g., the rising importance of white collar professional/technical jobs). Specifically, the data show the effect of changes in the distribution of jobs among occupations and industries on hourly compensation (wages and fringe benefits) and required education levels in recent years, as well as the effects anticipated by BLS employment projections. In the past, employment shifts towards low-paying industries have had an equal or more negative effect on overall compensation than the positive contribution of the shift to higher-paying occupations. For instance, industry job shifts between 1979 and 1986 lowered hourly compensation at a 3.20% (ten year) rate of change while occupation shifts raised hourly compensation at a 2.18% (ten year) rate of change.

An important conclusion from Table 3.44 is that both BLS projections show an extremely modest effect of occupation shifts on hourly compensation, raising compensation by just 0.24% to 0.37% over a 10 year period. In fact, the shift toward white collar work expected in the future will have a smaller effect on hourly compensation than the effect occupation changes have had in the prior 13 years (roughly 0.4% versus 2.5%). Or, in other words, the "rapid upscaling" to "high-skilled professions" suggested in some analyses represents a *slowdown* in the effect of occupational upgrading on hourly compensation. Plus, this positive contribution of the expected shift to higher-paying occupations over 12 or 14 years is less than the *annual* decline of real hourly compen-

Despite the widely held assumption that higher-paying white collar jobs are the wave of the future, there is little evidence that the deterioration of job quality and wages that took place in the 1980s will be reversed in the 1990s.

TABLE 3.45

The Effect of Occupation Employment Shifts on Skill and Education Requirements, 1973–2000

Skill Indices	1973–1979	1979–1986	1986–2000	1988–2000
	(Ten Year Rates of Change*)			
Handling Data	4.01%	5.07%	1.24%	1.31%
Verbal Aptitude	2.19	2.65	0.66	0.72
Length of Training	2.13	2.38	0.53	0.59
Intellectual Aptitude	2.02	2.35	0.55	0.63
General Educational Development (GED)	1.91	2.35	0.60	0.65
Handling People	1.71	2.45	0.72	0.72
Handling Things	–0.57	–2.08	–0.87	–0.68
Education				
Median Years Required	0.85%	1.11%	0.34%	0.38%
Shares of Employment Requiring: (Percentage Point Change*)				
Less than High School	–1.42	–1.51	–0.31	–0.37
High School Graduate	–0.92	–1.51	–0.55	–0.55
Some College	0.57	0.59	0.11	0.13
College Graduate or More	1.77	2.46	0.74	0.79

*To facilitate comparison of time periods, data have been converted to ten year rates of change—the change that would have occurred if the annual rates of change in each time period had continued for ten years.

"Rapid upscaling" to "high-skilled professions" suggested in some analyses represents a slowdown in the effect of occupational upgrading on hourly compensation.

sation for workers in each year of the 1980s.

The data in Table 3.44 also suggest that it is misleading to ignore the shift to lower-paying industries. The negative consequences of the expected shift to low-paying industries, a reduction of hourly compensation by 1.2% to 1.4% over 10 years, is three to five times larger than the positive benefits of expected occupation changes. The net result of the industry and occupation employment shifts will be to *lower* pay levels.

The effect of both industry and occupation employment shifts in raising education levels is rather small (Table 3.44). Even the largest rate of change found in the table (for occupation shifts in the 1979–1986 period) implies that in 1998,

126

the average change in educational attainment from the 1988 average of 12.76 years will only rise to 12.90 years. The projected shift in the occupation employment suggests a rise of just .04 extra years of schooling over ten years. Workers in the year 2000 might end up needing somewhat more education for somewhat lower wages.

The biggest factor in determining future pay levels is growth of hourly pay within particular occupations and industries. Given the trends of the 1980s and the slow growth in productivity that is projected for the future, it is unlikely that wages will be greater in the year 2000 than they were in 1980, even if real wages do grow in the 1990s.

In contrast to previous tables which examine the compensation and mean education implications of occupational upgrading, **Table 3.45** examines the expected changes (relative to past trends) in an array of job skill requirements due to occupational upgrading. These data show not only that the effect of expected future occupation shifts on skill levels is modest, but also that this effect will be smaller than in previous time periods. That is, when the effect of occupational change on skill levels in the 1973–79 or 1979–1986 periods are compared to the projections for 1986–2000 and 1988–2000, the future growth in skill levels is expected to occur at only one-third to one-quarter the pace of skill growth in the earlier periods. For example, skill levels in handling data went up at a ten year rate of 3.97% between 1973 and 1979 and a rate of 5.11% between 1979 and 1986, but are projected to rise in the future at rates only about one-third the 1973–79 rate and just one-quarter the 1979–1986 rate. These trends flatly contradict the popular notion that occupational upgrading will produce a future explosion in job skill requirements.

Analysis of future job trends shows that, contrary to the conventional wisdom, the move to a "service economy" will not automatically produce a highly skilled, well-paid job structure. This is because occupational upgrading trends are not large enough to generate a substantial rise in job skill levels or compensation. Furthermore, projected rates of occupational upgrading actually appear to represent a slow-down from upgrading trends in the past, trends that were themselves fairly modest. Thus, if previous growth in the service economy has not produced a highly skilled job structure, then future growth by itself is even less likely to do so.

Analysis of future job trends shows that, contrary to the conventional wisdom, the move to a "service economy" will not automatically produce a highly skilled, well-paid job structure.

CHAPTER 4

TABLE 4.1

Unemployment Rates

	Total	Male	Female	White	Black	Hispanic
1947	3.9%	4.0%	3.7%	N/A	N/A	N/A
1967	3.8	3.1	5.2	3.4%	N/A	N/A
1973	4.9	4.2	6.0	4.3	9.4%	7.5%
1979	5.8	5.1	6.8	5.1	12.3	8.3
1989	5.3	5.2	5.4	4.5	11.4	8.0

TABLE 4.2

Rates of Underemployment,* 1973–1989

	1973	1979	1989
	(000)	(000)	(000)
Civilian Labor Force	89,429	104,962	123,869
Unemployed	4,365	6,137	6,528
Discouraged Workers	689	771	859
Involuntary Part-Time	2,343	3,373	4,894
Total Underemployed*	7,397	10,281	12,281
Rate of Underemployment**	8.2%	9.7%	9.8%
Unemployment Rate	4.9	5.8	5.3

*Unemployed, discouraged, and involuntary part-time.

**Total underemployed workers divided by the sum of the labor force plus discouraged workers.

JOBS: WORSENING UNDEREMPLOYMENT

By the standards of the late 1970s and early 1980s, the 1989 unemployment rate of 5.3% was relatively low. Compared with the unemployment rates of the peak years of 1947, 1967, or 1973, however, 5.3% unemployment is well above average.

The unemployment rate by itself does not give us a complete picture of the labor market in which the average American attempts to find economic security. For instance, it does not reflect the deterioration of wages described in Chapter 3. Nor does it reflect the number of people working in part-time or temporary jobs because they cannot find full-time or permanent work. Neither does it reflect the expansion of low paying self-employment nor the growth of *over*employment, i.e., people having to work at more than one job in order to meet ordinary expenses. The trend toward part-time and temporary work and the growth of multiple jobholding has placed, along with unemployment, at least a fifth of the workforce in situations of labor market distress.

The trend toward part-time and temporary work and the growth of multiple jobholding has placed, along with unemployment, at least a fifth of the workforce in situations of labor market distress.

Unemployment and Underemployment

Table 4.1 gives a broad view of unemployment rates by race, sex, and age during various peak years in the business cycle since World War II. In peak years, the economy is at its strongest, and therefore unemployment is at its lowest. For every group, unemployment in 1989 was less than or equal to that in 1979, the prior cyclical peak. Relative to 1973 and earlier peak years, however, 1989 unemployment rates are above average.

Unemployment among minority workers continues to be roughly double that of white workers, as has been the case over the post-war period. The major shift in the 1980s has been a lowering of the unemployment rate for women relative to men.

A broader measure of the lack of success in the labor market is the rate of underemployment. This alternative measure includes unemployed workers but also includes people working part-time who want to work full-time ("involuntary" part-timers) and those who want to work but have been discouraged from searching for jobs by lack of previous success ("discouraged workers"). The rate of underemployment was essentially the same in 1989 as in 1979, 9.8%, despite a drop in unemployment (**Table 4.2** and

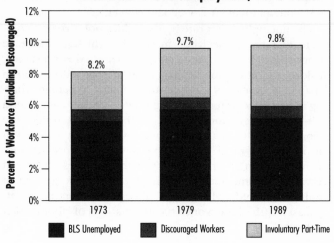

FIGURE 4A

Real Rates of Underemployment, 1973-1989

Percent of Workforce (Including Discouraged)

8.2% (1973) 9.7% (1979) 9.8% (1989)

BLS Unemployed   Discouraged Workers   Involuntary Part-Time

TABLE 4.3

Proportion of the Unemployed Who Receive Some Unemployment Insurance Payment

Year	Rate
1967	43%
1973	41
1979	42
1989	34

Figure 4A). The 1989 underemployment rate was substantially higher than the 5.3% unemployment rate primarily because of a 4.3% rate of involuntary part-time work. The 1989 underemployment rate, equivalent to the 1979 rate, 9.7%, was significantly higher than the underemployment rate of 8.2% in 1973.

Being unemployed was a bigger financial hardship in the 1980s than in earlier decades. As **Table 4.3** shows, in 1989, only 34% of the unemployed received unemployment insurance, a substantial drop from the financial protection available in prior years. Changes in the laws and administration of unemployment insurance at both the federal and state levels are primarily responsible for the lower coverage of unemployment insurance.

Job Creation: How Fast in the 80s?

The fact that unemployment dropped after 1982 led to the impression that the 1980s were a time of exceptional job creation. This inference is incorrect.

Table 4.4 presents the changes in three measures of employment growth over various periods since World War II: civilian employment, full-time equivalent employment (which combines part-time and full-time according to practices in each industry), and total hours worked. The trend is unmistakable: each measure of employment grew far more slowly from 1979 to 1988 than between 1973 and 1979. For instance, the rate at which civilian employment rose from 1979 to 1988, 1.68% annually, was more than 30% slower

Each measure of employment grew far more slowly from 1979 to 1988 than between 1973 and 1979.

TABLE 4.4

Employment Growth, 1947–1988

Period	Measures of Employment			Working-Age Employment	Labor Force Participation Rate
	Civilian Employment	Hours of Work	Full-Time Equivalent Employment		
	(Annual Rates of Growth)				(Percentage Point Annual Growth)
1947–67	1.33%	1.67%	1.83%	1.22%	.07%
1967–73	2.24	1.60	1.86	2.08	.20
1973–79	2.50	1.80	2.28	1.90	.48
1979–88	1.68	1.40	1.64	1.26	.24

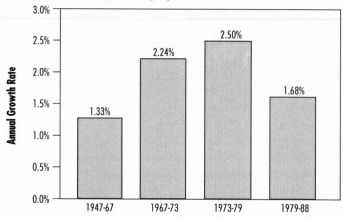

FIGURE 4B

Civilian Employment Growth, 1947-1988

Annual Growth Rate

- 1947-67: 1.33%
- 1967-73: 2.24%
- 1973-79: 2.50%
- 1979-88: 1.68%

. . . the lower unemployment of the later part of the 1980s has not been due to superior job creation . . . unemployment has fallen because fewer new jobs were demanded.

than the 2.5% annual employment creation rate prevailing between 1973 and 1979 (**Figure 4B**).

The last two columns of Table 4.4 show two reasons why unemployment has fallen despite *a much slower growth in job creation since 1979*. First, the working-age population has grown more slowly than it did in the period from 1967 to 1979. For instance, there were fewer new potential young workers in 1989 than in 1979, even though the overall population grew by 12%. In 1989, there were 32.2 million 16 to 24 year olds, a smaller number than the 37.0 million in 1979 or even the 33.5 million in 1973.

Second, the long-term rise in the proportion of the working-age population seeking work (the labor force participation rate) has also leveled off in recent years. As Table 4.4 shows, the annual percentage point increase in the labor force participation rate in the 9 years between 1979 and 1988 was only half as much as in the 6 years between 1973 and 1979. This reflects a slower increase in women's labor force participation since 1979.

These two trends, the smaller number of potential young workers and the slower labor force participation growth, have meant a slower growth in the number of people seeking work. Thus, the lower unemployment of the later part

132

of the 1980s has *not* been due to superior job creation. Instead, unemployment has fallen because fewer new jobs were demanded. The growth rate of new jobs actually slowed down, but the growth of new workers slowed down more.

The Growth in Part-Timers

As we have seen earlier, there has been a growth in underemployment due to more people working part-time who want full-time jobs. This section examines the growth of part-time work and the associated problems in more detail.

The expansion of part-time work is not *necessarily* a problem. Many workers prefer a part-time schedule because it allows time to pursue education, leisure, or family responsibilities. But large numbers of part-timers would prefer to work full-time. Part-timers generally have lower pay, lower-skilled jobs, poor chances of promotion, less job security, inferior benefits (such as vacation, health insurance, and pension) and lower status overall within their places of employment.

Table 4.5 shows that the share of total employment made up by full-timers has declined steadily from 1973 to 1989. At the same time, the share of jobs that are part-

There has been a growth in under-employment due to more people working part-time who want full-time jobs.

TABLE 4.5

Composition of Nonagricultural Employment, 1973–1988

| | Percent Part-Time | | | | |
Year	Total	Involuntary	Voluntary	Percent Full-Time	Total
1973	16.6%	3.1%	13.5%	83.4%	100.0%
1979	17.6	3.8	13.8	82.4	100.0
1988	18.4	4.7	13.7	81.6	100.0

Shares of Part-Time Job Growth, Voluntary and Involuntary, 1973–1988

| | Share of New Part-Time Jobs | | |
Years	Voluntary	Involuntary	New Part-Time Jobs (in thousands)
1973–79	66.3%	33.7%	3,055
1979–88	56.9	43.1	3,695

133

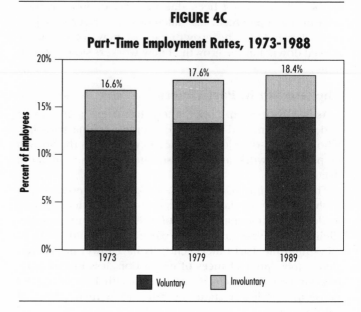

FIGURE 4C

Part-Time Employment Rates, 1973-1988

Percent of Employees

- 16.6% (1973)
- 17.6% (1979)
- 18.4% (1989)

■ Voluntary   □ Involuntary

. . . increase in the proportion of workers working part-time . . . has been entirely due to the increased rate at which workers are working part-time involuntarily.

time has increased from 16.6% in 1973 to 18.4% in 1988 (**Figure** 4C). This increase in the proportion of workers working part-time from 1979 to 1988 has been entirely due to the increased rate at which workers are working part-time *involuntarily*. It thus reflects the increased use of part-timers by employers and not the preferences of the work-force for shorter hours.

In 1988, involuntary part-time workers comprised 4.7% of the workforce, an increase of 0.9 and 1.6 percentage points of the workforce over, respectively, 1979 and 1973. Five million workers, on average, were involuntary part-timers in 1988, encompassing one-fourth of all part-time workers.

Table 4.6 presents the demographic breakdown of part-time workers, both voluntary and involuntary. *Voluntary* part-time workers are disproportionately women, teen-agers, and persons of retirement age. In 1988, 21.2% of employed women were voluntary part-timers, more than three times the 7.5% rate of voluntary part-time work among men. Roughly half of teenagers and persons over the age of 65 with jobs worked part-time voluntarily. These

134

demographic groups are the most willing to accept lower pay and status in order to obtain a reduced work schedule.

Involuntary part-time work affects those most vulnerable in the job market. Women, teens, and blacks are the groups most likely to be stuck in part-time work despite a preference for full-time jobs. These groups are the ones that are subject to discrimination in the job market and have weak bargaining power. In 1988, while women preferred part-time work more than men did, women were also 50% more likely (5.6% versus 3.9%) to be working part-time jobs although wanting a full-time job. Black workers are less likely to hold voluntary part-time jobs than whites, but 70% more likely to be working part-time involuntarily.

Involuntary part-time work affects those most vulnerable in the job market.

TABLE 4.6

Rate of Part-Time Employment for Various Workforce Groups, 1988

Nonagricultural Workforce Group	Percent Part-Time:		
	Involuntary	Voluntary	Total Part-Time
Men	3.9%	7.5%	11.4%
Currently married men	2.6	3.6	6.1
Single men*	6.3	14.3	20.7
Women	5.6	21.2	26.8
Currently married women	4.8	22.6	27.4
Single women*	6.5	19.4	26.0
By Age			
Age 16–19	10.5	53.7	64.3
Age 20–64	4.3	10.1	14.3
Age 65+	4.5	47.2	51.7
Black	7.2	9.8	17.0
Black men	6.5	6.7	13.2
Black women	7.9	12.8	20.7
White	4.4	14.2	18.5
White men	3.7	7.5	11.1
White women	5.3	22.5	27.7
All	4.7	13.7	18.4

*Never or no longer married.

135

TABLE 4.7

Age and Gender Composition of the Labor Force and Rate of Part-Time Employment, 1969 and 1988*

	1969		1988	
	Share of Total Employment	Percent Part-Time	Share of Total Employment	Percent Part-Time
All 16–21	12.8%	40.6%	10.6%	46.2%
Women 22–44	17.3	22.7	27.7	22.1
Women 45–64	13.2	22.5	11.3	24.1
Men 22–64	53.2	3.7	47.9	6.9
All 65+	3.5	41.0	2.5	51.7
Total	100.0	15.5	100.0	18.4

*All nonagricultural workers at work, both self-employed and wage and salaried.

TABLE 4.8

Rate of Involuntary, Voluntary, and Total Part-Time Work By Industry, 1969 and 1988*

	Percent Part-Time:					
	Involuntary		Voluntary		Total	
	1969	1988	1969	1988	1969	1988
Construction	4.4%	6.8%	4.2%	4.4%	8.6%	11.2%
Durable Manufacturing	1.4	1.6	1.8	2.4	3.2	4.0
Nondurable Manufacturing	3.4	3.7	4.4	4.6	7.8	8.3
Transport, Comm., Util.	1.8	3.1	6.0	5.6	7.8	8.7
Retail/Wholesale Trade	2.9	7.0	23.4	23.4	26.3	30.4
Finance	1.0	1.9	9.5	9.3	10.5	11.3
Pers. & Business Services	3.1	5.0	23.1	19.0	26.2	24.0
Public Administration	0.8	1.2	5.4	5.6	6.2	6.8
Mining	1.6	2.2	3.4	2.3	5.0	4.5
All Industries	2.5	4.0	13.0	13.3	15.5	17.8

*All nonagricultural wage and salary workers at work. Data limitations prevent the inclusion of self-employed workers in this table (they are included in Table 4.7).

136

A demographic explanation for the expansion of part-time jobs—the growth of women and younger workers in the labor force raises the need for part-time work—is not consistent with the available data. As shown in Table 4.5 above, the rise of part-time work is entirely due to the increased incidence of involuntary part-time work. Moreover for adult men, the group with the least preference for part-time work, the rate of part-time work rose from 3.7% in 1969 to 6.9% in 1988 (**Table 4.7**). In fact, the increase in part-time work can be almost fully explained by a rise in part-time work within each demographic group rather than any change in the age-gender composition of employment. If the rates of part-time work within each group had remained at their 1969 levels while the mix of employment, such as more women in the workforce, changed as it did from 1969 to 1988, then the overall rate of part-time work would only have risen from 15.5% in 1969 to 15.9% in 1988, far short of the actual rise to 18.4%. In other words, only 0.4% of the 2.9% rise in the incidence of part-time work can be attributed to changing demographic factors.

. . . job growth has been concentrated in service industries that intensively use part-timers.

The major reason for growing part-time work is that job growth has been concentrated in service industries that intensively use part-timers. In 1988, for instance, 30.4% of the retail/wholesale trade workforce and 24% of the service industry workforce were employed part-time (**Table 4.8**). As we saw in Chapter 3, roughly three-fourths of the net new jobs created between 1979 and 1989 were in these two industries. This shift of employment towards industries that provide low-wage, part-time employment can explain 1.7 of the 2.3 percentage point rise (or 74% of the increase) in the rate of part-time employment among nonagricultural wage and salary workers.

TABLE 4.9

Differences in Hourly Wages for Full-Time and Part-Time Workers, By Sex and Occupation, 1987

Sex and Occupation	Percent of All Part-Time Workers	Percent Working Part-Time	Average Wage (1987 Dollars)	
			Part-Time	Full-Time
Women				
All Workers	100.0%	26.0%	$ 8.03	$ 8.70
Professional, Managerial, and Technical	22.4	19.1	11.32	11.23
Sales	16.2	38.4	7.73	8.11
Clerical	25.6	22.4	7.70	8.19
Service	28.8	45.2	6.27	5.49
Craft, Operative, and Labor	7.0	14.9	6.71	7.01
Men				
All Workers	100.0%	4.7%	$12.46	$13.26
Professional, Managerial, and Technical	23.9	3.5	19.29	16.91
Sales	9.9	4.4	13.34	13.49
Clerical	8.2	6.8	8.60	12.08
Service	22.2	12.8	8.78	9.20
Craft, Operative, and Labor	35.8	3.9	10.84	11.34

A major problem associated with part-time employment is lower hourly pay received by part-time workers compared to equivalent full-time workers.

A major problem associated with part-time employment is lower hourly pay received by part-time workers compared to equivalent full-time workers. Except for professional men and women and some women service workers, part-time workers earn lower hourly wages than full-time workers in the same occupations (**Table 4.9**). The difference is greater for benefits, however (**Table 4.10**). For instance, only 25.6% of part-time female family heads are included in their employers' health plans compared to 74.1% of full-time female family heads. Similarly, men working in part-time jobs are only about half as likely (37.1% versus 79%) to be included in their employers' health plans.

138

Pay differentials are even greater when it comes to pensions. In each occupation group, workers with part-time jobs are far less likely than full-time workers to be enrolled in their employers' pension plans (Table 4.10).

The gap between part-time and full-time workers in the provision of health and pension benefits is as wide for women who are heads of households as it is for women in married-couple families (Table 4.10). It is also just as wide among professional women as among women in clerical or service occupations.

The gap between part-time and full-time workers in the provision of health and pension benefits is wider than the wage gap.

TABLE 4.10

Differences in Fringe Benefits, for Full-Time and Part-Time Workers, by Sex or Marital Status and Occupation, 1987

Sex or Marital Status and Occupation	Included in Pension Plan		Included in Health Plan	
	Part-Time	Full-Time	Part-Time	Part-Time
Female Family Heads				
All Workers	14.2%	50.2%	25.6%	74.1%
Professional, Managerial, and Technical	23.0	62.4	41.3	85.9
Sales	11.8	31.9	20.5	60.3
Clerical	20.6	55.9	36.8	82.1
Service	8.1	28.3	17.2	46.4
Craft, Operative, and Labor	18.8	45.2	22.8	69.1
Wives				
All Workers	17.9%	50.9%	17.8%	59.7%
Professional, Managerial, and Technical	26.2	64.0	23.5	68.0
Sales	12.0	29.7	16.4	44.7
Clerical	18.6	55.0	18.4	63.1
Service	13.4	27.6	12.1	37.2
Craft, Operative, and Labor	18.3	41.7	20.8	58.8
Husbands and Male Family Heads				
All Workers	18.3%	58.5%	37.1%	79.0%
Professional, Managerial, and Technical	24.5	67.6	43.6	86.1
Sales	18.5	44.2	38.7	75.3
Clerical	17.6	70.0	44.1	84.8
Service	12.9	55.6	27.8	71.8
Craft, Operative, and Labor	17.7	54.5	36.5	75.2

TABLE 4.11

Workweek Preference of 25- to 54-Year-Old Wage and Salary Workers, May 1985

	Percent of Workers Who Prefer:			
Group	Same Hours*	Fewer Hours*	More Hours*	Total
Hours at Work				
1 to 14	50.9%	4.6%	44.5%	100.0%
15 to 29	57.3	5.6	37.1	100.0
30 to 34	58.6	8.0	33.4	100.0
35 to 39	65.0	8.1	26.9	100.0
40	70.5	7.1	22.5	100.0
41 to 48	65.3	8.1	26.6	100.0
49 to 59	66.5	10.8	22.7	100.0
60 and over	63.9	16.3	19.8	100.0
Gender				
Men	66.5%	6.5%	28.0%	100.0%
Women	67.2	10.9	21.9	100.0

*At same hourly pay rate.

TABLE 4.12

Growth of Multiple Jobholding, All Workers, 1973–1989

			Percent of Workforce Who Hold Multiple Jobs Because of:	
Year	Number of Multiple Jobholders (000)	Multiple Jobholding Rate	Economic Hardship*	Other Reasons**
1973	4,262	5.1%	N/A	N/A
1979	4,724	4.9	1.8%	3.1%
1985	5,730	5.4	2.2	3.2
1989	7,225	6.2	2.8	3.4
Change				
1973–79	462	–0.2%	N/A	N/A
1979–85	1,006	0.5	0.4%	0.1%
1985–89	1,495	0.8	0.6	0.2

*To meet regular household expenses or pay off debts.

**Includes saving for the future, getting experience, helping a friend or relative, buying something special, enjoying the work, and so on.

The labor market also does not meet the needs of many workers who would prefer to work fewer hours (**Table 4.11**). For instance, from 7% to 8% of the workers working from 35 to 48 hours per week would prefer fewer hours of work each week, assuming they maintain their same *hourly* pay rate. This suggests that, relative to the preferences of millions of workers, employers are not providing enough opportunities for workers to have part-time jobs at pay rates equivalent to those paid full-time workers.

More Than One Job

The growth of part-time work reflects growing under-employment and deteriorating pay and opportunity in the economy. The growth of multiple jobholding—people working in at least two jobs—reflects the overemployment due to the deterioration of real wages since 1979, which persisted even during the recovery years from 1985 through 1989. This increased incidence of multiple jobholding between 1979 and 1989 due to economic hardship reasons was responsible for roughly 1.2 million additional multiple jobholders.

In 1989, 7.2 million workers held at least two jobs (**Table

The growth of multiple jobholding . . . reflects . . . deterioration of real wages since 1979 . . .

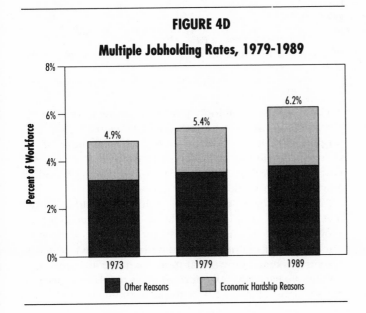

FIGURE 4D

Multiple Jobholding Rates, 1979-1989

141

TABLE 4.13

Growth of Multiple Jobholding By Sex, 1973-1989

Year	Number of Multiple Jobholders (000)	Multiple Jobholding Rate	Percent of Workforce Who Hold Multiple Jobs Because of:	
			Economic Hardship*	Other Reasons**
Women				
1973	869	2.7%	N/A	N/A
1979	1,407	3.5	1.5%	2.0%
1985	2,192	4.7	2.0	2.7
1989	3,109	5.9	2.9	3.0
Change				
1973-79	538	0.8	N/A	N/A
1979-85	785	1.2	0.5	0.7
1985-89	917	1.2	0.9	0.3
Men				
1973	3,393	6.6	N/A	N/A
1979	3,317	5.9	2.1	3.8
1985	3,537	5.9	2.3	3.6
1989	4,115	6.4	2.6	3.8
Change				
1973-79	- 76	-0.7	N/A	N/A
1979-85	220	0.0	0.2	-0.2
1985-89	578	0.5	0.3	0.2

*To meet regular household expenses or pay off debts.

**Includes saving for the future, getting experience, helping a friend or relative, buying something special, enjoying the work, and so on.

The growth of multiple jobholding has occurred primarily among workers who work at more than one job because of "economic hardship."

4.12). The rate of multiple jobholding grew from 4.9% in 1979 to 6.2% in 1989, an increase of 1.3 percentage points (**Figure 4D**). It is especially noteworthy that most of the growth of multiple jobholding occurred in the recovery years from 1985 to 1989, when an additional 1.5 million workers began working more than one job.

An analysis of the reasons for multiple jobholding shows that increased multiple jobholding reflects deteriorating economic performance, rather than enhanced opportunity. The growth of multiple jobholding has occurred primarily among workers who work at more than one job because of "economic hardship," the need to meet regular expenses or pay off debts (Table 4.12). Multiple jobholding due to eco-

142

nomic hardship increased by 1.0 percentage point from 1979 to 1989, accounting for more than three-fourths of the 1.3 percentage point rise in multiple jobholding. This same pattern holds even over the recovery years from 1985 to 1989, when increased economic hardship accounted for 0.6 percentage points of the 0.8 percentage point rise in the multiple jobholding rate. In contrast, the multiple jobholding rate for "other reasons" rose only 0.3% from 1979 to 1989, from 3.1% to 3.4%, and was responsible for about 350,000 more multiple jobholders.

There was a rapid increase in the multiple jobholding rate among women between 1979 and 1989, rising from 3.5% to 5.9% (**Table 4.13**). Economic hardship explains roughly 60% of this increase. Between 1985 and 1989, 75% of the rise in women's multiple jobholding is due to economic hardship. By 1989, a greater proportion of women (2.9%) than men (2.6%) worked more than one job in order to meet regular expenses or pay off debts.

Table 4.14 provides a demographic breakdown of those working more than one job for economic hardship reasons.

The share of women among those who worked more than one job because of economic hardship has rapidly increased.

TABLE 4.14

Distribution of Multiple Jobholders Experiencing Economic Hardship, 1979–1989

Sex/Marital Status	Distribution of Multiple Jobholders Who Have Economic Hardship Reasons*		
	1979	1985	1989
Total, 16 Years and Over	100.0%	100.0%	100.0%
Women	33.7	40.6	48.2
Married, Spouse Present	11.2	14.9	19.8
Other	22.5	25.7	28.5
Single	N/A	10.8	13.1
Widowed, Divorced, or Separated	N/A	14.9	15.5
Men	66.4	59.3	51.8
Married, Spouse Present	54.9	42.8	36.2
Other	11.6	16.5	15.6
Single	N/A	10.2	11.4
Widowed, Divorced, or Separated	N/A	6.4	4.2

*Workers who report they have multiple jobs in order to meet regular household expenses or pay off debts.

TABLE 4.15

Hours Worked By Multiple Jobholders, By Sex, 1989

| | | Percent of Multiple Jobholders Working: | | | | |
Sex	Average Weekly Hours	0–40 Hours	41–48 Hours	49–69 Hours	70+ Hours	Total
Total	52.0	17.6%	24.5%	43.9%	14.0%	100.0%
Male	55.8	9.3	23.9	48.4	18.5	100.0
Female	47.1	28.5	25.4	38.0	8.2	100.0

TABLE 4.16

The Use of Various Types of Contingent Labor

| | Percent of Surveyed Firms That Use Contingent Labor, By Type of Labor | | |
Survey	Internal Temporary Worker Pool	Temporary Agencies Help	Independent Contracting
1986*	36%	77%	63%
1989**	49	97	78

*Survey of 477 major companies.

**Survey of 521 major companies.

144

As suggested by Table 4.13, the share of women among those who worked more than one job because of economic hardship has rapidly increased so that by 1989 nearly half of these workers were women. In 1989, more than half of multiple jobholders were married (wives, 19.8%, husbands, 36.2%) and an additional fifth were widowed, divorced, or separated men or women. These data thus show that the hardship associated with and reflected by multiple jobholding is concentrated in working families and among adult workers.

The majority of those working multiple jobs in 1989 worked at least 49 hours per week (**Table 4.15**). Two-thirds of men working more than one job worked at least 49 hours per week while about 46% of women multiple jobholders did so. These data confirm that multiple jobholding does not simply reflect people combining two part-time jobs into the equivalent of one full-time job. Rather, multiple jobholders worked an average of 52 hours per week in 1989.

The Contingent Workforce

A significant portion of people in today's workforce have become "contingent workers." Workers can be hired on a temporary or "contingent" basis in a variety of ways. Some firms put workers directly on their payroll but assign them to an internal temporary worker pool. Employers also use temporary help agencies to obtain workers on a temporary basis, sometimes for long periods. Some businesses hire independent contractors to perform work that would otherwise be done by employees. All three types of contingent workers are frequently denied health insurance and pension coverage and have little access to promotions and better jobs.

Data drawn from surveys of major companies suggest that the use of contingent labor is widespread and rising (**Table 4.16**). In 1986, 36% of the surveyed firms had an internal temporary worker pool. A later survey (not of the same firms) shows that 49% of firms use their own temporary worker pool. The hiring of workers through temporary help agencies is now nearly universal among large companies. In the 1989 survey, 97% of the firms used temporary help agencies. Independent contracting is also widespread,

A significant portion of people in today's workforce have become "contingent workers."

TABLE 4.17

The Growth of Personnel Services Industry Employment, 1973–1989

	Personnel Industry Employment*			
	Number (000)		As Share of Total Employment	
Year	Total	Women	Total	Women
1973	256	133	0.3%	0.2%
1979	527	309	0.6	0.3
1982	555	354	0.6	0.4
1989	1,351	782	1.2	0.7

*This industry consists of temporary help agencies (75% of industry employment) and employment agencies (25% of industry employment).

FIGURE 4E

Temporary and Personnel Service Employment, 1973-1989

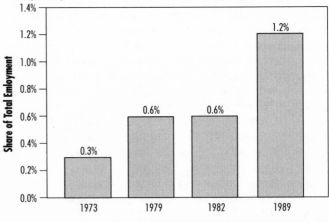

146

with 78% of the firms using this method in 1989. In the earlier survey, 63% of the firms hired independent contractors.

Unfortunately, these surveys do not have information on how many contingent workers these firms actually use. The only subgroup of contingent workers that is captured by government statistics is the workforce employed through temporary help agencies. Unfortunately, these data are not available for the years before 1982. For a longer perspective, however, it is possible to examine the growth of the entire personnel services industry, which consists primarily of workers hired through or working for temporary agencies (three-fourths of total) but also includes people working in employment agencies (**Table 4.17** and **Figure 4E**). There was an explosive growth in personnel services employment from 1979 to 1989, but especially between 1982 and 1989. Industry employment rose by 824,000 from 1979 to 1989, with 796,000 jobs added since 1982. As a result, the share of the workforce employed in the personnel services industry doubled, from 0.6% in 1982 to 1.2% in 1989. The industry share of total employment in 1989, 1.2%, was four times greater than its share in 1973, 0.3%. The increase in the proportion of the workforce in the personnel services industry from 1973 to 1989 (from 0.3% to 1.2%) meant an additional 1 million workers in the industry.

Women are more likely to be employed as temporary workers, partly because such work provides flexible hours but also because there is a higher incidence of temporary work in occupations dominated by women, such as clerical work. Moreover, "temping" is sometimes the only option available for work. In 1989, 782,000, or 58%, of the 1,351,000 workers in the personnel services industry were women.

Women are more likely to be employed as temporary workers . . .

TABLE 4.18

Growth in Temporary Help Industry Employment, 1982–89

| | Temporary Help Industry Employment | | | |
| | Number (000) | | As Share of Total Employment | |
Year	Total	Women	Total	Women
1982*	401	256	0.4%	0.3%
1989	1,032	618	0.9	0.7

*Earlier data not available.

TABLE 4.19

Elements of the Marginal Workforce*

	Number of Workers (in thousands)
Temporary Help Services**	944
Leased Workers**	120
At-home Workers***	2,243
8 hours/week or more	1,992
35 hours/week or more	1,067

*Data are from different sources and reflect the situation in the 1985–87 period.

**1987

***1985

The available information on temporary help industry employment since 1982 is presented in **Table 4.18**. These data confirm that the growth in the overall personnel services industry is primarily due to more workers employed through temporary help agencies. An additional 0.5% of the workforce, or 575,000 more workers, were employed through temporary help agencies in 1989 compared to 1982. Most of the increase was among women.

Other types of marginal workers (**Table 4.19**) include "leased employees" who work for one firm but are leased to another, and workers employed at home (so employers can reduce their overhead and avoid labor regulations such as minimum wage, overtime, and safety protections). These workers, along with those employed by "temp" agencies, are the statistically visible portion of this new marginal workforce; many others—such as new immigrants—escape detection.

An additional 0.5% of the workforce were employed through temporary help agencies in 1989 compared to 1982.

Self-Employment

A significant portion of total employment consists of self-employed workers, those whose primary job is working in their own business, farm, craft, or profession. Individual independent contractors, discussed above, would be considered self-employed.

In 1989, self-employment represented 7.5% of total employment, up from 7.1% in 1979 (**Table 4.20**). The greatest

TABLE 4.20

The Growth of Self-Employment

Year	Self-Employment as Share of Total Employment* Among:		
	All Workers	Men	Women
1948	12.1%	N/A	N/A
1967	7.3	8.8%	4.9%
1973	6.7	8.2	4.4
1979	7.1	8.8	4.9
1989	7.5	9.0	5.8

*Nonagricultural industries.

TABLE 4.21

Self-Employment (1983 Dollars) and Paid Employment Earnings

	Median Annualized Earnings of Full-Time Year-Round Workers	
	Men	Women
Self-Employed Workers	$13,520	$ 3,767
Paid Employees	20,039	12,079
Self-Employed Workers' Earnings as Percent of Paid Employees' Earnings	67%	31%

growth in self-employment has been among women workers, who earn far less in self-employment than in regular paid employment. An additional 1.4% of women workers were considered self-employed in 1989 compared to 1973. The rate of self-employment among men is higher than among women but has risen more slowly.

Much of self-employment is disguised underemployment. Self-employed women earn only 31% as much as women wage and salary workers, the growth of self-employment means lower earnings for millions of women (**Table 4.21**). Self-employed men earn one-third less than men who are paid as wage and salary workers. So, the growth of male self-employment means depressed earnings for millions of men.

Much of self-employment is disguised under-employment.

CHAPTER 5

TABLE 5.1

Median Net Worth by Family Income, 1983
(1983 Dollars)

Family Income	Percent of Families	Median Net Worth
Less than $5,000	9%	$ 514
5,000–7,499	8	2,140
7,500–9,999	7	2,725
10,000–14,999	14	11,575
15,000–19,999	13	15,383
20,000–24,999	11	22,820
25,000–29,999	9	28,876
30,000–39,999	13	45,981
40,000–49,999	7	63,941
50,000+	10	130,851

TABLE 5.2

Percent Distribution of Wealth and Income, 1983

Family Income Group	Shares of Total		
	Net Financial Assets	Net Worth	Income
Upper 2%	54%	28%	14%
Next 8%	32	29	19
Bottom 90%*	14	43	67
All	100	100	100

*20 percent of families had a zero or negative net worth; 54 percent of families had a zero or negative net value of financial assets.

WEALTH: A FINANCIAL BOOM ONLY FOR THE FEW

S tagnant incomes and falling wages are only part of the decline in the well-being of working Americans. A family's wealth also affects its standard of living, as well as its ability to cope with financial emergencies. For example, financial assets, such as money in a bank account, can help a family make ends meet during periods of illness or unemployment. Tangible assets, such as a home or a car, can directly affect a family's standard of living.

The distribution of wealth is even more concentrated at the top than the distribution of income. In addition, the typical black family with a given income has a tiny fraction of the wealth of a white family with the same income. There are similar racial differences controlling for family type as well.

In the 1980s, the financial assets owned primarily by the wealthy grew considerably, while tangible assets, which are spread out more evenly, increased only slightly. This caused the distribution of wealth to become yet more unequal. In particular, we project that the average net worth of the richest 0.5% of families rose 6.7% between 1979 and 1989, while the average net worth of families in the bottom 90% actually fell by 8.8% (Table 5.11). This means that the gap in overall financial security between the rich, on the one hand, and the middle class and the poor, on the other, has widened even further. In addition, there has been a striking increase in the wealth gap between older and younger families.

In the 1980s, the financial assets owned primarily by the wealthy grew considerably, while tangible assets, which are spread out more evenly, increased only slightly.

Wealth More Unequal Than Income

The distribution of wealth is considerably less equal than the distribution of income. Thus, the typical low income family has a net worth well *below* its annual income, while the typical high income family has a net worth that *exceeds* its income (**Table 5.1**).

The concentration of wealth among very high income families is dramatic. **Table 5.2** and **Figure 5A** reveal that in 1983, the latest year for which such data is available, the top 2% of families, ranked by income, earned 14% of total income, yet owned 28% of total net worth and a remarkable 54% of net financial assets. Net worth is the value of one's assets, minus one's debts. For a typical family this might be the value of its house, car, other consumer goods,

153

Distribution of Income, Net Worth, and Net Financial Assets, 1983

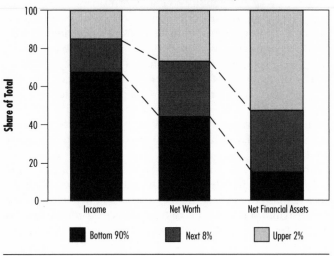

TABLE 5.3

Selected Holdings of American Families, 1983

Asset Class	Super Rich (Top 0.5%)	Very Rich (Next 0.5%)	Rich (90–99%)	Rest (0–90%)	Total
Assets Held Primarily by the Wealthy					
Corporate Stock	46.5%	13.5%	29.3%	10.7%	100.0%
Bonds	43.6	7.5	39.3	9.7	100.0
Business Assets (net)	40.1	11.5	39.3	9.0	100.0
Assets and Liabilities Held Primarily by the Non-Wealthy					
Real Estate	15.3%	4.2%	29.5%	50.9%	100.0%
Liquid Assets*	9.5	5.6	32.0	52.9	100.0
Insurance	6.5	3.5	20.8	69.2	100.0
Debt	10.4	3.3	18.9	67.5	100.0

*Money in checking and savings accounts, money market accounts, IRAs, Keoghs, CDs.

154

and bank accounts, less the amount owed on its mortgages and credit cards. Net financial assets are *financial* assets minus debts. For the same family, this would be the bank account balance, minus mortgage and credit card debts.

At the bottom of the distribution, 20% of families had a zero or negative net worth and fully 54% of families had zero or negative net financial assets (Table 5.2). Although most of the latter are not poor, their lack of financial assets indicates that more than half of American families are living from paycheck to paycheck with little or nothing in the bank in case of a loss of job or other serious financial emergency.

The concentration of financial assets at the top implies that American businesses are owned and financed primarily by the very wealthiest families. In 1983, for example, the top 0.5% of wealth holders owned 46.5% of all corporate stocks, while the bottom 90% owned only 10.7% (**Table 5.3**). The top 0.5% also owned 43.6% of bonds and 40.1% of private business assets, while the bottom 90% owned only 9.7% of bonds and 9.0% of business assets. The bottom 90%, moreover, are stuck with 67.5% of the debt.

Wide Gaps Between the Races

We already know that blacks and other minorities tend to have lower incomes than whites. Yet blacks lag even further behind in the accumulation of wealth. The wealth of a typical black family is just a fraction of the wealth of a typical white family *at the same income level* (**Table 5.4**). This is particularly true among low income families: in 1984, black households with less than $900 in income per

TABLE 5.4

Median Net Worth by Race and Monthly Household Income, 1984

(1984 Dollars)

Monthly Income	Median Net Worth		Black/White Ratio
	Blacks	Whites	
Less Than $900	$ 88	$ 8,443	.01
900 to 1,900	4,218	30,714	.14
2,000 to 3,999	15,977	50,529	.32
4,000 or more	58,758	128,237	.46

TABLE 5.5

Median Net Worth by Type of Household, 1984

(1984 Dollars)

Household Type	Median Net Worth		Black/White Ratio
	Blacks	Whites	
All Households	$ 3,397	$39,135	.09
Married Couples	13,061	54,184	.24
Female Head	671	22,500	.03
Male Head	3,022	11,826	.26

TABLE 5.6

Growth of Household Wealth, 1949–1989

	Annual Growth of Household* Net Worth Per Adult			
	1949–67	1967–73	1973–79	1979–89
Total	3.3%	0.7%	1.9%	1.5%
Tangible Assets	3.9	3.6	3.9	0.6
Net Financial Assets	3.0	-1.0	0.4	2.3

*Includes all households, personal trusts, and nonprofit organizations.

For each type of family, there are large wealth gaps between blacks and whites.

month had only 1% of the wealth of white households with the same incomes. Even black households with incomes over $4,000 per month had only 46% of the wealth of equivalent white households.

This racial difference is not simply the result of differences in family structure: for each type of family, there are large wealth gaps between blacks and whites (**Table 5.5**). At the extreme, black female-headed households own just 3% of the wealth of white female-headed households.

156

Household Wealth: Financial Assets Boomed, Tangibles Slowed

A basic measure of aggregate wealth is *household net worth*, which is just the total assets of all households, minus their debts. Household net worth per adult increased 1.5% per year between 1979 and 1989 (**Table 5.6** and **Figure 5B**). This rate was greater than the 0.7% annual rate in the 1967–73 period, but less than the 1.9% rate of 1973–79 and well under the 3.3% annual growth of 1949–67.

Not all household assets increased in value at the same rate. Financial assets boomed, but tangible assets grew much more slowly. Since the wealthy own most of the financial assets in the country, these developments have benefitted them in particular. Growth of net financial assets per adult

Financial assets boomed, but tangible assets grew much more slowly.

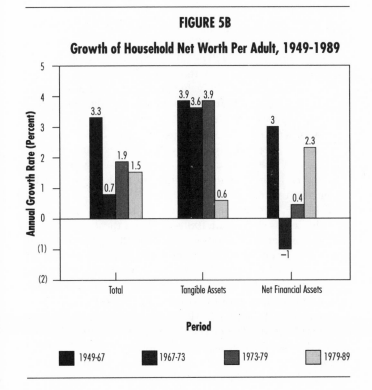

FIGURE 5B

Growth of Household Net Worth Per Adult, 1949-1989

157

TABLE 5.7

Growth of Tangible Asset Values, 1949-1989

	Annual Growth Per Adult*			
	1949–67	1967–73	1973–79	1979–89
Adjusted for Overall Inflation in Economy				
Owner-occupied housing and land	3.9%	4.3%	5.0%	0.6%
Consumer durables	3.5	2.4	2.2	0.9
Adjusted for Specific Inflation of Housing and Durables				
Owner-occupied housing**	N/A	2.2%	1.3%	0.8%
Consumer durables	4.9%	4.5	3.6	2.6

*Nonprofit organizations excluded.
**Land excluded.

was 2.3% per year in the 1979–89 period. Although this rate was less than the 3.0% growth rate of 1949–67, it considerably exceeded the –1.0% yearly decline of 1967–73 and the 0.4% annual growth of 1973–79.

On the other hand, the value per adult of tangible assets, such as housing and land, automobiles, appliances, and so on, barely grew at all: just 0.6% per year. This was considerably slower than the annual growth rates of 3.9%, 3.6%, and 3.9%, respectively, in the three preceding periods. Since tangible assets are spread out more evenly than financial assets, their stagnation mainly affected the bulk of the population who are not wealthy.

Table 5.7 looks more closely at the slow growth of tangible assets during the 1980s. It shows the annual growth rates of owner-occupied housing and land, on the one hand, and of consumer durables such as automobiles and appliances, on the other. Adjusted for overall inflation, the values of both housing and consumer durables per adult grew much more rapidly in previous periods than in the current period (lines 1–2). Housing and land per adult grew at a rapid clip of 5% per year between 1973 and 1979, then slowed to only 0.6% per year during the 1979–89 period. Annual growth of consumer durables per adult also fell, from 2.2% in 1973–79 to 0.9% in 1979–89.

Tangible assets . . . stagnation mainly affected the bulk of the population who are not wealthy.

158

Since these growth rates are corrected for overall inflation rather than for specific price changes, they can be
influenced by unusual changes in prices of housing or consumer durables. For example, housing prices boomed in the
1970s and slumped in the 1980s; this may explain the high
growth in 1973–79 and the stagnation in 1979–89. In other
words, even though housing and land per adult did not
increase greatly in value during the 1980s, real improvements in housing quality and quantity may have continued
apace. We can get at this issue by adjusting housing and
consumer durables by their own price inflation rates rather
than by the overall inflation rate. The resulting growth rates
indicate the rate at which housing and consumer durables
per adult became better and more plentiful in each period.

Housing prices boomed in the 1970s and slumped in the 1980s.

Figure 5C and the latter half of Table 5.7 show these
rates. Even using the specific inflation measures, real rates

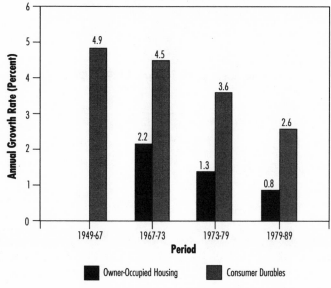

FIGURE 5C

**Growth of Tangible Assets Per Adult Adjusted for Specific
Inflation of Housing and Consumer Durables, 1949-1989**

Owner-Occupied Housing   Consumer Durables

159

FIGURE 5D

Household Debt Burden, 1949–1989

Debt as Percent of Assets (Left Scale)

Debt as Percent of Personal Income (Right Scale)

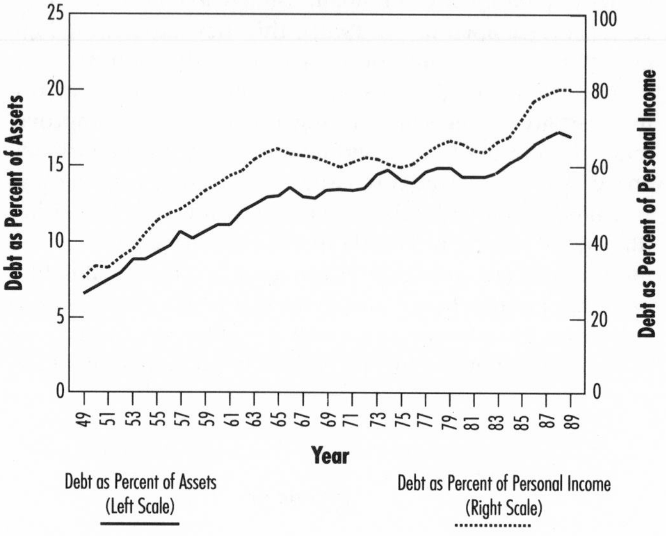

TABLE 5.8

Household Debt Burden, 1949–1989

	Debt as Percent of:		
Year	Personal Income	Total Assets*	Assets Less Pension Funds
1949	30.3%	6.9%	7.0%
1967	62.5	13.1	13.9
1973	61.8	14.5	15.6
1979	66.8	14.9	16.3
1989	80.2	17.1	19.9

*Financial assets (including pension funds and insurance), real estate, and consumer durables.

160

of growth still fall off substantially in the current period. Housing per adult grew at only 0.8% per year in the 1979–89 period, after growing 2.2% in 1967–73 and 1.3% in 1973–79. Consumer durable growth also slowed to 2.6% per year in 1979–89, following annual growth rates of 4.9%, 4.5%, and 3.6% in the three previous periods.

Debt Soared, Hurting Low Income Families

At the same time that tangible assets, the main assets of working people, have grown more slowly, household debt has skyrocketed. Two measures of the total debt burdens of households, debts as a percent of assets and as a percent of personal income, have each grown markedly in the 1980s after a long period of relative stability (**Figure 5D**). Household debt lept from 66.8% of personal income in 1979 to 80.2% in 1989, and from 14.9% of household assets in 1979 to 17.1% in 1989 (**Table 5.8**). Since the asset totals include pension funds, which are not generally accessible before retirement, we also present debt as a percent of assets excluding pension funds. This percentage rose even more, from 16.3% in 1979 to 19.9% in 1989 (Table 5.8).

This increased indebtedness reflects financial strain among low income families in particular. As **Table 5.9** shows, low income families have the largest debt servicing burdens of all, and their burdens grew the most between 1970 and 1983, the years for which the most reliable data are available. The lowest fifth of families had an average yearly debt payment of 24% of income in 1970, compared to 14% for the average family overall. The yearly burden for the lowest fifth grew to 34% in 1983, while burdens among upper income families actually fell off slightly.

Household debt has skyrocketed . . . reflecting financial strain among low income families in particular.

TABLE 5.9

Annual Household Debt Servicing Burdens as Percents of Household Incomes

| Year | Household Income Fifths | | | | | All |
	Lowest	Second	Middle	Fourth	Highest	
1970	24%	17%	16%	16%	11%	14%
1983	34	20	16	14	10	13

TABLE 5.10

The Changing Distribution of Wealth, 1963–1989

(1989 Dollars)

	Super Rich (Top 0.5%)	Very Rich (Next 0.5%)	Rich (90–99%)	Rest (0–90%)	Total
Distribution of Net Worth					
1963 (actual)	28.5%	9.0%	35.3%	27.2%	100.0%
1979 (projected)	27.8	8.8	36.4	27.0	100.0
1983 (actual)	28.1	9.0	35.0	27.9	100.0
1989 (projected)	29.2	9.1	37.5	24.3	100.0
Average Net Worth Per Household ($000)					
1963 (actual)	$5,441	$1,707	$374	$29	$ 95
1979 (projected)	7,009	2,223	509	38	126
1983 (actual)	6,238	1,988	431	34	111
1989 (projected)	7,476	2,332	533	35	128
Percent Change					
1963–1979	28.8%	30.2%	36.3%	31.3%	32.2%
1979–1989	6.7	4.9	4.7	-8.8	1.6
Average Assets Per Household ($000)					
1963 (actual)	$5,644	$1,765	$405	$45	$114
1979 (projected)	7,622	2,416	571	60	156
1983 (actual)	6,826	2,173	491	56	139
1989 (projected)	8,271	2,582	613	63	166
Average Debt Per Household ($000)					
1963 (actual)	$ 204	$ 58	$ 31	$17	$ 19
1979 (projected)	613	193	62	22	29
1983 (actual)	587	185	59	21	28
1989 (projected)	795	250	80	29	38

TABLE 5.11

Distribution of Wealth by Age, 1962–1983

(1989 Dollars)

Age of Family Head	Average Household Wealth In:			% Change, 1973–83	% Change, 1962–83
	1962	1973	1983		
Under 25	$ 12,466	$ 27,444	$ 16,924	-38.3%	35.8%
25–34	35,304	63,653	57,455	- 9.7	62.7
35–44	80,600	98,415	144,639	47.0	79.5
45–54	108,718	115,954	275,849	137.9	153.7
55–59	192,374	126,632	289,880	128.9	50.7
60–64	139,114	133,218	307,929	131.1	121.3
65 and over	159,237	171,934	266,461	55.0	67.3
All	104,981	108,138	175,317	62.1	67.0

The Result: Even Greater Inequality

After a decade of booming financial assets, almost stagnant tangible asset values, and rising debt burdens, it would be surprising if the wealthy did not own a rather larger share of net wealth in 1989 compared to 1979. Although the most recent suitable survey of household wealth took place in 1983, it is possible to project the distributions of wealth in 1979 and 1989. According to the projections, the share of the richest 0.5% increased from 27.8% of wealth in 1979 to 29.2% in 1989 (**Table 5.10** and **Figure 5E**). Because the shares of the next 0.5% and the 90–99% group also increased, the projected share of the bottom 90% sank from 27.0% in 1979 to 24.3% in 1989. This entire shift occurred during the period of economic recovery between 1983 and 1989. Projected average net worth per household in the bottom 90% decreased by 8.8% between 1979 and 1989, from $38,000 to $35,000, while the average super rich household experienced a projected gain of 6.7%, from $7,009,000 to $7,476,000.

The projected share of the bottom 90% sank from 27.0% in 1979 to 24.3% in 1989.

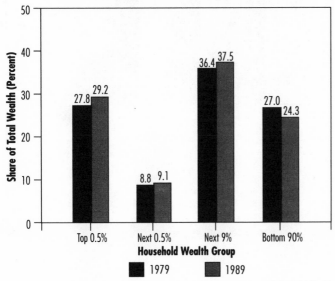

FIGURE 5E

Shares of Household Wealth (Projected), 1979-1989

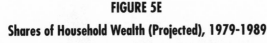

163

TABLE 5.12

Growth of National Wealth, 1949–1989

	Annual Growth of National Net Worth Per Adult			
	1949–1967	1967–1973	1973–1979	1979–1989
Total: Governments, Businesses and Households	2.9%	3.1%	3.9%	–0.6%
Businesses and Households Only*	2.3	2.6	3.7	0.2

*Including net foreign corporate stock owned by Americans.

FIGURE 5F

Growth of National Net Worth Per Adult, 1949-1989

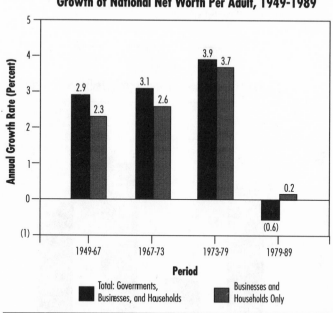

Young Families Lost Out

From 1973 to 1983, the age distribution of wealth also became strikingly more unequal, in parallel with the age distribution of income (**Table 5.11**). During this period, the wealth of the average young household plummeted, while the average wealth of older households increased considerably. For example, the average wealth of households headed by persons under 25 years of age fell 38.3% from 1973 to 1983, while the wealth of households whose heads were 45 to 54 increased by 153.7%.

National Net Worth Stagnates

Household net worth does not include the net worth of businesses and governments. One broader measure of aggregate wealth is national net worth, which is the combined net worth of businesses, governments, and households. After increasing 2.9% per year between 1949 and 1967, 3.1% in the 1967–73 period, and 3.9% in 1973–79, national net worth per adult actually *fell* in the 1980s, at an annual rate of –0.6% (**Table 5.12** and **Figure 5F**).

The federal government's burgeoning debt was one cause of the sudden drop in national net worth. However, even when the public sector is left out, the annual growth of the net worth per adult in the private sector—businesses and households—was virtually nil between 1979 and 1989: a tiny 0.2% (Table 5.12, Figure 5F). This is far less than the growth of earlier periods, and particularly disappointing after the 3.7% annual growth rate of the previous period.

From 1973 to 1983, the age distribution of wealth also became strikingly more unequal.

165

CHAPTER 6

TABLE 6.1

Percent in Poverty, 1959–1988

Year	Poverty Rate	Number in Poverty (000)
1959	22.4%	39,490
1967	14.2	27,769
1973	11.1	22,973
1979	11.7	26,072
1989	12.8	31,534

TABLE 6.2

Poverty Rates when Noncash Benefits Are Included

Year	Current Definition	Adding Food and Housing Benefits	
		At Market Value	At Recipient Value
1979	11.7%	9.7%	10.0%
1987*	13.4	12.0	12.4
Point Increase, 1979–1987	1.7	2.3	2.4

*Latest data available using 1979 methods.

166

POVERTY: FALLING WAGES, TORN SAFETY NET

Although per capita income and median family income have grown since 1979, the well-being of those at the bottom of the income scale has deteriorated. The poverty rate has actually increased since 1979, and more of the poor now have incomes below half of the poverty line. Poverty rates have increased most among children and persons in female-headed families. Decreased governmental aid and lower wages are largely to blame for the increase in poverty since 1979. Among female-headed families, cuts in benefits raised the poverty rate by 8.6 percentage points between 1979 and 1988.

Among married-couple families, poverty is due primarily to low wages. Most of these families also receive no government benefits. The reasons for poverty among female-headed families are more complex. Women on welfare suffer from low government benefits and child support levels. The costs of working also often outweigh the benefits, because of low wages, high child care expenses, and the rapid phaseout of government aid as earnings increase. The vast majority of female family heads in 1989 were either divorced (36.4%), widowed (23.9%), or married to absent husbands (17.1%). Only a small fraction, 22.6%, of female family heads in 1989 had never been married (Table 6.31).

Worse by Any Measure

Poverty has been getting worse since 1979, no matter how you measure it. As **Table 6.1** shows, poverty at the peaks of successive business cycles has been increasing since reaching a low of 11.1% in 1973. This trend reverses the rapid improvement that took place between 1959 and 1973. In 1989, an additional 5.5 million people were living in poverty compared with 1979.

The official measure of poverty includes governmental cash benefits but not food and housing benefits. Including these benefits may reduce the *absolute* level of poverty, but it makes the *increase* in poverty since 1979 even greater than before. **Table 6.2** uses two ways to value food and housing benefits: market value, which is what the benefits would actually cost if purchased, and recipient value, which is an estimate of what a real family would be willing to pay to get the benefits. Using either method, food and housing benefits decrease the poverty level in each year, as we

Decreased governmental aid and lower wages are largely to blame for the increase in poverty since 1979.

167

TABLE 6.3

The Market Value of Medicare in the Six Largest States, 1987

	Elderly Couple Covered by Medicare		
State	Market Value of Medicare Coverage	Poverty Threshold	Market Value as a Percent of Poverty Threshold
California	$6,224	$6,865	90.7%
New York	5,124	6,865	74.6
Texas	4,628	6,865	67.4
Pennsylvania	5,634	6,865	82.1
Florida	5,648	6,865	82.3
Illinois	5,066	6,865	73.8

TABLE 6.4

Poverty Income Deficits, 1973–1988

	Mean Income Deficits*	
Year	Per Family Member	Persons Not in Families
Deficits		
1973	$1,162	$2,608
1979	1,266	2,553
1989	1,416	2,836
Percent Changes		
1973–79	8.9%	–2.1%
1979–89	11.9	11.1

*The dollar gap between actual incomes and the poverty line.

The poverty level does not reflect today's high cost of health insurance.

would expect. However, poverty rose by 2.3 or 2.4 points between 1979 and 1987—well over the 1.7 point increase that is based on the official definition of poverty.

Some have even suggested that medical benefits should be included in the definition of income, but the case for this is weak since the poverty level does not reflect today's high cost of health insurance. For example, as **Table 6.3** shows, the cost of health insurance equivalent to Medicare for an elderly couple living in California was $6,224 in 1987, while the poverty level itself was only $6,865. If the market value

168

of medical benefits were included in income, a couple who received Medicare and had a total cash income of just $700 over the entire year would not be considered poor.

The Poor Are Poorer

Not only are there more poor; the poor are also poorer. This can be seen by examining poverty income deficits, which indicate how far the income of the average poor family or individual falls below the poverty line (**Table 6.4**). Income deficits have increased markedly since 1979, by 11.9% for family members and by 11.1% for persons not living in families.

Another measure of the depth of poverty is the percentage of the poor who have incomes below half of the poverty line. In 1989, 38% of the poor had incomes below half of poverty, compared to 32.9% in 1979 (**Figure 6A**). A smaller proportion of the poverty population have incomes close to the poverty line: the percentage with incomes between 75% and 100% of the poverty line fell from 37.4% in 1979 to 34.3% in 1989.

Not only are there more poor; the poor are also poorer.

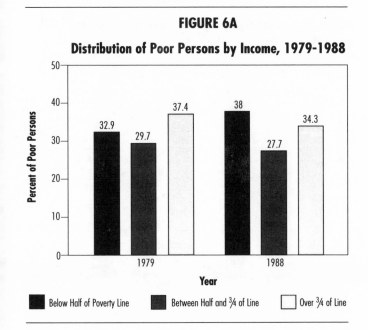

FIGURE 6A

Distribution of Poor Persons by Income, 1979-1988

■ Below Half of Poverty Line ■ Between Half and ¾ of Line □ Over ¾ of Line

TABLE 6.5

Poverty by Age and Race/Ethnic Group, 1988

Age	Total	White	Black	Hispanic
Under 3 years	23.5%	17.6%	54.3%	41.3%
3–5	21.6	16.7	46.0	37.6
6–11	19.8	15.0	43.8	36.5
12–17	16.1	11.9	36.5	31.8
18–21	15.3	12.4	29.8	27.0
22–44	10.6	8.4	22.7	20.9
45–54	7.4	6.1	17.4	17.0
55–59	9.7	7.6	28.6	17.4
60–64	9.5	7.5	27.0	18.8
65+	11.4	9.6	30.8	20.6
Total	12.8	10.0	30.7	26.2

FIGURE 6B

Poverty by Age and Race/Ethnic Group, 1988

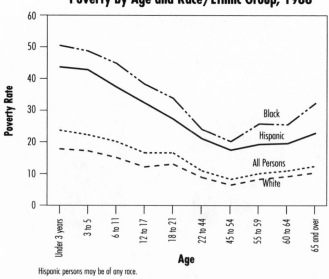

Hispanic persons may be of any race.

170

Some Groups Are Much Poorer Than Others

Which groups are most at risk to be poor? As **Table 6.5** and **Figure 6B** show, minorities are two or three times as likely to be poor; and within each race/ethnic group, children are the age group most likely to be poor. Half (54.3%) of all black children and 41.3% of Hispanic children live in poverty. **Table 6.6** shows also that 14.4% of women were poor in 1989, versus 11.2% of men. This difference begins in adulthood; thus, it reflects inequalities in pay, together with the fact that most single-parent families are headed by women.

Poverty Higher, by Race and Gender

Although minorities are much more likely to be poor than whites, poverty among whites increased between 1979 and 1989 yet eased slightly among blacks. **Table 6.7** shows that poverty among whites rose from 9% in 1979 to 10% in

Minorities are two or three times as likely to be poor; and within each race/ ethnic group, children are the age group most likely to be poor.

TABLE 6.6

Poverty by Age and Sex, 1988

Age	Male	Female
Under 16 years	20.0%	20.3%
16–21	13.6	17.1
22–44	7.9	12.7
45–54	5.9	8.9
55–59	7.8	11.4
60–64	8.4	10.5
65+	7.8	14.0
Total	11.2	14.4

TABLE 6.7

Poverty Rates by Race/Ethnic Group, 1967–1988

Year	All	White	Black	Hispanic
1967	14.2%	11.0%	39.3%	N/A
1973	11.1	8.4	31.4	21.9%
1979	11.7	9.0	31.0	21.8
1989	12.8	10.0	30.7	26.2

FIGURE 6C

Poverty Rates by Race/Ethnic Group, 1959–1988

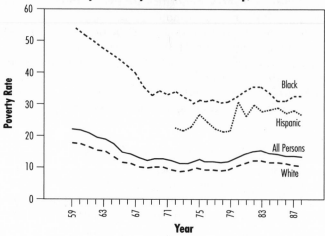

TABLE 6.8

Poverty by Sex, 1973–1989

Year	Male	Female
1973	9.6%	12.5%
1979	10.0	13.2
1989	11.2	14.4

TABLE 6.9

Poverty Among the Elderly and All Persons Before and After Cash Transfers, 1967–1988

	Poverty Rate Among:			
	All Persons		The Elderly*	
Year	Before Transfers	After Transfers	Before Transfers	After Transfers
1967	19.4%	14.3%	58.3%	29.7%
1973	19.0	11.1	58.0	16.1
1979	20.4	11.6	58.9	15.1
1988	21.2	13.0	52.0	12.0

*Persons aged 65 and over.

1989, while black poverty fell from 31% in 1979 to 30.7% in 1989 (see also **Figure 6C**). Hispanics experienced a large increase during the same period, from 21.8% to 26.2%. In addition, **Table 6.8** shows that although more women are poor than men, men and women have had comparable increases in poverty since 1979.

Poverty Among the Elderly

Figure 6D contrasts child poverty with poverty among the elderly and all persons. As this Figure shows, poverty among the elderly has fallen dramatically since 1967. **Table 6.9** and **Figure 6E** examine the reasons for this decrease by contrasting the "before-transfer" poverty rate, which is the rate that would prevail if there were no government cash assistance, with the actual or "after-transfer" poverty rate, which includes such assistance. The reduction in poverty among the elderly has come largely from expanded government transfer payments, particularly between 1967 and 1973. During this period, the before-transfer poverty rate dipped very slightly, from 58.3% to 58%, but higher Social Security benefits virtually halved after-transfer poverty, from 29.7% to 16.1%. In 1988, more than half of the

The reduction in poverty among the elderly has come largely from expanded government transfer payments, particularly between 1967 and 1973.

FIGURE 6D

Poverty Rates Among Children and the Elderly, 1959–1988

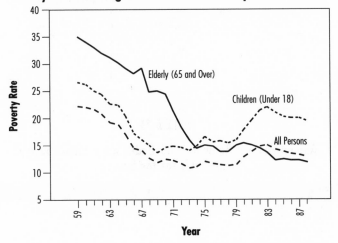

173

FIGURE 6E

Poverty Among the Elderly and All Persons Before and After Cash Transfers, 1967–1988

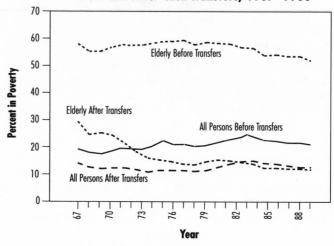

TABLE 6.10

The Poor and the Near-Poor

Year	Poverty Rate		Percent Between Poverty Level and 125% of Poverty Level	
	All	Elderly	All	Elderly
1969	12.1%	25.3%	5.3%	9.9%
1973	11.1	16.3	4.7	10.5
1979	11.7	15.2	4.7	9.5
1989	12.8	11.4	4.5	7.7

TABLE 6.11

Annual Poverty Rates in 1986 Under Alternative Poverty Thresholds for the Elderly

Measure	Elderly Persons	Non-Elderly Persons	All Persons
Official Threshold	12.4%	13.7%	13.6%
Same Threshold for Elderly as for Nonelderly	15.3	13.7	13.9

174

elderly would have been poor without government transfer programs. The effect of government benefits in 1988 was to reduce the poverty rate among the elderly from 52% to just 12%.

On the other hand, poverty rates for the elderly are still higher than the rates for adults (Table 6.5 and Figure 6B). Moreover, because of their dependence on Social Security, many of the elderly are just above the poverty line and are therefore vulnerable to cuts in benefits. **Table 6.10** shows that fully 7.7% of the elderly are above but within 25% of the poverty line, in contrast to 4.5% of the general population.

Furthermore, the relatively low rate of elderly poverty is due in part to a *lower definition of poverty*. When the poverty lines were first developed in the 1950s, the poverty line for the elderly was set lower than that for equal-sized younger families, since the elderly need fewer "calories." Many experts question whether the lower poverty line is still realistic today, given, for example, the high cost of medical care. As **Table 6.11** shows, if nonelderly poverty thresholds are applied to the elderly, their poverty rate in 1986 rises from 12.4% to 15.3%, which is greater than the 1986 poverty rate for the nonelderly, 13.7%.

Many of the elderly are just above the poverty line and are therefore vulnerable to cuts in benefits.

Higher Poverty Among Children

Figure 6D shows that children have suffered severely in recent years. Poverty among children has been increasing since 1969, and at a far faster rate than among the total population. Child poverty increased from 14.2% in 1973 to 16.2% in 1979, and then to 19.6% in 1988 (**Table 6.12**).

TABLE 6.12

Poverty Rates of Children under Age 18*

Year	Total	White	Black	Hispanic
1967	16.3%	11.3%	47.4%	N/A
1973	14.2	9.7	40.6	27.8%
1979	16.2	11.6	40.9	27.8
1989	19.0	14.1	43.2	35.5

*In families and unrelated subfamilies.

175

TABLE 6.13

Poverty Rates for Children under 18 in Female-Headed Families, 1967–1988

Year	White	Black	Hispanic
1967	46.9%	76.6%	N/A
1973	42.1	67.2	68.7%
1979	38.6	63.1	62.2
1989	42.8	62.9	65.0

TABLE 6.14

Effects of Transfers and Taxes on Poverty

| | | Percent of Pre-Transfer/Pre-Tax Poor Persons Removed from Poverty By: | | |
	Number of Pre-Transfer Pre-Tax Poor in Category (000)	Social Insurance (Including Social Security)	Means-Tested Cash, Food, and Housing Benefits, and Federal Taxes*	Total: All Taxes and Benefits
All Persons				
1979	41,695	33.2%	15.0%	48.2%
1988	49,145	31.1	9.4	40.5
Point change, 1979–88		− 2.1	− 5.6	− 7.7
Persons in Single-Parent Families with Related Children under 18				
1979	11,480	9.7%	30.0%	39.7%
1988	14,149	6.9	15.9	22.8
Point change, 1979–88		− 2.8	−14.1	−16.9
Persons in Married-Couple Families with Related Children under 18				
1979	10,030	17.9%	15.1%	33.0%
1988	11,156	16.3	8.1	24.4
Point Change, 1979–88		− 1.6	− 7.0	− 8.6

*Percent removed by means-tested benefits includes only those not already removed by non-means-tested benefits.

176

Moreover, child poverty has grown considerably within each of the three main racial/ethnic groups. Hispanic children suffered a particularly large increase, from 27.8% in 1979 to 35.5% in 1989. Poverty among white and black children also increased considerably, by about 2 to 3 percentage points each.

Poverty is particularly high among children in female-headed families (**Table 6.13**). In 1989, 42.8% of white children in female-headed families were poor, as were 62.9% of black children and 65% of Hispanic children. Rates among whites and Hispanics were higher than in 1979.

Government Benefit Cutbacks Increased Poverty

The increase in poverty in the 1980s was due partly to declining governmental aid to the poor, in the form of more restrictive rules and lower benefits. In the next three tables, we use a definition of poverty that includes food and housing benefits in income and deducts federal taxes. This permits a more comprehensive examination of the impact of government policies on the poor in the 1979–88 period.

Table 6.14 shows the percent of the poor who were removed from poverty in 1979 and 1988 by governmental programs. Between 1979 and 1988, the percent of poor persons removed from poverty by social insurance declined by 2.1 points, while the percentage removed by means-tested benefits and the tax system declined by 5.6 points, from 15% to 9.4%. Among families with children, the changes are even greater. Government taxes and benefits removed 39.7% of persons in female-headed families with children from poverty in 1979, but only 22.8% in 1988. Among married-couple families with children, government policies removed 33% of poor persons in such families from poverty in 1979, but only 24.4% in 1988.

The increase in poverty in the 1980s was due partly to declining governmental aid to the poor . . .

Poverty Among Families With Children Before and After Cash Transfers, 1967–1988

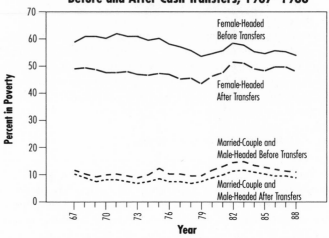

TABLE 6.15

Poverty Rates* Using Different Income Definitions, 1979–1988

Family Relationship	Market Income Before Transfers	Plus Social Insurance (Including Social Security)	Plus Means-Tested Cash Transfers	Plus Food and Housing Benefits	Less Federal Taxes	Poverty Rate Reduction Due to Government Taxes and Benefits
						(1)–(5)
	(1)	(2)	(3)	(4)	(5)	
All Persons						
1979	19.1%	12.8%	11.6%	9.6%	9.9%	9.2%
1988	20.2	13.9	13.0	11.6	12.0	8.2
Point change,						
1979–1988	1.1	1.1	1.4	2.0	2.1	– 1.0
Persons in Single-Parent Families with Related Children under 18						
1979	50.0%	45.1%	40.2%	30.0%	30.1%	19.9%
1988	49.5	46.0	43.7	38.3	38.2	11.3
Point change,						
1979–1988	– 0.5	0.9	3.5	8.3	8.1	– 8.6
Persons in Married-Couple Families with Related Children under 18						
1979	9.4%	7.7%	7.1%	5.9%	6.3%	3.1%
1988	10.5	8.8	8.3	7.5	7.9	2.6
Point change,						
1979–1988	1.1	1.1	1.2	1.6	1.6	– 0.5

*Rates are based on adding benefits to income cumulatively, from left to right.

Figure 6F shows graphically the before- and after-transfer poverty rates among persons in nonelderly families with children between 1967 and 1988. Only cash transfers are included in this figure, and the effects of taxes are ignored. Both pre- and post-transfer poverty among persons in female-headed families have long been much higher than the rates in other families. In addition, the gap between pre- and post-transfer poverty within female-headed families visibly narrows after the mid-1970s, which reflects reduced governmental assistance in recent years.

Table 6.15 looks at the effects of government programs from a different angle. The poverty rates in this table are based on adding benefits to income cumulatively, from left to right. The third row in each group shows the *increase* in poverty between 1979 and 1988 using each successive definition of income. The final column shows the percent of each group, poor and nonpoor, who were removed from poverty in each year by all government benefits and federal taxes taken together.

The third row for each group in Table 6.15 shows that each additional government benefit removed proportionately fewer people from poverty in 1988 than in 1979. The final column shows that benefits and taxes decreased the overall poverty rate by 9.2 points, from 19.1% to 9.9%, in 1979, but by a slightly lower 8.2 percentage points, from 20.2% to 12.0%, in 1988. The reduced effectiveness of benefits and taxes is more striking for single-parent families with children: government programs decreased the poverty rate for persons in such families by 19.9 points in 1979, from 50% to a still high 30.1%, but by only 11.3 points in 1988, from 49.5% to 38.2%.

Among persons in married-couple families with children, benefits and taxes decreased poverty by 3.1 points in 1979, but by a slightly lower 2.6 points in 1988. These numbers are not as striking as those for single-parent families because poverty within married-couple families is lower to begin with.

. . . each additional government benefit removed proportionately fewer people from poverty in 1988 than in 1979.

179

TABLE 6.16

Contributions to Increase in Poverty, 1979–1988

	Increases* in Poverty Rate Due to:		
Family Relationship	Market Income and Demographics	Government	Total
All Persons	1.1	1.0	2.1
Persons in Single-Parent Families with Related Children under 18	–0.5	8.6	8.1
Persons in Married-Couple Families with Related Children under 18	1.1	0.5	1.6

*Point changes, i.e., the 1988 rate minus the 1979 rate.

TABLE 6.17

Work Experience of the Poor, 1989

	1989
Number of poor aged 15+ (thousands)	20,474
Percent not employable*	33.9%
Percent employable and worked	41.1%
Percent employable and did not work	25.0%
Percent of poor workers who worked:	
Year-Round**	34.1%
Full-Time, Year-Round	22.4%

 * "Employable" poor are those who are not retired, ill, disabled, or in school. Those who are keeping house are in the employable group.
** At least 50 weeks.

Table 6.16 uses the figures in Table 6.15 to show the contributions of different factors to the increase in the poverty rate between 1979 and 1988. For example, the 1.1 point increase due to market income and demographics is drawn from the third row of column 1 of Table 6.15, which gives the change in the poverty rate as measured using only cash income before transfers. The 1.0 point increase due to government comes from the third row of column six of Table 6.15, which gives the change in poverty rate reduction due to taxes and benefits. The data in Table 6.16 that refer to specific family types also come from corresponding parts of Table 6.15.

As Table 6.16 shows, the increase in the poverty rate for all persons, a rise of 2.1 percentage points, was due about equally to market incomes and demographics, on the one hand, and to reduced governmental assistance on the other. ("Demographics" refers to factors such as changes in family structure and size.) However, single-parent and married-couple families were affected differently by these two factors. The poverty rate for persons in single-parent families with children went up by a large 8.1 points; all of this increase and then some (8.6 percentage points) was due to changes in taxes and benefits between 1979 and 1988. On the other hand, most poor married-couple families do not receive government benefits, so program cutbacks haven't hurt them as much: of the 1.6 percentage point increase in poverty among such families, 1.1 points were due to changes in market incomes and demographics, and a smaller component (0.5 points) was due to reductions in government assistance.

Work and Poverty

We have shown that changes in government programs have pushed more people below the poverty line. But what makes people dependent on these programs to begin with? Some may think that many of the poor are able-bodied yet do not want to work. However, in 1989, 33.9% of poor persons aged over 15 were not employable because they were retired, ill, disabled, or in school (**Table 6.17**). Another 41.1% worked at least some of the time. Only 25% of poor persons aged over 15 were employable yet did not work at all during 1989. (Starting with Table 6.17, we return to the official definition of poverty, which excludes food

Only 25% of poor persons aged over 15 were employable yet did not work at all during 1988.

181

FIGURE 6G

Poverty by Family Relationship, 1959–1988

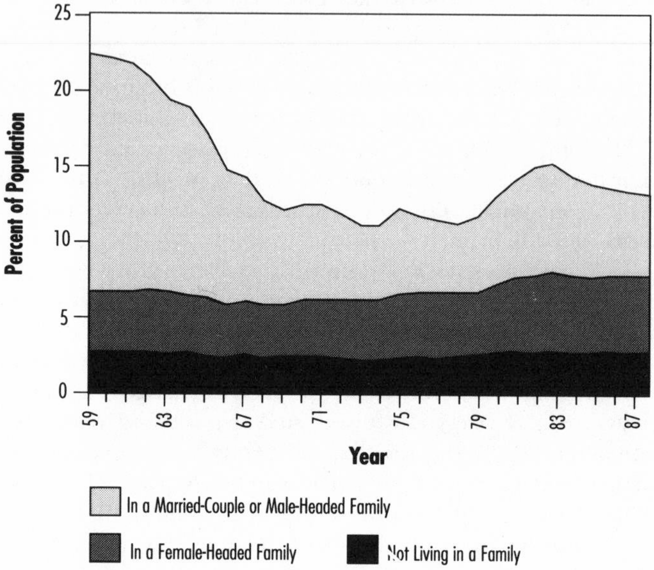

Legend:
- In a Married-Couple or Male-Headed Family
- In a Female-Headed Family
- Not Living in a Family

TABLE 6.18

Changing Family Structure and Poverty, 1959–1989

Year	Percent of Persons in:				Poverty Rate of Persons in:			
	Female-Headed Families	Married-Couple and Male-Headed Families*	Not Living in Families	Total	Female-Headed Families	Married-Couple and Male-Headed Families*	Not Living in Families	All Persons
1959	8.0%	85.9%	6.1%	100.0%	49.4%	18.2%	46.1%	22.4%
1967	9.1	84.2	6.7	100.0	38.8	9.6	38.1	14.2
1973	10.5	80.7	8.8	100.0	37.5	6.0	25.6	11.1
1979	12.1	76.2	11.7	100.0	34.9	6.4	21.9	11.7
1989	13.2	72.5	14.3	100.0	35.9	7.3	19.2	12.8

*Including unrelated subfamilies since 1979.

and housing benefits and does not deduct federal taxes.)

Working year-round, or even year-round and full-time, is not sufficient for obtaining an above-poverty income. In 1989, 22.4% of poor working adults worked full-time, year-round, while 34.1% worked at least 50 weeks and remained poor. The main reason that work is not a sufficient cure for poverty is the large and growing proportion of jobs that pay poverty-level wages. This trend was examined in Chapter 3.

The Role of Family Structure

Family structure is an important dimension in the analysis of poverty. In particular, female-headed families are poor for different reasons than male-headed and married-couple families. This is reflected in **Figure 6G**. The percent of persons who are poor and in married-couple and male-headed families has been very volatile. The sharp swings in poverty among these families reflect changes over the business cycle. On the other hand, the percent of persons who are poor and in female-headed families has risen fairly steadily since the late 1960s; it has not gone up and down with swings in the economy. This suggests that different economic conditions and factors explain poverty in female-headed families.

Because poverty rates differ considerably by family type, changes in family structure may also help explain changes in poverty rates at successive business cycle peaks. In 1988, persons in female-headed families were the most likely to be poor (35.9% poor), followed by persons not in families (19.2%) and persons in married-couple and male-headed families (7.3%) (**Table 6.18**). This is important because shifts in family structure have increased the proportions of persons who are in families that are more vulnerable to poverty. Between 1959 and 1989, there was a steady decline in the proportion of persons in married-couple and male-headed families, from 85.9% to 72.5% (Table 6.18). This was coupled with a rising proportion in female-headed families, from 8.0% in 1959 to 13.2% in 1989, and an increasing percentage not in families, from 6.1% to 14.3%.

Working year-round, or even year-round and full-time, is not sufficient for obtaining an above-poverty income.

183

TABLE 6.19

Contributions of Changes in Family Structure
to Changes in the Poverty Rate

Period	Change in Poverty Rate	Predicted Change Due to Family Structure*	Difference: Change Due to Other Factors**
1959–67	–8.2	0.5	–8.7
1967–73	–3.1	1.0	–4.1
1973–79	0.6	1.1	–0.4
1979–89	1.1	0.7	0.4

*Effect on overall poverty rate of changes in proportions of persons in female-headed families, married-couple and male-headed familes, and not in families.

**Effect on overall poverty rate of changes in poverty rates within these three main demographic groups, primarily due to changes in market incomes, government cash assistance, family size, and the interactions of various factors.

TABLE 6.20

Poverty Rates for Female-Headed Families

Year	All	White	Black	Hispanic
1973	32.2%	24.5%	52.7%	N/A
1979	30.4	22.3	49.4	49.2%
1989	32.2	25.4	46.5	47.5

TABLE 6.21

Increase in Poverty in Female-Headed Families, 1973–1989

| Year | Race | | | Total | Number (000) |
	White	Black	Other*		
Percent of Poor Female-Headed Families Who Are in Each Racial Group:					
1973	54.3%	44.4%	1.3%	100.0%	2,193
1979	51.0	46.7	2.3	100.0	2,645
1989	53.0	43.5	3.5	100.0	3,504
Share of Total Increase:					
1973–79	35.4%	57.5%	7.1%	100.0%	452
1979–89	59.1	33.8	7.1	100.0	859

*Includes Asians, Pacific Islanders, American Indians, Aleuts, and Eskimos.

Table 6.19 compares the actual changes in the overall poverty rate with how shifts in family structure alone would have changed it. The difference, in the third column, is that part of the change in the overall poverty rate that is due to changes in each group's poverty rate. Changes in poverty rates within groups are probably due mainly to changes in income, including government assistance, and family size.

In the first three periods, family structure shifts pushed the overall poverty rate up, while other changes, which probably included rising incomes and smaller families, lowered it (Table 6.19). But in the 1979–1989 period, factors other than family structure actually *increased* the overall poverty rate by 0.4 points. The main reason for this is that poverty among female-headed families has been rising since 1979, while poverty in married-couple and male-headed families has been increasing since 1973 (Table 6.18). The poverty rate for persons in female-headed families rose from 34.9% to 35.9% in the 1979–1989 period. In married-couple and male-headed families, poverty increased from 6.0% to 6.4% in the 1973–79 period, and then to 7.3% in 1989. In contrast, poverty among each type of family decreased, often considerably, in earlier periods.

Poverty in female-headed families is often portrayed as a minority problem. However, **Table 6.20** shows that although poverty rates among minority female-headed families are higher than among white families, they decreased somewhat between 1979 and 1988 while poverty among white female-headed families increased from 22.3% to 25.4%. Moreover, whites have consistently made up the majority of poor female-headed families (**Table 6.21**). And although blacks accounted for most (57.5%) of the increase of poor female-headed families between 1973 and 1979, whites accounted for 59.1% of the increase in the 1979–1989 period (Table 6.21). Clearly, poverty among single mothers is a problem for families in all race/ethnic groups.

Despite the increasing proportion of persons in female-headed families and the high rate of poverty in such families, the majority of the poor are actually not in such fami-

Whites have consistently made up the majority of poor female-headed families.

TABLE 6.22

Family Relationships of Poor Persons by Race/Ethnic Group, 1989

Family Relationship	Race/Ethnic Group			All
	White	Black	Hispanic	
Not in Family	25.0%	16.1%	12.0%	21.9%
In Family	75.0	83.9	88.0	78.1
Female-Headed, No Husband	28.3	60.3	35.9	37.8
Other	46.7	23.7	52.1	40.2
Total	100.0	100.0	100.0	100.0
Number of Persons (000)	20,245	9,178	5,293	30,832

TABLE 6.23

The Reasons for Poverty in Married-Couple Families, 1987

Reasons for Poverty	Percent of Poor Married-Couple Families
Low hourly earnings	64.3%
Parents worked hours equivalent to a full-time, full-year worker*	44.0
Parents worked less than FT/FY hours but still would have been poor even if they had worked FT/FY hours**	20.3
One or both parents ill, disabled, or retired***	21.8
Other reason(s)	13.9
Parents worked less than FT/FY hours and would not have been poor if had worked more**	4.9
Neither parent worked	9.0
TOTAL	100.0

*Defined as 1,750 hours of work annually.

**Computed by determining the average wage by dividing annual earnings by total annual hours, multiplying this average wage by 1,750 hours to get potential annual earnings, and comparing these figures to the poverty line for the family.

***Includes 2.9 percent in which other parent worked FT/FY, 6.8 percent in which someone worked but not FT/FY, and 12.1 percent in which neither parent worked.

lies. **Table 6.22** shows that only 37.8% of poor persons, including single persons, were in female-headed families in 1989. A higher proportion, 40.2%, were in married-couple and male-headed families. A significant fraction of poor persons, 21.8%, were not living in families at all. This does vary by race: 60.3% of poor blacks are in female-headed families, while only 28.3% of poor whites and 35.8% of poor Hispanics are. Thus, female-headed families are important, but are not the whole story.

Married-Couple Family Poverty: A Low-Wage Problem

What causes poverty in married-couple families? The answer for most such families is *wages that are too low*. In addition, poor married-couple families usually do not receive governmental assistance. **Table 6.23** presents the labor market experiences of poor married-couple families in 1987. As it shows, fully 64.3% of these families either had a full-time, full-year worker or earned wages that still would have left them in poverty if they had had such a worker. Another 21.8% were poor because of illness, disability, or retirement. Very few—4.9%—were poor because they did not work *enough*. Another 9% were poor and did not work at all; at least some of these families would not have earned enough to avoid poverty if they had worked.

Table 6.24 shows that many married-couple families who do avoid poverty can do so only by sending both spouses into the workforce: poverty rates for married-couple families in each ethnic group would have been over

What causes poverty in married-couple families? The answer for most such families is wages that are too low.

TABLE 6.24

Role of Part-Time Spousal Earnings in Poverty Avoidance, 1985

Race/Ethnicity	Currently in Poverty	Would Be in Poverty Without Spouses' Part-Time Earnings
White	4.8%	8.5%
Black	16.7	25.9
Hispanic	13.6	21.4

TABLE 6.25

Percent of Poor Married-Couple Families Without Benefits and Medical Protection, 1984

Types of Families	Percent Receiving No Government Benefits	Percent with No Medical Protection
Full-time working poor	54%	36%
Partially employed or unemployed poor	21	38
Disabled or retired poor	7	16
All poor two-parent families	33	33

TABLE 6.26

Work Status of Poor Female Heads of Families, 1989

Work Status	Distribution of Poor Female Heads of Families with Children
Total	100.0%
Worked	42.8
50 to 52 weeks	14.5
Full time	9.7
49 weeks or less	28.3
Healthy, Did Not Work	48.1
Keeping house	39.7
Going to school	3.2
Unable to find work	4.4
All other reasons	0.8
Ill, Disabled, or Retired	9.1
Ill or disabled	7.4
Retired	1.7

half again as large without part-time spousal earnings. Given the costs of child care, this is not always an option for families with young children.

Inadequate wages may be due in part to a shortage of good job training; as we will show Chapter 9, the U.S. spends relatively little on training and placement. Moreover, the real value of the minimum wage has fallen considerably since its high point in the late 1960s (Chapter 3). Even after the current two-step increase, which will restore the minimum wage to its real 1986 value, families of two or more members with one minimum wage worker will still be below the poverty line. The minimum wage is relevant to married-couple families because a majority of minimum wage workers in 1986 were adults. The minimum wage also affects the wages just above it, and many who work at the minimum wage or slightly above have family responsibilities.

> *. . . the social benefit system does not assist working poor married-couple families.*

Another problem is that the social benefit system also does not assist working poor married-couple families. For example, 54% of full-time working poor married-couple families received no government benefits in 1984 (**Table 6.25**). A shocking 36% of such families had no health insurance either—almost as many as the 38% of partially employed or unemployed poor married-couple families who lacked health insurance.

Female-Headed Families: Can't Afford to Work

Now let us consider female-headed families. In contrast to married-couple families, only 42.8% of poor single mothers worked at all in 1989, and most of these worked part-time (**Table 6.26**). Another 9.1% did not work because they were ill, disabled, or retired. Finally, 48.1% of healthy poor single mothers did not work at all. Some 39.7% did not work because of family responsibilities, while another 4.4% wanted to work but could not find a job.

The evidence is that single mothers who do work do so because the benefits outweigh the costs. For example, single mothers who work tend to have better educations, and thus can expect higher earnings. They are also less likely to have a large number of young children, and therefore face lower child care costs. In 1984, 51% of nonworking single mothers were high school dropouts, compared to 28% of part-time or part-year workers and 17% of full-time, full-year

189

TABLE 6.27

Comparison of Selected Characteristics
of All Healthy Female Family Heads (Poor and Non-poor)
by Level of Work, 1984

	Worked Full-time, Full-year	Part-time or Part-year	Did Not Work
Education of Head	100%	100%	100%
Under 12 years	17	28	51
High school only	43	42	35
Over 12 years	40	30	14
Wage Rate	100	100	100
Under $4.00/hr.	12	37	—
$4.00–$4.99/hr.	12	16	—
$5.00–$5.99/hr.	13	14	—
$6.00–$6.99/hr.	12	9	—
$7.00/hr. and over	51	24	—
Number of Children	100	100	100
One or Two	87	78	65
Three or More	13	22	35
Age of Youngest Child	100	100	100
Under 6	24	41	54
6–12	35	32	25
Over 12	41	27	21

workers (**Table 6.27**). In addition, 37% of part-time or part-year working single mothers earned less than $4.00 per hour 1984, compared to 12% of full-time, full-year workers.

Having several young children clearly increases the costs of child care that a single mother would face if she worked, and in the extreme case may make working impossibly expensive. A large portion of nonworkers, 35%, had three or more children, compared to 22% of part-timers and 13% of full-timers (Table 6.27). The children of nonworkers also tend to be younger: 54% of nonworkers had at least one child under six years old, compared to 41% of part-timers and 24% of full-timers.

Since low wages are part of the problem, the above arguments about the causes of married-couple poverty apply to some extent to poverty in female-headed families as well; that is, wages are too low and there is a lack of adequate job training. Single mothers also suffer from low child support levels and poor enforcement. Only 55% of divorced moth-

Having several young children may make working impossibly expensive.

190

ers, 33.7% of separated mothers, and 13.6% of never-married mothers received any child support in 1987 (**Table 6.28**). In addition, **Table 6.29** shows that AFDC and Food Stamp benefits are low in 1990 compared to 1980 and are phased out quickly as a single mother's earnings increase. This rapid phaseout just adds to the costs a single mother faces if she works for a living. As Table 6.29 indicates, even relatively low earnings can disqualify a single mother for Medicaid after 12 months in many states; since many low-paid jobs have no medical benefits, losing Medicaid may be an intolerable expense. Finally, child care expenses also add

AFDC and Food Stamp benefits are low in 1990 compared to 1980 and are phased out quickly as a single mother's earnings increase.

TABLE 6.28
Receipt of Child Support by Single Mothers,* 1987

Marital Status of Mother	Child Support Award in Place	Award in Place and Received Some Payment	Average Payment Received by Those With Some Payment
Divorced	77.2%	55.0%	$3,073
Separated	54.8	33.7	2,745
Never Married	19.7	13.6	1,632
Total	51.1	35.2	2,800

*This data is for women who were living with their own children under age 21 from an absent father, as of Spring 1988 (for the year 1987).

TABLE 6.29
Effect of Wages on AFDC, Food Stamps, and Medicaid for a Mother of Two Children, 1980–1990
(1988 Dollars)

Wages as % of Poverty Level	AFDC and Food Stamps		Number of States That Don't Provide Medicaid* (1988)
	1980	1990	
0	$7,071	$6,611	9
50	5,427	4,225	31
75	4,353	2,837	46
90	3,702	2,256	51
100	3,142	1,836	51
125	1,990	1,134	51

*In many states, Medicaid income limits are higher for pregnant women and young children. As of April 1990, states must wait 12 months after earnings rise to end Medicaid coverage.

191

TABLE 6.30

AFDC Levels and Single Motherhood

| Year | AFDC and Food Stamp Benefits* (1988 $) | Female-Headed Families as % of Families | Indices (1960=100) | |
			AFDC and Food Stamp Benefits	Female-Headed Families as % of Families
1960	$ 7,652	9.8%	100	100
1964	7,525	10.2	98	104
1968	8,123	10.6	106	108
1972	10,133	11.5	132	117
1976	9,888	13.1	129	133
1980	8,529	14.6	111	148
1984	7,918	16.0	103	162
1988	8,019	16.4	105	167

*Family of four with no income.

Figure 6H

Unmarried Births and Benefit Levels by State, 1980

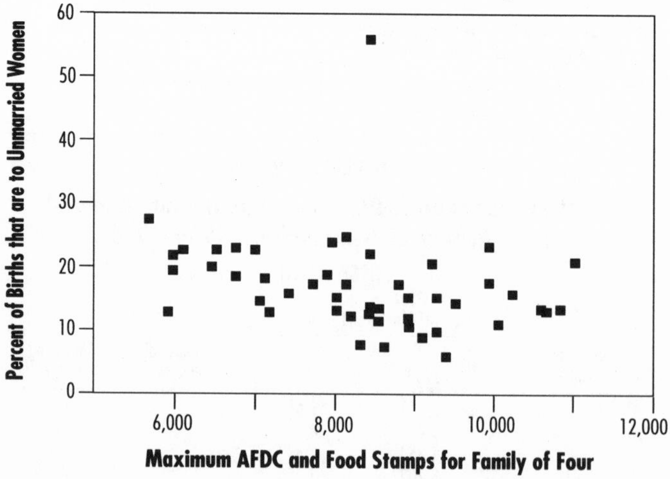

Maximum AFDC and Food Stamps for Family of Four

to the costs of working—particularly for mothers with several young children.

Poor Female-Headed Families Increase

We have seen that the proportion of persons in female-headed families has increased steadily since 1959 (Table 6.18). Some have claimed that this trend is due in part to increases in AFDC and Food Stamp benefits. However, there is little evidence for this view. **Table 6.30** shows that the percent of families that are female-headed has risen steadily since 1960, yet AFDC and Food Stamp benefit levels first increased from 1964 to 1972 and then fell considerably from 1972 to 1988. If rising welfare benefits were responsible for the increase in female-headed families, falling welfare benefits should have led to a decrease, or at least to a significant slowdown. Furthermore, as **Figure 6H** indicates, a cross-state comparison also shows no relationship between welfare benefits levels and births to unmarried women. Thus, the increase in female-headed families does not appear to have been caused by higher welfare benefits.

Never-married women constitute a small minority of female heads of families.

The stereotypical female family head has had a number of children out of wedlock and has never been married. But in fact, never-married women constitute a small minority of female heads of families. The number of never-married female family heads has indeed grown rapidly: by 62.5% in the 1973–79 period and by 84.4% in the 1979–1989 period **(Table 6.31)**. However, the number of divorced female fami-

TABLE 6.31

Marital Status of Female Family Heads, 1973–1989

	Marital Status of Female Family Heads:*					
Year	Married, Husband Absent	Widowed	Divorced	Never Married	Total	Total Number (000)
1973	23.9%	37.7%	25.9%	12.6%	100.0%	6,535
1979	21.0	29.8	33.0	16.2	100.0	8,220
1989	17.1	23.9	36.4	22.6	100.0	10,890
Percent Increase in Number of Families:						
1973–79	10.6%	−0.4%	60.2%	62.5%		25.8%
1979–89	8.1	6.0	46.4	84.4		32.5

*Women without dependents are not regarded as family heads.

TABLE 6.32

Percent in Poverty Using Standard and Experimental Deflators

Year	Using CPI-U (Current Definition)	Using CPI-U-X1
1974*	11.2%	10.5%
1979	11.7	10.5
1989	12.8	11.4
Increase		
1979–89	1.1%	0.9%

*Earliest available using CPI-U-X1.

TABLE 6.33

Poverty Rates Under Alternative Thresholds, 1987

	Poverty Rate
Official threshold	13.5%
Threshold indexed by CPI-U-X1	12.0
Housing consumption standard*	23.4
Updated multiplier standard**	25.9

*Based on Fair Market Rents and Housing Affordability guidelines used in the Section 8 subsidized housing program.

**Calculated using the same general methods as the original Orshansky standard, but with a "multiplier" updated to reflect the changing share of food in family budgets.

ly heads has also increased quickly: by 60.2% in 1973–79 and 46.4% in 1979–1989. As a result, never-married women still made up only 22.6% of female heads of families in 1989. Another 36.4% of female family heads were divorced, 23.9% were widowed, and 17.1% were married to absent husbands.

The increasing proportion of poor persons living in female-headed families therefore does not simply reduce to a greater number of out-of-wedlock births. Other factors, including higher divorce rates, are at least as important. Moreover, one should question the greater economic vulnerability of female-headed families. Why is it that women who live independently from men cannot obtain either high enough wages or generous enough benefits to keep themselves and their families out of poverty? An explanation of the feminization of poverty must address this issue, in addition to the increased number of female-headed families.

Measuring Poverty

Since houses are assets that appreciate and can be resold at a profit, many analysts claim that it is not appropriate to include the whole cost of buying a home when measuring inflation. Because of this, since 1983 the housing component of the CPI-U has been based on home rental costs rather than on home purchase prices. Before 1983, the statistician has a choice of using the old index, which includes home purchase prices, or an experimental price index, the CPI-U-X1, which is based instead on estimates of rental costs for the period 1967–83.

We did not use this experimental index for several reasons. First, most data about poverty—particularly historical data— use only the CPI-U. It would have been inconsistent to have used the CPI-U-X1 for some things and the CPI-U for others. Second, since the two indices have been the same since 1983, using the CPI-U-X1 would not significantly change the story of what has happened in the 1980s. To illustrate, **Table 6.32** shows that the increase in poverty since 1979 using the experimental index, 0.9 points, has been nearly as great as the official increase of 1.1 points. The choice of index actually makes a greater difference for the 1974–79 period, during which there was no increase in poverty using the CPI-U-X1 but there was a 0.5 point increase using the CPI-U.

We also agree with other researchers that conversion to the CPI-U-X1 should be just one part of a comprehensive revision of the definition of poverty. Poverty should be redefined because the costs of housing and medical care have increased faster than the general price level and make up a larger part of the expenses of the poor than is reflected in the CPI-U. As **Table 6.33** shows, an updated poverty line that reflects this increase in housing costs would raise the 1987 poverty rate for all persons from 13.5% to 23.4%. Another shortcoming of the current poverty concept that we have already noted is that lower poverty lines are used for elderly households. This is probably no longer realistic, given, among other things, the high cost of medical care.

Poverty should be redefined because the costs of housing and medical care have increased faster than the general price level and make up a larger part of the expenses of the poor than is reflected in the CPI-U.

CHAPTER 7

TABLE 7.1

Median Income of Young Families By Race, 1973–1989

(1989 Dollars)

| | Income of Young Families* | | | |
| | Median | | | |
Year	All	White	Black	Hispanic
1973	$31,544	$32,635	$20,832	N/A
1979	32,457	33,708	19,468	$22,691
1989	30,873	32,804	16,849	21,324
Annual Rates of Change				
1973–79	0.5%	0.5%	– 1.1%	N/A
1979–89	–0.5	–0.3	– 1.4	–0.6
Total Change (Percent)				
1973–79	2.9%	3.3%	– 6.5%	N/A
1979–89	–4.9	–2.7	–13.5	–6.0

*Families with head of household aged 25–34.

YOUNG FAMILIES

T he economic position of the typical young family deteriorated during the 1980s. This is because the factors that adversely affect working families (real wage erosion, the need to work longer hours) affected young workers and families the most. The boom in capital income, which was the most positive result of the 1980s, was of little help to young families since they generally have little savings. Because young families depend almost entirely on labor earnings for their income, they were affected quite significantly by the fall in real wages during the 1980s. Moreover, the shifts in employment toward low-wage industries, the effects of the large trade deficits, and the erosion of union membership have all affected young workers more than older workers. This is because young workers were more likely to be laid off from or unable to find jobs in the better paying industries that were shrinking in the 1980s.

The income deterioration among young families was most acute for the 55% of young families headed by a worker with no more than a high school diploma and for young black families.

The slight income growth among young married couples with children was entirely due to the increased annual earnings of wives, primarily because they worked more hours per week and more weeks each year.

Young Families' Incomes Decline

Our analysis of young families and workers focuses on the population aged 25–34. For the most part, people in this group have completed their formal education and are in the process of forming families and having children.

The economic fortunes of these young families declined in the 1980s (**Table 7.1**). Between 1973 and 1979, the median family income of young families *grew* by 2.9%, or 0.5% annually, but *fell* 4.9% between 1979 and 1989, an erosion of 0.5% each year. In 1989 the typical (median) young family had $671 less income than its counterpart 15 years earlier in 1973.

From 1979 to 1988, the median income of young families fell for whites, blacks, and Hispanics, although minority family incomes fell at least twice as fast as those of white families. The incomes of young black families have been falling since 1973: by 1989, their median income was $3,983, or 19%, less than in 1973.

The economic position of the typical young family deteriorated during the 1980s. The factors that adversely affect working families affected young workers and families the most.

197

TABLE 7.2

Median Family Income of Young Families
By Educational Attainment and Race, 1973–1987

Head of Household Educational Attainment, By Race	Real Median Family Income, Head of Household Aged 25–34			Distribution of Families By Race and Education	Percent Change	
	1973	1979	1987	1987	1973–79	1979–87
	(1989 Dollars)					
All Races	$31,544	$32,457	$30,906	100.0%	2.9%	−4.8%
< 4 Yrs HS*	24,365	20,917	17,292	15.5	14.2	−17.3
4 Yrs HS	30,389	30,200	28,009	42.5	−0.6	−7.3
1–3 Yrs Col	34,167	34,707	34,163	20.4	1.6	−1.6
4+ Yrs Col	42,220	42,005	46,554	21.6	−0.5	10.8
White	$32,635	$33,708	$33,199	100.0%	3.3%	−1.5%
< 4 Yrs HS*	26,916	23,726	20,790	14.6	−11.9	−12.4
4 Yrs HS	31,030	31,334	29,894	42.5	1.0	−4.6
1–3 Yrs Col	34,594	35,443	35,765	20.2	2.5	0.9
4+ Yrs Col	42,657	42,181	47,903	22.7	−1.1	13.6
Black	$20,832	$19,468	$16,721	100.0%	−6.5%	−14.1%
< 4 Yrs HS*	13,761	12,531	8,333	21.6	−8.9	−33.5
4 Yrs HS	23,070	19,371	15,351	47.5	−16.0	−20.8
1–3 Yrs Col	30,063	25,864	23,156	20.3	−14.0	−10.5
4+ Yrs Col	33,898	35,469	35,240	10.7	4.6	−0.6
Hispanic	N/A	$22,691	$21,623	100.0%	N/A	−4.7%
< 4 Yrs HS*	N/A	17,697	15,230	42.0	N/A	−13.9
4 Yrs HS	N/A	24,512	23,560	33.3	N/A	−3.9
1–3 Yrs Col	N/A	28,630	28,172	16.7	N/A	−1.6
4+ Yrs Col	N/A	41,455	44,225	8.1	N/A	6.7

*Less than 4 years of high school.

The greatest deterioration in income has been among families headed by someone with a high school education or less (**Table 7.2** and **Figure 7A**). The median family income of a young family headed by a high school graduate in 1987 (the latest year for which data are available) was 7.3% less than in 1979, and 7.8% less than in 1973. Thus, in 1987 a young family headed by a high school graduate started out with an annual income $2,300 below the income level of a comparable family in 1973. In contrast, the median income of a family headed by a college graduate was 10.8% higher in 1987 than in 1979. Unfortunately, this income growth benefitted only the 21.6% of young families with a college educated household head.

The decline in income was greatest among black families, especially those headed by someone with a high school degree or less, a group encompassing 69.1% of young black families in 1987. A young black family headed by a high school graduate in 1987 had a median income 20.8% less than in 1979 and one-third, or $7,719, lower than the level

In 1987 a young family headed by a high school graduate started out with an annual income $2,300 below the income level of a comparable family in 1973.

FIGURE 7A

Median Income of Young Families by Education, 1973-1987

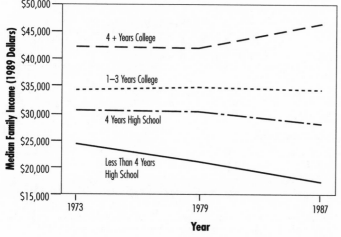

199

FIGURE 7B

Median Income of Young Families Headed by High School Graduates, by Race, 1973-1987

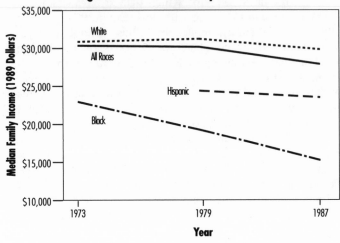

TABLE 7.3

Young Family Income Growth, By Type of Family, 1973-1987

| | Mean Family Income Growth* | | | |
| | Percent Change | | Annual Rate | |
Family Type	1973–79	1979–87	1973–79	1979–87
Families With Children				
Married Couple	6.7%	2.0%	1.1%	0.2%
Single Mothers	11.6	– 9.2	1.8	-1.2
Single Fathers	-17.3	-12.1	-3.2	-1.6
Families Without Children				
Married Couple	7.9%	4.5%	1.3%	0.6%
Single Men	-0.3	1.0	-0.1	0.1
Single Women	0.2	5.9	0.0	0.7
All Families	5.2	2.0	0.8	0.2

*Mean income of families with head of household aged 25–34, adjusted for family size. Due to rising inequality over the 1980s, mean income growth will exceed median income growth.

in 1973 (**Figure 7B**). It was only among blacks that young families headed by a college graduate were not economically better off in 1987 than in 1979.

Income Changes By Family Type

Table 7.3 presents the income growth of various types of young families since 1973. Families are categorized by whether they are composed of a married couple, a single man or woman, or include children. These data differ from those of previous tables because income growth is adjusted for changes in family size and is measured as a change in the average, not median, income. These two differences lead to an overstatement of the change in the economic well-being of a typical or median young family. As discussed in Chapter 1, adjusting family income data for changes in family size means that a couple that decided, out of economic necessity, not to have any children is said to be better off than a couple with slightly more income that decided to have children. Moreover, mean income will always increase faster than median income whenever high income families experience greater than average income growth, as was the case in the 1980s. For instance, the mean, or average, young family income fell 0.5% between 1979 and 1988, whereas the median income of young families fell 4.8%, a difference of 4.3 percentage points of growth. Since income inequality rose only slightly in the 1970s, there was not much divergence between mean and median income growth.

Nevertheless, average incomes for young families, adjusted for family size, grew by just 2% from 1979 to 1987, even less than the 5.2% growth between 1973 and 1979. Given the overall differences between mean and median income growth in this period, it seems likely that the size-adjusted median income of young families fell between 1979 and 1987.

Mean income growth was slower in the later period than in the earlier period for young married couples (with or without children) and for single mothers. In the 1979–1987 period, only young single women fared better than in the earlier period *and* had increasing incomes.

It was only among blacks that young families headed by a college graduate were not economically better off in 1987 than in 1979.

201

TABLE 7.4

Composition of Young Families By Family Type, 1973–1987

Family Type	Family Composition Head of Household Aged 25–34			Income Relative to Average*	Annual Weeks Worked by Family Members
	1973	1979	1987	1987	1987
Families With Children	66.0%	55.9%	50.3%		
Married Couple	56.5	43.9	37.5	94%	77.4
Single Mothers	9.1	11.2	11.3	38	28.6
Single Fathers	0.4	0.8	1.5	64	41.2
Families Without Children	34.0%	44.1%	49.7%		
Married Couple	15.5	14.9	14.1	159%	90.8
Single Men	11.7	18.3	22.1	108	44.4
Single Women	6.8	10.9	13.6	98	45.2
All Families	100.0	100.0	100.0	100	61.6

Mean Family Income in 1987 With Family Type Composition of**:

	1973	1979	1987
Mean Family Income (Actual 1987=100)	100.6	100.0	100.0

* Mean family income in 1987, adjusted for family size, as percent of average.

**Shows the effect of changes in the distribution of families on mean family income. For instance, the change in the composition of families between 1973 and 1979 lowered mean family income by 0.6%.

Fewer young families include children, down from 66% in 1973 to 50.3% in 1987.

Table 7.4 examines the changes in the make-up of young families from 1973 to 1987. The major trend was that fewer young families included children, down from 66% in 1973 to 50.3% in 1987. The biggest decline was the proportionate shrinkage of married couples with children. In contrast, there was a growing portion of families consisting of a young single man or woman.

The young families with the most income were the married couple families with no children. These families had incomes 59% greater than average in 1987. These higher incomes, however, were the result of working more weeks per year than other families, more adult workers than single men or women, and no child care responsibilities. Generally, the types of families with the highest incomes were those with the greatest potential for work and with the greatest number of weeks worked (except single men, who work less than average but earn more than average).

Table 7.4 (bottom panel) also shows that changes in the composition of young families did not appreciably affect overall income growth among them after 1973. This suggests that the major demographic change affecting young family incomes has been the trend toward fewer families with children and fewer children per family. These computations also show that the lack of growth in the incomes of young families reflects difficulty in obtaining income and not a demographic shift toward single-person households or single-parent families. That is, the demographic factors with the greatest impact are occurring *within* family types (such as having fewer children) and not *among* family types.

The Earnings Slowdown

Because young families rely on labor earnings much more than other families, they have been particularly vulnerable to the fall in real wages and the shift toward low-wage jobs in the 1980s. Labor earnings provide 94.3% of the average young family's income compared to 73% of the average family's income (Table 1.13 and **Table 7.5**). This is because young families have minimal savings and few other sources of wealth to provide them with capital income and, except

Because young families rely on labor earnings much more than other families, they have been particularly vulnerable to the fall in real wages and the shift toward low-wage jobs in the 1980s.

TABLE 7.5

Sources of Income for Young Families*

| Family Type | Sources of Income,** 1987 | | | | |
	Earnings	Government Transfers	Capital Income	Other	Total
Families With Children					
Married Couples	95.6%	1.8%	2.2%	0.4%	100.0%
Single Mothers	73.8	16.5	2.4	7.3	100.0
Single Fathers	90.0	6.3	3.3	0.0	100.0
Families Without Children					
Married Couples	95.7%	1.0%	3.1%	0.0%	100.0%
Single Men	94.8	1.5	3.3	0.0	100.0
Single Women	94.7	1.2	3.3	0.7	100.0
All Families	94.3	2.1	2.8	0.7	100.0

*Head of household aged 25–34.

**Mean family income, adjusted for family size.

TABLE 7.6

Young Family Income Growth, By Type of Income, 1973–1987

Time Period	Earnings	Government Transfers	Capital Income	Total Income
		(Annual Rate of Growth)		
1973–79	0.7%	0.4%	5.6%	0.8%
1979–87	0.3	–2.3	1.7	0.2

*Mean income, adjusted for family size, of families with head of household aged 25–34.

TABLE 7.7

Earnings Growth in Families With Children By Family Type and Earner, 1973–1987

	Married Couple		Single Mother		Single Father	
Earner	73–79	79–87	73–79	79–87	73–79	79–87
Annual Earnings Growth (Percent)						
All Earners	6.0%	2.2%	31.1%	–7.7%	–15.5%	–11.5%
Adult Men	–0.3	–5.0	N/A	N/A	–15.6	–10.9
Adult Women	42.6	32.3	31.4	–7.8	N/A	N/A
Weekly Earnings Growth (Percent)						
All Earners	–2.9%	–5.1%	5.4%	–0.4%	–11.7%	–2.1%
Adult Men	–0.4	–3.6	N/A	N/A	–11.8	–2.5
Adult Women	7.7	8.4	5.4	–1.0	N/A	N/A
Change In Annual Weeks Employed (Percent)						
All Earners	7.5%	6.9%	21.7%	–9.3%	–5.9%	–10.9%
Adult Men	–1.0	–1.7	N/A	N/A	–6.4	–7.2
Adult Women	30.1	23.6	22.3	–9.2	N/A	N/A
Change In Annual Weeks Employed (Number of Weeks)						
All Earners	5.1	5.0	5.6	–2.9	–2.9	–5.0
Adult Men	–0.5	–0.8	N/A	N/A	–3.0	–3.1
Adult Women	5.2	5.3	5.6	–2.8	N/A	N/A

for single mothers, do not receive much government assistance. Thus, changes in young family income growth reflect the success or failure of young workers in the labor market. Since, as we have seen in Chapter 3, the wages of young workers fell more than those of any other group in the 1980s, it follows that young family incomes fared poorly.

From 1979 to 1987 total family earnings of young families grew by just 0.3% annually, or less than 3% overall, (**Table 7.6**). This was less than half as fast as the 0.7% annual earnings growth in the 6 years from 1973 to 1979. Young families also experienced much slower growth in capital income in the 1979–1987 period than in the 1973–79 period. After 1979 there was a rapid acceleration of capital income growth among all families. However, since capital income has been an insignificant income source for young families, the financial boom of the 1980s did little to help their income growth. Similarly, the 2.3% annual reduction in government transfers between 1979 and 1987 had little effect on young families since they receive very little in transfers. The cutbacks in government assistance, however, do help explain the rapid income decline among young single-mother families, a group that depends on government assistance for 16.5% of its total income.

Since capital income has been an insignificant income source for young families, the financial boom of the 1980s did little to help their income growth.

Working More at Lower Wages

Given that young family income growth is overwhelmingly determined by changes in total labor earnings, it is worthwhile to examine earnings growth more closely. **Tables 7.7** and **7.8** present information on the growth of total annual earnings, average weekly wages, and the number of weeks worked for each type of young family and for the principal earners (adult men and women in these families). These data allow us to assess each family type, changes in family earnings in each time period, and the role of major earners. Moreover, these data allow us to identify how changes in weekly wages and the number of weeks worked have affected overall earnings growth.

For young married couples with children, total family earnings in 1987 were 2.2% higher than in 1979, a growth of only 0.3% annually (Table 7.7). In contrast, total earnings for these families grew 6% between 1973 and 1979. During both periods, earnings growth occurred despite a *fall* in average weekly earnings of 5.1% and 2.9%, respectively, in

205

TABLE 7.8

Earnings Growth in Families Without Children
By Family Type and Earner, 1973–1987

| | Families Without Children | | | | | |
| | Married Couple | | Single Men | | Single Women | |
Earner	73–79	79–87	73–79	79–87	73–79	79–87
Annual Earnings Growth (Percent)						
All Earners	6.4%	5.1%	−0.6%	1.7%	0.1%	5.8%
Adult Men	3.0	0.2	−0.6	1.7	N/A	N/A
Adult Women	11.6	10.2	N/A	N/A	0.1	5.8
Weekly Earnings Growth (Percent)						
All Earners	0.6%	2.3%	−3.1%	0.6%	−0.5%	5.2%
Adult Men	0.6	−0.2	N/A	N/A	−0.5	5.2
Adult Women	5.7	10.3	−3.1	0.6	N/A	N/A
Change In Annual Weeks Employed (Percent)						
All Earners	4.8%	2.5%	−0.1%	0.7%	1.5%	1.0%
Adult Men	2.0	1.3	−0.1	0.7	N/A	N/A
Adult Women	6.8	−1.3	N/A	N/A	1.5	1.0
Change In Annual Weeks Employed (Number of Weeks)						
All Earners	4.1	2.3	0.0	0.3	0.7	0.5
Adult Men	0.9	0.6	0.0	0.3	N/A	N/A
Adult Women	2.4	−0.5	N/A	N/A	0.7	0.5

An average young married couple family with children in 1987 had a higher income than in earlier years because the adults worked more at lower wages.

the 1979–1987 and 1973–79 periods (**Figure 7C**). Declines in average weekly earnings reflect both that the weekly wages of the husbands in these families fell (3.6% from 1979 to 1987) and that the wives, who tend to earn less than the husbands, were performing a greater fraction of the total weeks worked by family members. For instance, the wives in young married couple families with children worked an average of 10.5 more weeks a year in 1987 than in 1979, whereas the husbands worked 1.3 fewer weeks, or 60% more.

The overall increase in weeks employed by young married-couple families with children, 10.1 weeks more in 1987 than in 1973, is clearly the only reason overall earnings have increased since 1973. In other words, an average young married-couple family with children in 1987 had a higher income than in earlier years because the adults worked more at lower wages. In particular, the wives in these families were employed for 23.6% more weeks in 1987 than in 1979. The resulting greater annual earnings of the women in these families was responsible for all of their income growth in the 1979 to 1987 period, a subject discussed in the next section.

Between 1973 and 1979, the annual earnings of single mothers rose 31.4%. In contrast, their annual earnings fell by 7.8% between 1979 and 1987. This pattern of earnings growth primarily reflects the 22.3% increase in the number of weeks single mothers were employed in 1979 compared to 1973, and a subsequent 9.2% drop in weeks employed by 1987. In addition, the weekly wages of single mothers rose in the earlier period by 5.4% but fell 0.4% during the second period.

Earnings growth in childless married-couple families also was lower in the 1979 to 1987 period than in the prior six years, 5.1% versus 6.4% annual growth (Table 7.8). The men in these families earned no more in 1987 than in 1973 (up 0.2%) but worked slightly more, an additional 1.5 weeks. The main contribution to earnings growth in these

Wives in these families were employed for 23.6% more weeks in 1987 than in 1979.

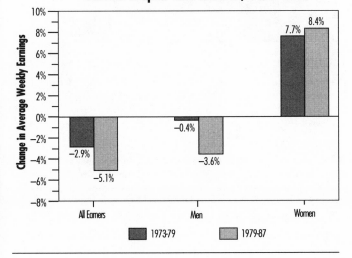

FIGURE 7C

Total Change in Weekly Earnings in Young Married Couples with Children, 1973-1987

Change in Average Weekly Earnings

All Earners: −2.9% (1973-79), −5.1% (1979-87)
Men: −0.4% (1973-79), −3.6% (1979-87)
Women: 7.7% (1973-79), 8.4% (1979-87)

■ 1973-79   ▨ 1979-87

TABLE 7.9

Effect of Young Wives' Earnings Growth on Married-Couple Earnings,* 1979–1987

		Change in Family Income**	
Time Period	Actual	Not Including Increased Earnings of Wives	Difference: Effect of Increased Wives' Earnings on Family Income
1973–79	6.7%	1.0%	5.7%
1979–87	2.0	–3.7	5.7

*Married couples with children, head of household aged 25–34.

**Mean family income, adjusted for family size.

FIGURE 7D

Effect of Wives' Earnings Growth on Incomes of Young Married Couples with Children, 1979-1987

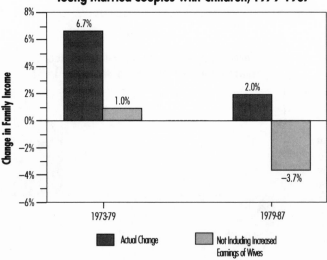

208

families was the increased number of weeks the wives were employed (up 5.5 from 1973 to 1987) and their higher weekly wages (up 10.3%).

The fastest earnings growth in the 1979 to 1987 period was among single women, whose weekly wages rose 5.2% and who worked slightly more, a half a week, by the end of this period. Single men worked about the same amount and had equivalent annual earnings in 1987 as in 1973.

The Role of Wives' Earnings

As mentioned earlier, the only reason that the overall earnings of young married-couple families with children were higher in 1987 than in 1973 was the increased earnings of the wives in these families. As seen in Chapter 1, the total gain in family income among all ages of married-couple families with children was due to the wives' greater earnings. Among young married couples with children, the increased earnings of wives were not only responsible for the income gains but also prevented a *lowering* of incomes (**Table 7.9**). For instance, increased wives' earnings allowed family income to rise by 2.0% rather than fall 3.7% between 1979 and 1987, a difference of 5.7 percentage points of growth (**Figure 7D**).

Among young married couples with children, the increased earnings of wives were not only responsible for the income gains but also prevented a lowering of incomes.

TABLE 7.10

Factors Explaining Young Wives' Increased Annual Earnings,* 1979–1987

Year	Percent of Wives With Earnings	Average Weeks Employed Wives With Earnings	Average Weeks Employed All Wives**
1973	51.7%	33.5 weeks	17.3 weeks
1979	62.5	36.1	22.5
1987	68.4	40.7	27.9
Change			
1973–79	10.8%	2.6%	5.2%
1979–87	5.9	4.7	5.3
Changes (Total Percent)			
1973–79	20.9%	7.7%	30.1%
1979–87	9.4	12.9	23.6
Changes (Annual Rate*)**			
1973–79	1.8%	1.2%	4.4%
1979–87	0.7	1.5	2.6

*In married-couple families with children, head of household aged 25–34.

**Includes changes in the percentage of wives with earnings and change in weeks employed by wives with earnings, i.e., the weeks employed by the average wife is the product of the percent with earnings and the weeks employed by wives with earnings.

***Annual changes in percent of wives with earnings is in percentage points per year.

TABLE 7.11

Contribution of Increased Weekly Wages and Weeks Worked to Annual Earnings Growth of Young Wives,* 1973–1987

Years	Annual Growth in Wives': Earnings	Annual Growth in Wives': Weeks Employed**	Annual Growth in Wives': Weekly Wage	Contribution to Wives' Annual Earnings Growth: More Weeks Employed**	Contribution to Wives' Annual Earnings Growth: Higher Weekly Wage	Contribution to Wives' Annual Earnings Growth: Total
1973–79	5.9%	4.5%	1.2%	76.6%	23.4%	100.0%
1979–87	3.5	2.6	1.0	73.4	26.6	100.0

*Married-couple families with children, adjusted for family size, head of household aged 25–34.

**Includes changes in the percentage of wives with earnings and changes in weeks worked by wives with earnings.

210

The wives in these families are contributing greater annual earnings because more are working, those employed are working more weeks, and the real weekly wages of working wives have risen (**Table 7.10**). For instance, the average wife in these families was employed for 27.9 weeks in 1987, 10.6 more weeks than the average in 1973 (**Figure 7E**). The greater number of weeks employed reflects the greater percentage of wives who were earners (68.4% in 1987, up from 51.7% in 1973) and the increase in weeks worked by them (40.7 weeks in 1987, up from 33.5 weeks in 1973). These two factors led to a 30.1% and 23.6% increase, respectively, in the number of weeks the average wife was employed in the 1973–79 and 1979–1987 periods.

As shown in **Table 7.11** and **Figure 7F**, the real weekly wages of working wives also increased over these same periods (1.3% and 0.9% annually) but rose more slowly than the increase in employed weeks (4.6% and 2.6% annually). The result is that roughly three-fourths of the total rise in the annual earnings of wives in young married-couple families with children was due to wives being employed for

Roughly three-fourths of the total rise in the annual earnings of these wives was due to being employed for more weeks per year, with one-fourth due to higher real weekly wages.

FIGURE 7E

Weeks Employed of Wives in Young Married Couples With Children, 1973-1987

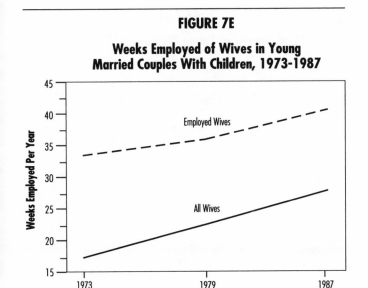

211

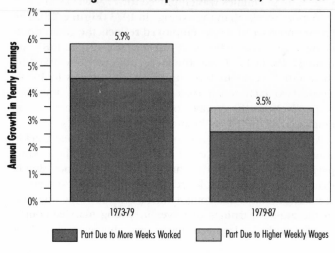

FIGURE 7F

Components of Increased Earnings of Wives in Young Married Couples with Children, 1973-1987

Annual Growth in Yearly Earnings

- 5.9% (1973-79)
- 3.5% (1979-87)

■ Part Due to More Weeks Worked   ▢ Part Due to Higher Weekly Wages

TABLE 7.12

Wage Growth of Young Workers, 1979–1987

	Full-Time Equivalent Wage*		Change, 1979–1987	
	1979	1987	Dollars	Percent
	(1987 Dollars)			
Aged 16–24				
All	$11,170	$ 9,778	$–1,392	–12.5%
Black Women	9,899	8,060	–1,839	–18.6
Black Men	10,643	8,914	–1,729	–16.2
White Women	10,526	9,455	–1,071	–10.2
White Men	12,316	10,400	–1,916	–15.6
Aged 25–34				
All	$18,317	$17,000	$–1,317	–7.2%
Black Women	13,509	13,000	–509	–3.8
Black Men	18,139	14,222	–3,917	–21.6
White Women	15,198	15,392	194	1.3
White Men	22,808	20,500	–2,308	–10.1

*Annual wage working full-time, full-year at average hourly wage.

more weeks per year, with one-fourth due to higher real weekly wages. The lack of available data on hours worked per week prevents a thorough assessment of the relative roles of annual hours versus hourly earnings on wives' earnings growth. However, given the trend toward more hours per week among women workers, it is fair to estimate that at least 75% of earning growth among young wives with children is due to greater hours of work and less than 25% is due to higher wage rates.

Lower Wages, More Poverty Level Jobs

As we have seen, young families are nearly entirely dependent on labor earnings for their incomes. Since real wages in young families have been falling, these families have been faced with the choice of working more to maintain or improve their incomes or having their real incomes decline. This section looks more closely at the wage trends among young workers. Wages for workers aged 25–34 have declined considerably in real terms. Moreover, the shift toward lower paying jobs has been greatest among young workers, especially among men.

Table 7.12 presents the changes in full-time equivalent wages in the 8 years from 1979 to 1987 for young workers by race and gender. The average young worker aged 25–34 earned 7.2% less in 1987 than in 1979. Astonishingly, young black workers earned 21.6% less. Young white workers also experienced a significant wage reduction of 10.1%. Young white women fared better, with a modest wage growth of 1.3%, while black women's wages fell by 3.8%. As a result of the deep wage decline among black men, in 1987 there was almost wage equality between black men and women aged 25–34, with black women earning only 9% less than black men.

Real wages have fallen even more for the youngest group of workers, those aged 16–24, whose overall real wage fell 12.5% between 1979 and 1987. Real wages fell by at least 10% in each race/gender group among these youngest workers.

The average young worker aged 25–34 earned 7.2% less in 1987 than in 1979. Astonishingly, young black workers earned 21.6% less.

213

TABLE 7.13

Shares of Young Workers by Wage Level By Age, 1979–1987

	Share of Workers Earning:*				
	Less Than the Poverty Line	Poverty to Two Times Poverty	Two Times to Three Times Poverty	Three Times Poverty and Above	Total
All Workers					
1979	25.7%	39.7%	20.4%	14.2%	100.0%
1987	31.5	37.9	17.9	12.7	100.0
Change	5.8	–1.8	–2.5	–1.5	0.0
Aged 16–24					
1979	46.5%	41.8%	8.9%	2.9%	100.0%
1987	62.1	31.7	4.4	1.7	100.0
Change	15.7	–10.1	–4.4	–1.2	0.0
Aged 25–34					
1979	17.7%	43.7%	26.1%	12.5%	100.0%
1987	25.9	45.1	20.1	8.8	100.0
Change	8.2	1.4	–5.9	–3.6	0.0

*Defined according to whether someone working full-time, year-round at a particular hourly wage can maintain a family of four at once, twice, or three times the poverty threshold.

The rapid fall in wages among young workers is reflected in the rapid shift toward low-wage employment among these workers (**Table 7.13**). Between 1979 and 1987, the proportion of workers aged 25–34 who earned poverty level wages grew from 17.7% to 25.9%, adding 8.2% of the young workforce to the ranks of low-wage earners. A parallel trend was the 9.5% drop of young workers aged 25–34 who earned at least twice the poverty wage. Overall, there has been an expansion of low-wage earners and a contraction of high-wage earners among the young (**Figure 7G**).

The rapid fall in wages among young workers is reflected in the rapid shift toward low-wage employment among these workers.

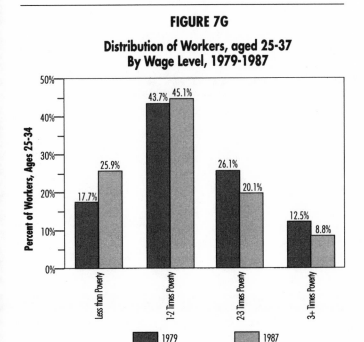

FIGURE 7G

Distribution of Workers, aged 25-37
By Wage Level, 1979-1987

TABLE 7.14

Shares of Workers By Wage Level, Aged 16–24, 1979–1987

Workers, Aged 16–24	Share of Workers Earning:*				
	Less Than the Poverty Line	Poverty to Two Times Poverty	Two Times to Three Times Poverty	Three Times Poverty and Above	Total
Black Women					
1979	58.3%	36.4%	3.8%	1.6%	100.0%
1987	71.1	26.1	2.2	0.7	100.0
Change	12.8	−10.3	−1.6	−0.9	0.0
Black Men					
1979	50.1%	36.3%	10.0%	3.6%	100.0%
1987	65.6	28.5	3.6	2.4	100.0
Change	15.5	−7.8	−6.5	−1.2	0.0
White Women					
1979	51.6%	41.7%	5.0%	1.7%	100.0%
1987	64.8	29.6	4.1	1.5	100.0%
Change	13.3	−12.1	−0.9	−0.3	0.0
White Men					
1979	39.6%	43.1%	13.3%	4.1%	100.0%
1987	57.0	35.5	5.4	2.1	100.0
Change	17.4	−7.6	−7.9	−2.0	0.0

*Defined according to whether someone working full-time, year-round at a particular hourly wage can maintain a family of four at once, twice, or three times the poverty threshold.

There was a great shift toward low-paying jobs among the youngest workers, aged 16–24 (**Table 7.14**). The rapid expansion of poverty level employment among these workers occurred among each gender/race group. Even among white men in this age range, 57% were earning poverty level wages in 1987, up from 39.6% in 1979. Among the other groups, roughly two-thirds or more of the workers had poverty-level jobs in 1987.

Among workers aged 25–34, there was a rapid expansion of the fraction working at poverty level wages within each race and gender group (**Table 7.15** and **Figure 7H**). The greatest shift toward low-wage work occurred among young black men, whose rate of poverty level work nearly

Among workers aged 25–34, there was a rapid expansion of the fraction working at poverty level wages within each race and gender group.

TABLE 7.15

Shares of Workers By Wage Level, Aged 25–34, 1979–1987

Workers, Aged 25–34	Share of Workers Earning:*				
	Less Than the Poverty Line	Poverty to Two Times Poverty	Two Times to Three Times Poverty	Three Times Poverty and Above	Total
Black Women					
1979	31.6%	47.4%	16.4%	4.5%	100.0%
1987	41.4	46.2	10.1	2.2	100.0%
Change	9.8	–1.2	–6.3	–2.3	0.0
Black Men					
1979	18.4%	44.6%	26.2%	10.8%	100.0%
1987	34.0	45.9	14.3	5.8	100.0
Change	15.6	1.3	–11.9	–5.0	0.0
White Women					
1979	24.9%	53.0%	17.0%	5.1%	100.0%
1987	30.6	48.0	16.3	5.1	100.0
Change	5.7	–5.0	–0.8	0.0	0.0
White Men					
1979	9.3%	35.0%	35.4%	20.3%	100.0%
1987	16.3	43.1	26.7	13.8	100.0
Change	7.0	8.1	–8.6	–6.5	0.0

*Defined according to whether someone working full-time, year-round, at a particular hourly wage can maintain a family of four at once, twice, or three times the poverty threshold.

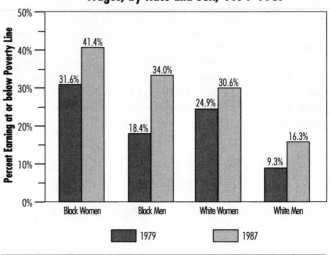

FIGURE 7H

Percent of Workers, Aged 25-34, Earning Poverty Wages, by Race and Sex, 1979-1987

doubled from 18.4% in 1979 to 34.0% in 1987. Within each group there was a shrinkage of workers earning high wages of more than twice the poverty wage. There has been a general shift downward in the wage structure of young workers, regardless of race and gender.

Explaining the Fall in Young Workers' Wages

There are two major reasons why the wages of young noncollege educated workers fell so much during the 1980s relative to the wages of young college graduates. First, these workers were increasingly employed in low-paying industries and were thus much less likely to be covered by a union contract. Second, there was a somewhat faster growth in the number of young high school educated workers relative to college graduates, a factor that can be expected to lower the wages of high school graduates relative to college graduates. These factors are further examined below.

Young workers were increasingly employed in low-paying industries and were thus much less likely to be covered by a union contract.

218

Table 7.16 presents the basic information on the labor market position of young, white, male workers aged 25–34 in 1973, 1979 and 1987. The data focus on white male workers in order to concentrate on issues unrelated to discrimination. The focus is on workers aged 25 to 34 years old because these workers should have completed their schooling and military service.

The annual wage of a full-time, year-round, high school graduate fell 8.6% from 1979 to 1987. In contrast, the wage of a full-time, year-round, college graduate rose by 9.2% in that same time period. As a result, the wage gap between high school and college graduates doubled from 16% in

The annual wage of a high school graduate fell 8.6% from 1979 to 1987, while that of a college graduate rose by 9.2%.

TABLE 7.16

Education Wage Gaps Among White Male Full-Time, Full-Year Workers, Aged 25–34, 1973–1987

	1973	1979	1987	Percent Change	
				1973–79	1979–87
Annual Earnings (Full-Time, Full-Year) (1987 Dollars)					
Less Than High School	$20,128	$18,693	$15,922	-7.1%	-14.8%
High School Graduate	24,718	23,440	21,420	-5.2	-8.6
College Graduate	30,034	27,583	30,132	-8.2	9.2
Wage Gap*				(Percentage Pt Change)	
College Graduate/High School Graduate	20%	16%	33%	-4	17
Employment-to-Population Ratio					
Less Than High School	88%	80%	77%	-8	-3
High School Graduate	94	89	89	-5	0
College Graduate	94	94	94	0	0
Relative Supply					
Ratio of College Graduates to High School Graduates	0.66	0.90	0.76	0.24	-0.14

*Percentage by which (log) earnings of college graduates exceed those of high school graduates, controlling for age, region, and marital status.

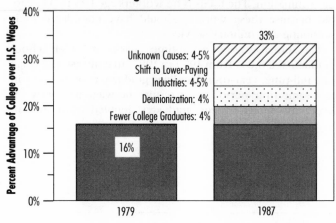

FIGURE 71

College Wage Advantage Among Workers Aged 25-34, 1979-1987

Percent Advantage of College over H.S. Wages

- Unknown Causes: 4-5%
- Shift to Lower-Paying Industries: 4-5%
- Deunionization: 4%
- Fewer College Graduates: 4%

33%

16%

1979   1987

TABLE 7.17

Effect of Industry Employment Shift on Education Differentials, 1979-1987*

| | | Change Due to: | |
By Method	Change in College/High School Wage Gap, 1979-87	Industry Employment Shift	Other Reasons
Regression Method	17%	4%	13%
Shift-Share Method	18	5.5	12.5

*White, male, full-time, full-year workers, aged 25-34.

220

1979 to 33% in 1987 (**Figure 7I**). Our analysis attempts to explain the rise in this wage gap.

It is noteworthy that the erosion of earnings among both high school graduates and high school dropouts did not lead to greater employment opportunities relative to college graduates. In fact, the opposite happened. The proportion of the noncollege educated population with jobs was lower in 1987 than in 1973, particularly for high school dropouts. Thus, falling real wages were not accompanied by the benefits of increased employment opportunities.

The first possible cause of the rising college/high school wage gap is demographic changes leading to a relative abundance of one type of worker. As Table 7.16 show, the ratio of college graduates fell between 1979 and 1987, partly reversing this ratio's rise in the 6 years between 1973 and 1979. Thus, the supply of noncollege educated workers had expanded relative to the supply of college educated workers. Given no changes in the relative usage (or demand) of high school versus college graduates, the relative increase of high school educated workers impeded their wage growth. Thus, an increase in the relative supply of high school graduates can partially explain the rise in the wage gap between high school and college graduates.

Table 7.17 presents an analysis of the effect of the employment shift toward lower wage industries on the college/high school wage gap. The data show that, by two different methods, the shift to lower wage industries increased the wage gap by 4 to 5.5 percentage points, explaining from 24% to 30% of the total 17 percentage point rise in the wage gap. This result reflects, as we saw in Chapter 3, that the employment expansion of low-wage industries has adversely affected less educated workers more than college educated workers. Industry shifts are thus an important factor in why noncollege educated workers have earned relatively lower wages in recent years.

The erosion of earnings among both high school graduates and high school dropouts did not lead to greater employment opportunities.

TABLE 7.18

Effect of Deunionization on Average Earnings By Education, White Male Workers, Aged 25–34, 1980–88

Workers Aged 25–34 By Education	Fall in Proportion Unionized 1980–88*	Union Premium in 1980**	Effect of Deunionization on Average Earnings***
Less Than High School	–13%	20%	–3%
High School Graduate	–13	30	–4
College Graduate	–6	–2	0

*Holding constant industry shares.

**Percentage (in log points) by which union wages exceed nonunion wages, controlling for worker characteristics.

***In log points.

TABLE 7.19

Explanation for Increased College/High School Wage Gap Among White Male Workers Aged 25–34, 1979–1987

Item	Contribution to Change in College/High School Wage Gap
Change in College/High School Wage Gap	17%
Explanatory Factors	
Industry Shifts*	4–5
Shift in Relative Labor Supply	4
Deunionization	4
Overall Change Accounted for	12–13
Percent of Overall Change Accounted for	71–76

*Range of results with two methods, shown in Table 7.17.

Another important factor is the large decline in the rate of unionization among noncollege educated workers (**Table 7.18**). Between 1980 and 1988, the unionization rate among both high school dropouts and graduates dropped 13 percentage points (independent of industry shifts), or more than twice as much as the 6 percentage point drop in unionization among young college graduates. Since less educated workers gain significantly from unions (their wages are 20% to 30% more than those of comparable nonunion workers) the large drop in unionization lowered their average wage about 3% to 4%. The drop in unionization among college graduates had no effect on their wages since these workers received insignificant union premiums. Thus, the wage gap between college and high school graduates rose by 4 percentage points due to the deunionization that occurred between 1980 and 1988.

Table 7.19 and Figure 7I bring together all of the factors that have been identified as increasing the college/high school wage gap. The increase in the relative number of high school graduates can explain a 4 percentage point rise in the wage gap. The deunionization and industry shift factors explain another 8 to 9 percentage points of the increase in the wage gap. Together, these factors explain from 71% to 76% of the total 17 percentage point rise in the college/high school wage gap. Over half of the rise (three-fourths of the explainable rise) in the wage gap can be attributed to changes in the types of jobs available to non-college educated workers while only one-fourth is attributable to demographic or supply-side factors.

The changes in the types of jobs available to high school educated workers—explained by the industry shift and deunionization—are not likely to be reversed in the future. However, recent increases in college enrollments can be expected to expand the supply of college educated workers relative to high school graduates. Given these trends, the college/high school wage gap among young workers can be expected to decline, but only by a small amount.

Deunionization and industry shift . . . explain from 71% to 76% of the total 17 percentage point rise in the college/high school wage gap.

CHAPTER 8

TABLE 8.1

Home Ownership Rates By Age of Household Head, 1973–1989

Age of Household Head	Home Ownership Rate in:			Point Change:	
	1973	1980	1989	1973–80	1980–89
Under 25	23.4%	21.3%	17.6%	-2.1	-3.7
25–29	43.6	43.3	35.4	-0.3	-7.9
30–34	60.2	61.1	53.6	0.9	-7.5
35–39	68.5	70.8	63.9	2.3	-6.9
40–44	72.9	74.2	70.8	1.3	-3.4
45–54	76.1	77.7	75.3	1.6	-2.4
55–64	75.7	79.3	80.2	3.6	0.9
65–74	71.3	75.2	78.2	3.9	3.0
75+	67.1	67.8	70.3	0.7	2.5
Average for All Households	64.4	65.6	63.9	1.2	-1.7

HOUSING, HEALTH CARE, AND EDUCATION: LOSING ACCESS TO THE BASICS

ntil now we have defined well-being in terms of resources: income, earnings, wealth, and so on. We have found that the resources of American families have, on the whole, grown slowly since 1979 and have become much more unequally distributed. In this chapter, we examine well-being in terms of what these resources *buy*. In particular, we consider access to three basic goods: housing, health care, and education. These three goods are crucial to family well-being and, in the case of education, to creating equal opportunity for new generations. We find that, because the costs of these goods have soared, fewer can afford them, and the gaps have grown between those who can and those who cannot.

Housing

As a result of high interest rates and home prices in the 1980s, the percentage of households owning their own homes dropped, particularly among young households. In addition, the burden of housing costs for renters rose. Families with children have been squeezed particularly hard by rising housing costs.

Home Ownership Down Among Under-55s

Home ownership has been the foundation of economic security for the American family for many years. In the 1980s, this foundation weakened. Between 1973 and 1980, the overall home ownership rate *increased* by 1.2 percentage points (**Table 8.1**). However, during the 1980–89 period, it *fell* by 1.7 points.

Ownership rates fell for all households headed by someone under 55 years old, and in particular for households in their prime childbearing years. Home ownership among the 25–29 age group fell from 43.3% to 35.4%, a decline of 7.9 points. For households with heads aged 30–34, home ownership fell 7.5 percentage points. The 35–39 age group experienced a decline of 6.9 percentage points.

Ownership rates increased slightly among households with heads over 55, and particularly among retirees. This may be because many older households had already purchased homes before the run-up in home prices during the

The percentage of households owning their own homes dropped, particularly among young households.

225

TABLE 8.2

Burdens of Buying Homes and Renting, 1967–1989

	Housing Expenses as Percent of Income for:	
	Prime First-Time Home Buyers*	Renters
At Business Cycle Peaks:		
1967	21.2%	24.4%
1973	24.3	23.3
1979	36.0	25.8
1989	33.1	29.1
Period Averages:		
1967–73	22.5	23.7
1974–79	29.9	24.9
1980–89	37.2	29.1

*Married-couple renters aged 25 to 29.

FIGURE 8A

Housing Cost Burdens for Renters and Prime First-Time Buyers, 1967–1989

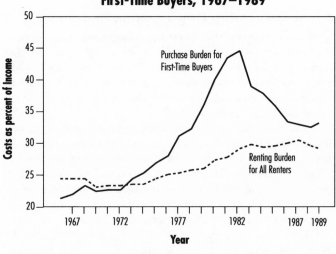

226

1970s and because the incomes of older families have risen relative to those of younger families.

Housing Costs Outstrip Incomes

In the 1980s, high interest rates and home prices made purchasing a home considerably less affordable than in the early 1970s. These developments have affected renters as well.

Table 8.2 and **Figure 8A** show rental costs and first-time home purchasing costs as a percent of income between 1967 and 1989. The total burden for first-time home buyers is the expense of the median-priced home, expressed as a percentage of the median income of married-couple renters aged 25–29. (These families are selected because they are especially likely to be considering the purchase of a first home.) The burden for renters is the yearly expense of renting, expressed as a percentage of the median income of all renters.

The first part of Table 8.2 gives housing burdens at the peaks of successive business cycles. Fueled by volatile mortgage interest rates, the burden for first-time buyers rose from 24.3% of income in 1973 to 36.0% in 1979 (Table 8.2). As Figure 8A shows, the burden reached a high (44.5%) in 1982, then dropped with declining interest rates through 1988. In 1989, the burden rose again, to 33.1%.

The housing burden for first-time buyers *averaged* 37.2% throughout the 1980–89 period (Table 8.2, last line). Since home ownership rates respond slowly to changing costs, the high home purchasing burdens of the early and mid-1980s help explain the depressed ownership rates of 1989.

In contrast to home purchasing costs, which have come down significantly from their peak, the rental burden has dipped only slightly from a high in 1987 (Figure 8A). Median rental expenses were 29.1% of income in 1989, compared with 25.8% in 1979 and with even lower levels in 1967 and 1973 (Table 8.2). Their average during the 1980–89 period was also 29.1%, up from 24.9% in the 1974–79 period.

In the 1980s, high interest rates and home prices made purchasing a home considerably less affordable than in the early 1970s.

227

TABLE 8.3

Median Incomes of Renters and Owners, 1967–1989

1989 Dollars

	Median Incomes of:			Renters' Income as Percent of
Year	All Owners	All Renters	Young Renters	Owners' Income
1967	$27,361	$17,684	$26,694	64.6%
1973	29,720	18,607	27,653	62.6
1979	30,686	16,768	25,488	54.6
1989	34,000	16,900	26,000	49.7

TABLE 8.4

Households Paying Over 25% of Income for Housing, By Household Size, 1970–1987

A. By Household Size

	Household Size					
Year	1	2	3	4	5	6+
1970	53.1%	32.4%	20.4%	18.5%	15.7%	15.4%
1979	50.8	35.5	27.9	22.5	21.6	21.3
1987	51.4	36.9	36.6	34.2	36.5	40.4

B. Small vs. Large Households; All Households

Year	Small (1–2 Persons)	Large (3+ Persons)	All Households
1970	37.9%	17.8%	24.0%
1979	39.6	23.6	28.5
1987	40.8	36.6	37.9

Richer Owners, Poorer Renters

At the same time that homes have become more expensive and less affordable for young families, the incomes of owners and renters have moved further apart. This trend is probably the reflection of increased income inequality in the economy at large. Since 1967, the median renter's income has declined from $17,684 to $16,900, while the median home owner's income has risen from $27,361 to $34,000 (**Table 8.3**). As a result, renters' incomes fell from 64.6% of owners' incomes in 1967 to only 49.7% in 1989.

Families with Children Most Affected

The higher costs of both owning a home and renting have hit families with children the hardest. **Table 8.4** shows the percent of households paying over 25% of their incomes for housing—the conventional measure of housing affordability—in the 1970–87 period, broken down by size of household. Between 1970 and 1987, the percent of small (1–2 person) households paying over 25% of income for housing rose slightly, from 37.9% to 40.8%. In the same period, the proportion of large (3 + persons) households facing such burdens more than doubled, from 17.8% to 36.6%.

The higher costs of both owning a home and renting have hit families with children the hardest.

229

TABLE 8.5

Shelter Poverty, By Household Size
1970–1987

A. By Household Size

Year	Household Size					
	1	2	3	4	5	6+
1970	39.3	27.3%	20.2%	26.3%	31.2%	43.5%
1979	28.9	24.5	27.2	29.2	37.8	50.2
1987	27.0	24.9	27.9	31.3	42.1	54.7

B. Small vs. Large Households; All Households

Year	Small (1–2 Persons)	Large (3+ Persons)	All Households
1970	30.5%	29.1%	29.6%
1979	25.7	34.7	31.9
1987	25.5	37.3	33.7

FIGURE 8B

Shelter Poverty by Household Size, 1970-1987

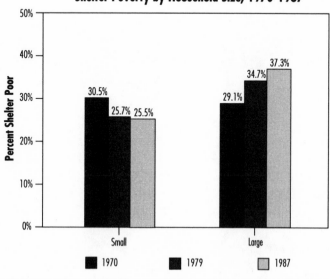

One shortcoming of the conventional measure of housing affordability is that paying over 25% of income for housing may not be a hardship for some households (i.e., those with high incomes). A better measure is "shelter poverty" (**Table 8.5** and **Figure 8B**). A household is "shelter poor" if, after housing expenses, it does not have enough to pay for a minimum amount of non-housing necessities, as defined by the U.S. Bureau of Labor Statistics.

As Table 8.5 shows, fully 33.7% of households were "shelter poor" in 1987. In other words, just over a third of American households could not buy enough food, clothing, and other necessities after paying for housing. The shelter poverty rate was higher in 1987 than in either 1970 or 1979, when it was 29.6% and 31.9%, respectively.

Table 8.5 and Figure 8B also more clearly demonstrate the differing fortunes of large and small households. Large households saw a substantial increase in their shelter poverty rate in the 1970–87 period, from 29.1% to 37.3%. This implies a deterioration in the living standards of families with children. On the other hand, small households actually experienced a decrease in shelter poverty from 30.5% to 25.5%.

Health Care

Like housing expenses, the cost of health care has risen substantially. Americans spend more on health care than anyone else in the world, in part because doctors' fees are high. However, higher spending in the U.S. has not resulted in better health for the average American.

The American health insurance system also has problems. Many people are uninsured and are thus vulnerable to medical and financial disaster. In addition, coverage deteriorated in the 1980s as employers reacted to international competition and rising health costs by scaling back on coverage. Most other advanced countries have avoided these problems by providing comprehensive public health care.

TABLE 8.6

OECD Spending on Health, 1960–1987

Country	Total Health Expenditure at Percent of Gross Domestic Product in:				Rank in 1987 (out of 24)
	1960	1970	1980	1987	
Australia	4.6%	5.0%	6.5%	7.1%	15
Austria	4.6	5.4	7.9	8.4	6
Belgium	3.4	4.0	6.6	7.2	14
Canada	5.5	7.2	7.4	8.6	3
Denmark	3.6	6.1	6.8	6.0	21
Finland	3.9	5.7	6.5	7.4	12
France	4.2	5.8	7.6	8.6	3
West Germany	4.7	5.5	7.9	8.2	7
Greece	3.2	4.0	4.3	5.3	23
Iceland	1.2	4.3	6.4	7.8	8
Ireland	4.0	5.6	8.5	7.4	12
Italy	3.3	4.8	6.8	6.9	16
Japan	2.9	4.4	6.4	6.8	18
Luxembourg	N/A	4.1	6.8	7.5	10
Netherlands	3.9	6.0	8.2	8.5	5
New Zealand	4.4	5.1	7.2	6.9	16
Norway	3.3	5.0	6.6	7.5	10
Portugal	N/A	N/A	5.9	6.4	19
Spain	2.3	4.1	5.9	6.0	21
Sweden	4.7	7.2	9.5	9.0	2
Switzerland	3.3	5.2	7.3	7.7	9
Turkey	N/A	N/A	N/A	3.5	24
United Kingdom	3.9	4.5	5.8	6.1	20
United States	**5.2**	**7.4**	**9.2**	**11.2**	**1**
U.S. Rank	2	1	2	1	
OECD Average (excluding Turkey, Portugal, and Luxembourg)	3.81%	5.35%	7.11%	7.55%	
U.S. as Multiple of OECD Average	1.36	1.38	1.29	1.48	

Spending and Costs Are Higher in the U.S.

Table 8.6 shows health care expenditures between 1960 and 1987 for countries in the Organization for Economic Cooperation and Development (OECD), an association that includes most of the advanced industrial countries. In 1987, the U.S. spent 11.2% of GDP on health care, the highest proportion in the OECD. The U.S. now spends 1.48 times the OECD average, up from 1.38 in 1970 and 1.29 in 1980. As the third to last row in Table 8.6 indicates, the U.S. has consistently spent either the highest or the second highest percent of GDP on health care since 1960.

One reason that Americans spend more on health care than people in other countries is that medical fees are much higher in the U.S. **Table 8.7** compares total fees of physicians for a sample of procedures in Germany, France, Japan, and the U.S. in 1984. The fees for Germany, France, and Japan in Table 8.7 are adjusted to represent what their fees

One reason that Americans spend more on health care than people in other countries is that medical fees are much higher in the U.S.

TABLE 8.7

Medical Service Fees, 1984

1984 Dollars

| Procedure | U.S. Fee | Adjusted Fees* | | | Ratio of U.S. Fee to Average of Fees in Other 3 Countries |
		Germany	France	Japan	
1. GP Home Visit	$ 31	$ 16	$ 16	$ 13	2.1
2. 1st consultation with major exam.	72	11	19	9	5.6
3. Cholecsytectomy	1,754	160	182	506	6.2
4. Total Hysterectomy	1,754	178	228	386	6.7
5. Appendectomy	1,135	95	114	237	7.6
6. Examination of urine	5	N/A	24	15	0.3
7. Prothrombin time test	7	N/A	5	3	1.8
8. Total cholesterol dosage	5	N/A	3	4	1.4
9. Thorax radiography	41	29	24	N/A	1.5
10. Colon radiography	155	52	88	N/A	2.2
11. Radiography of lombasacral column	93	49	36	N/A	2.2
12. Electroencephalogram	125	38	159	32	1.6
13. Electrocardiogram	45	16	18	9	3.1
14. Bronchoscopy	413	38	68	20	9.8
15. Rectosigmoidoscopy	72	58	23	6	2.5

*Adjusted for differences in per capita GNP.

TABLE 8.8

Health Indicators in U.S. and in Average OECD Country*

Indicator	Year	U.S. Rank (Out of 23)	U.S. Level	OECD Average
Infant Mortality Rate**	1970	15	2.00	2.05
	1980	17	1.26	1.14
	1986	21	1.04	0.87
Perinatal Mortality Rate**	1970	12	2.30	2.29
	1980	14	1.32	1.28
	1986	15	1.03	0.99
Female Life Expectancy at Birth	1960	12	73.3	72.9
	1980	15	76.7	77.5
	1986	15	78.3	78.8
Male Life Expectancy at Birth	1960	16	66.7	67.8
	1980	18	69.6	70.9
	1986	15	71.3	72.3

*Excluding Turkey.

**Infant mortality is deaths of infants less than one year old, as a percent of all live births. Perinatal mortality is fetal deaths occurring after 28 weeks of pregnancy, plus infant deaths occuring prior to 7 days after birth, as a percent of all live births and fetal deaths.

TABLE 8.9

Number and Percent of the Population Under Age 65 Without Health Insurance, 1979–1986

	1979	1983	1984	1985	1986
Number Uninsured (millions)	28.4	34.8	36.8	36.7	36.8
Percent Uninsured	14.6%	16.9%	17.7%	17.6%	17.5%

234

would be if the per capita income of each country were the same as in the U.S. Only one of the procedures is less expensive in the U.S. Other U.S. fees are between 1.4 and 9.8 times the average of the other 3 countries.

. . . Yet Health Indicators Lag

It may be argued that medical care in the U.S. is more expensive because it is the finest in the world. Yet it seems unlikely, for example, that an American appendectomy is of such high quality that it is worth $1,135, compared to $237 in Japan, $114 in France, and $95 in Germany (Table 8.7). In addition, despite our high fees and large expenditures on health, the average American is actually less healthy than the citizen of the average OECD country, and the U.S. has been falling further behind in this respect.

Table 8.8 shows four basic health indicators in the U.S. and in the average OECD country (excluding Turkey): the infant mortality rate, the perinatal mortality rate, and the life expectancies of females and males at birth. As the second column shows, the U.S. rank, low to begin with, has dropped for each of the main indicators except male life expectancy. Our infant mortality rate was 15th out of 23 in 1970, 17th in 1980, and 21st in 1986; the latter part of this decline occurred even as the U.S. was extending its lead in spending. The perinatal mortality rate and female life expectancies are also ranked lower than in earlier years.

. . . And Many Lack Insurance

Not only is health care very expensive in the U.S.; many Americans also lack health insurance and are thus exposed to great medical and financial risks. While large numbers of Americans are uncovered during the entire year, many others have coverage only part of the time. Young adults, children, minorities, and workers with gaps in employment are the groups most likely to lack continuous coverage. Moreover, workers in the service sector and in small firms are much less likely to receive insurance than other workers.

The uncovered population increased substantially between 1979 and 1986. In 1979, 28.4 million persons, or 14.6% of the population, lacked health insurance for the entire year (**Table 8.9**). By 1986, the uninsured population had increased to 36.8 million (17.5%).

Despite our high fees and large expenditures on health, the average American is actually less healthy than the citizen of the average OECD country.

235

TABLE 8.10

Breaks in Health Insurance During a 28-Month Period
(1985–87 Period)

Group	Percent Covered Less Than 28 Months
All	28.1%
Race/Ethnic Group	
White	26.4
Black	37.7
Hispanic*	52.0
Age	
Under 18	34.5
18–24	51.9
25–44	27.7
45–64	19.9
65 and over	0.7
Work Experience	
Worked Full-Period, Full-Time	14.0
Worked Full-Period, Part-Time	25.4
Worked with Interruptions	44.7

*Persons of Hispanic origin may be of any race.

Part-time and part-year workers are also vulnerable to loss of health insurance.

Many others have health insurance only part of the time. **Table 8.10** gives the percent of persons who lacked coverage for one or more months during a 28-month period between February 1985, and August 1987. Fully 28.1% of the population had unprotected periods, compared to 17.5% who lacked coverage throughout all of 1986. Young adults and children are particularly likely to go through uncovered periods. Over half (51.9%) of young adults aged 18–24, as well as 34.5% of children under 18, were uncovered for a month or more (see also **Figure 8C**).

Part-time and part-year workers are also vulnerable to loss of health insurance. While 14.0% of full-period, full-time workers had uncovered periods, 25.4% of part-time workers had these periods, as did 44.7% of those who had gaps in employment (Table 8.10). Minorities are also at greater risk. Among whites, 26.4% had uncovered periods, compared to 37.7% of blacks and fully 52.0% of Hispanics.

236

One of the main reasons that many people lack health insurance or go though uncovered periods is that a large and increasing proportion of jobs do not provide coverage. As **Table 8.11** shows, 75.6% of full-year, full-time workers received health insurance from their employers, compared to only 44.9% of part-year, full-time workers and to even smaller percentages of part-time workers.

A large and increasing proportion of jobs do not provide coverage.

FIGURE 8C

Gaps in Health Insurance, by Age, 1985-1987

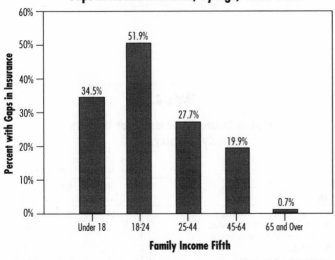

TABLE 8.11

Workers Receiving Health Insurance From Own Job, By Job Status, 1986

Job Status	Percent Receiving Insurance From Own Job
Full-Year, Full-Time	75.6%
Full-Year, Part-Time	24.9
Part-Year, Full-Time	44.9
Part-Year, Part-Time	11.3

TABLE 8.12

Health Insurance Coverage of Workers, By Firm Size, 1988

Firm Size	Percent Receiving Insurance from:			
	Own Job	Other Source	Not Insured	Total
Under 25 Employees	26.8%	49.9%	23.3%	100.0%
25-99	52.2	30.8	17.0	100.0
100-499	62.6	25.7	11.7	100.0
500-999	66.6	22.5	10.9	100.0
1,000 or More	67.3	24.8	7.9	100.0

TABLE 8.13

Health Insurance Coverage of Workers, By Industry, 1988

Industry	Percent Receiving Insurance from:			
	Own Job	Other Source	Not Insured	Total
Agriculture, Forestry, and Fisheries	16.8%	54.8%	28.4%	100.0%
Personal Services, Including Household	19.9	53.1	27.0	100.0
Entertainment and Recreation Services	28.5	51.5	20.0	100.0
Retail Trade	31.2	48.6	20.2	100.0
Business and Repair Services	40.1	39.2	20.7	100.0
Construction	44.2	28.5	27.3	100.0
Professional and Related Services	56.2	35.2	8.6	100.0
Finance, Insurance, and Real Estate	63.5	28.7	7.8	100.0
Wholesale Trade	63.8	24.7	11.5	100.0
Manufacturing, Nondurable Goods	69.1	18.5	12.4	100.0
Public Administration	72.2	17.4	10.4	100.0
Mining	73.0	17.7	9.3	100.0
Transportation, Communications, and Public Utilities	73.7	20.9	5.4	100.0
Manufacturing, Durable Goods	76.8	13.5	9.7	100.0

Employees of small firms are much less likely to receive insurance than workers in large firms. In 1988, only 26.8% of workers in firms of under 25 employees received health insurance from their employers (**Table 8.12**). Some had other sources of insurance, but 23.3% of these employees were uninsured. On the other hand, 67.3% of workers in firms of at least 1,000 employees received health insurance, and only 7.9% of these employees were uninsured.

Service sector firms are much less likely to provide health insurance than other firms. The most generous industry in 1988 was durable goods manufacturing, in which 76.8% of workers received health insurance from their employers (**Table 8.13**). On the other hand, firms in personal services, entertainment and recreation services, and retail trade provide only 19.9%, 28.5%, and 31.2% of their workers with health insurance, respectively. If coverage rates in these industries do not improve, their rapid growth threatens a further deterioration in the proportion of Americans who are covered by health insurance.

The rapid growth [of the service sector] threatens a further deterioration in the proportion of Americans who are covered by health insurance.

Insurance Costs Rose for Workers

In response to skyrocketing health insurance premiums, some employers stopped offering health insurance in the 1980s. Others raised deductibles or copayments, or required their workers to contribute a larger share of the premiums.

TABLE 8.14

Overall Inflation vs. Health Insurance Inflation 1965-1988

	Annual Inflation Rates	
Period	Overall	Health Insurance
1965–1980	5.6%	5.2%
1980–1988	4.6	10.6

FIGURE 8D

Health Insurance Prices vs. Overall Price Level, 1965-1988

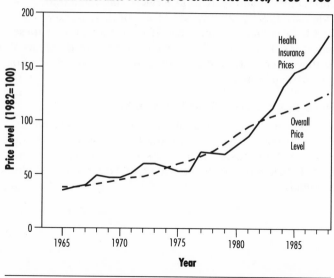

Between 1980 and 1988, health insurance premiums shot up at an annual rate of 10.6%.

In the 1965–80 period, health insurance premiums rose 5.2% per year, slightly less than the overall rate of inflation (**Table 8.14** and **Figure 8D**). However, between 1980 and 1988, premiums shot up at an annual rate of 10.6%, which was more than double the overall inflation rate of 4.6%.

The results were dramatic. Between 1970 and 1980, the share of private health insurance premiums paid by employers rose from 70.0% to 79.7% (**Table 8.15**). But by 1987, employers had cut back to only 69.5%, which was less than in 1970.

In the short period between 1982 and 1988, even many full-time workers in firms of over 250 employees lost coverage or had to contribute more towards their premiums. The proportion of such workers who had health insurance dropped from 97% in 1982 to 92% in 1988 (**Table 8.16**). Strikingly, the proportion whose employers payed the entire premium for personal health insurance fell 20 percentage points, from 71% to 51%. Given the short time period of only 6 years, this is a very significant change. The proportion of workers whose employers were willing to finance all of their family insurance also fell considerably, from 46% to 34%.

In the short period between 1982 and 1988, even many full-time workers in firms of over 250 employees lost coverage or had to contribute more towards their premiums.

TABLE 8.15

Employer vs. Employee Spending on Private Health Insurance Premiums, Billions of 1989 Dollars
1965–1987

| Year | Total Spending (Billions) | Percent Paid By: | | |
		Employer	Employee	Total
1965	$ 25.2	56.8%	43.2%	100.0%
1970	35.8	70.0	30.0	100.0
1975	50.1	74.4	25.6	100.0
1980	73.8	79.7	20.3	100.0
1984	98.2	76.5	23.5	100.0
1987	115.4	69.5	30.5	100.0

TABLE 8.16

Medical Benefits for Full-Time Workers in Large Firms*
1982–1988

| Year | Percent Who Receive Medical Insurance | Percent Whose Firms Pay Entire Premium for: | |
		Personal Insurance	Family Insurance
1982	97%	71%	46%
1988	92	51	34
Change, 1982–88	–5	–20	–12

*The above figures exclude most of the service industries, such as health and education services, and include only establishments that employ at least 250 workers in the mining, construction, retail trade, and some manufacturing and transportation industries.

TABLE 8.17

Public Health Coverage in OECD Countries,* 1987

Country	Percent of Population Covered for:		
	Inpatient Care	Ambulatory Care	Medical Goods
Australia	100%	100%	100%
Austria	99	99	99
Belgium	98	93	93
Canada	100	100	34
Denmark	100	100	100
Finland	100	100	99
France	99	98	98
West Germany	92	92	92
Greece	100	100	100
Iceland	100	100	100
Ireland	100	37	40
Italy	100	100	100
Japan	100	100	100
Luxembourg	100	100	100
Netherlands	73	67	61
New Zealand	100	100	100
Norway	100	100	100
Portugal	100	100	100
Spain	97	97	97
Sweden	100	100	100
Switzerland	99	99	99
United Kingdom	100	100	100
United States	**43**	**43**	**10**
Number with 100% Coverage	15	14	12

*No data available for Turkey.

In contrast to the American system, in which most health insurance is provided by employers, a majority of OECD countries have comprehensive systems of public health insurance. **Table 8.17** shows the percent of persons in each OECD country who are covered by public health insurance. Of the 23 countries for which information is available, the U.S. ranks last in percent covered for each category of expense: inpatient care, ambulatory care, and medical goods. The majority of countries cover all of their citizens against each type of expense. Even poor countries such as Portugal and Greece provide comprehensive coverage.

Opportunities among American students are very unequal.

Education

In addition to adequate housing and health care, another crucial part of our expectations as Americans is equal opportunity for our children. We place great emphasis on the education system to achieve this goal. However, opportunities among American students are very unequal. Partly because of greater poverty, many American children have poor skills by international standards. Spending on public schools is also low and uneven. Moreover, the growing gap between public and private college fees has transformed higher education into a two-tiered system. And while the education of minority students has improved, many students still lack access to higher education and advanced degrees.

TABLE 8.18

Science Test Scores for 14-Year-Olds, 1983–86

| Country | 14-Year-Olds | | | |
	Grade Tested	Average Test Score	Percent of Age Group in School	Mean Age, in Years and Months
Australia	8,9,10	17.8	98%	14:5
Canada (English)	9	18.6	99	15:0
England	9	16.7	98	14:2
Finland	8	18.5	99	14:10
Hong Kong	8	16.4	99	14:7
Hungary	8	21.7	98	14:3
Italy	8,9	16.7	99	14:7
Japan	9	20.2	99	14:7
Netherlands	9	19.8	99	15:6
Norway	9	17.9	99	15:10
Poland	8	18.1	91	15:0
Sweden	8	18.4	99	14:9
United States	**9**	**16.5**	**99**	**15:4**

TABLE 8.19

Mathematics Test Scores for 8th Graders, 1981–82

Country or Province	Mean Percent Correct, All Items
Average	47.4%
Belgium	
Flemish	53.2
French	51.4
Canada	
British Columbia	51.6
Ontario	49.0
England and Wales	47.2
Finland	46.8
France	52.5
Hong Kong	49.4
Hungary	56.0
Israel	45.0
Japan	62.1
Luxembourg	37.5
Netherlands	57.1
New Zealand	45.5
Scotland	48.4
Sweden	41.8
United States	**45.3**

244

U.S. Students Falling Behind: Poverty May Be One Reason Why

The average scores of American students on science and mathematics tests are poorer than scores of children in other countries. **Table 8.18** gives scores of 14- and 15-year-olds on a standard test of science achievement in the 1983–86 period. The average score for American students was 16.5. Only Hong Kong has an average score lower than the U.S. In addition, **Table 8.19** gives scores of 8th graders on an international mathematics test in 1981 and 1982. The average U.S. score of 45.3 exceeds scores in only three of the other countries.

Table 8.20 suggests one possible reason for the lower average scores of American students (see also **Figure 8E**). Among children with the most advantaged upbringings, 42.5% to 48.5% scored in the top fourth of students on tests of mathematics, reading, and science in 1988. On the other hand, among students with disadvantaged backgrounds, only 7.9% to 9.1% were in the top fourth on the same tests. This suggests that American children may have lower average skills in mathematics and science partly because, as we will see in Chapter 9, more of them are poor.

American children may have lower average skills in mathematics and science partly because more of them are poor.

TABLE 8.20

Effects of Family Background on Scores of 8th Graders, 1988

Test Subject and Score Group	Family Background		
	Disadvantaged	Average	Advantaged
Mathematics	100.0%	100.0%	100.0%
Lower Fourth	44.3	23.8	9.3
Second Fourth	30.8	26.9	16.1
Third Fourth	17.0	27.0	26.2
Upper Fourth	7.9	22.3	48.5
Reading	100.0%	100.0%	100.0%
Lower Fourth	44.0	24.2	11.1
Second Fourth	29.1	27.0	16.9
Third Fourth	18.5	25.8	26.3
Upper Fourth	8.4	23.0	45.7
Science	100.0%	100.0%	100.0%
Lower Fourth	42.3	24.7	11.1
Second Fourth	29.2	25.5	16.9
Third Fourth	19.3	27.3	29.4
Upper Fourth	9.1	22.6	42.5

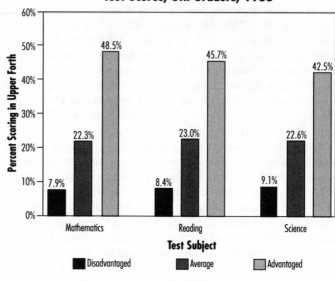

FIGURE 8E
Effects of Family Background on Test Scores, 8th Graders, 1988

Percent Scoring in Upper Forth

- 48.5% — Mathematics, Advantaged
- 22.3% — Mathematics, Average
- 7.9% — Mathematics, Disadvantaged
- 45.7% — Reading, Advantaged
- 23.0% — Reading, Average
- 8.4% — Reading, Disadvantaged
- 42.5% — Science, Advantaged
- 22.6% — Science, Average
- 9.1% — Science, Disadvantaged

Test Subject

■ Disadvantaged ■ Average ▨ Advantaged

TABLE 8.21
Country Education Expenditures, 1985

Country	Education Spending as Percent of GDP
Sweden	7.0%
Austria	5.9
Switzerland	5.8
Norway	5.3
Belgium	4.9
Denmark	4.8
Japan	4.8
Canada	4.7
West Germany	4.6
France	4.6
Netherlands	4.5
United Kingdom	4.5
Italy	4.2
United States	**4.1**
Australia	3.9
Ireland	3.8

K–12 Education: Investing Less Than Other Major Countries

In addition to greater poverty, another obstacle to equal opportunity for American children is low and uneven spending on grades K–12. **Table 8.21** shows spending on grades K–12 as a percent of GDP in the U.S. and in a number of other industrial countries. (The percentages are adjusted for differences in enrollments.) U.S. public and private spending, at 4.1% of GDP, is one of the lowest among the countries listed.

Resources are also distributed very unequally among public schools. For example, some states spend much more on public schools than others, even after correcting for different enrollments and costs of living. **Table 8.22** gives state

Another obstacle to equal opportunity for American children is low and uneven spending on grades K-12.

TABLE 8.22

Public School Expenditures Per Pupil, 1988–89
Adjusted for Cost of Living Differences Between States

State	Adjusted Spending Per Pupil 1988/89	Percent of U.S. Average
Highest Ten States		
New York	$5,723	135%
Alaska	5,684	134
New Jersey	5,355	126
Connecticut	5,350	126
Wyoming	5,154	121
Vermont	5,127	121
Rhode Island	4,955	117
Pennsylvania	4,910	116
Delaware	4,891	115
Wisconsin	4,888	115
Lowest Ten States:		
Tennessee	$3,400	80%
Hawaii	3,300	78
Oklahoma	3,255	77
Arkansas	3,176	75
Kentucky	3,065	72
Idaho	2,987	70
Louisiana	2,980	70
Mississippi	2,925	69
Alabama	2,842	67
Utah	2,680	63
U.S. Average	4,246	100

TABLE 8.23

Public and Private College Costs, 1967–1988

(1989 Dollars)

| | Average Tuition, Room and Board for: | | | | |
| | Public 4-Year College | | Private 4-Year Colleges | | |
School Year Period	Dollars	Percent of Parents' Median Income*	Dollars	Percent of Parents' Median Income*	Private Costs as Multiple of Public Costs
1966–67	$3,907	12.1	$ 8,195	25.4	2.1
1972–73	4,311	11.0	9,076	23.1	2.1
1978–79	3,838	9.0	9,060	21.3	2.4
1987–88	4,899	11.1	13,840	31.3	2.8

*Based on median family income for families with heads aged 45–54.

FIGURE 8F

Public and Private College Costs, 1967-1988

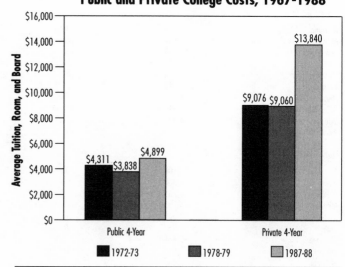

248

spending per public school pupil in the 1988–89 school year, adjusted for differences in costs of living. Spending on education ranged from 63% of the national average, in Utah, to 135%, in New York. In addition, there are sharp disparities in spending between districts *within* many states.

Higher Education: A Two-Tiered System

The rapid growth of private college fees in the 1980s raised new financial barriers for low- and middle-income families who would send their children to private colleges. This is troubling because many private colleges provide their graduates with better employment opportunities and connections than public colleges. The cost of a year at the average private 4-year college shot up from $9,060 in 1978–79 to $13,840 in 1987–88 (**Table 8.23 and Figure 8F**). This was 2.8 times the annual cost at the average public 4-year college, compared to 2.4 in 1978–79 and 2.1 in 1972–73.

Some financial aid is available for low income students. However, federal financial aid is meager and has not kept pace with college fees. The average award in 1980–81, not including student loans, was 33.5% of the average cost of attendance at a private university (**Table 8.24**). In 1988–89, it amounted to only 20.9%. The average award

The rapid growth of private college fees in the 1980s raised new financial barriers for low- and middle-income families.

TABLE 8.24

Federal Student Aid

(1988 Dollars)

	1980–81	1988–89
Average Federal Aid		
Pell Grant	$1,204	$ 1,339
College Work-Study	1,101	901
Supplemental Educational Opportunity Grant	701	684
TOTAL	$3,006	$ 2,924
Average College Costs		
Private University	$8,969	$13,977
Public University	3,703	4,822
Average Aid as Percent of Costs		
Private University	33.5%	20.9%
Public University	81.2	60.6

TABLE 8.25

Parental Contributions to College Costs
at Stanford University 1990–91

1990–91 Tuition, Room and Board at Stanford:* $20,210

| | Parental Contribution if Net Worth is: | | | |
| | $20,000 | | $75,000 | |
Disposable Income**	Dollars	Percent of Income	Dollars	Percent of Income
$ 15,000	$ 0	0.0%	$ 1,227	8.2%
20,000	1,138	5.7	2,395	12.0
30,000	4,124	13.7	6,336	21.1
40,000	8,763	21.9	11,036	27.6
50,000	13,463	26.9	15,736	31.5
60,000	18,163	30.3	20,210	33.7
75,000	20,210	26.9	20,210	26.9
150,000	20,210	13.5	20,210	13.5
250,000	20,210	8.1	20,210	8.1

*Tuition is $14,280 and room and board are $5,930.

**Income after federal income and payroll taxes, and state/local taxes.

FIGURE 8G

Parental Contributions to College Costs
Stanford University, 1990-1991

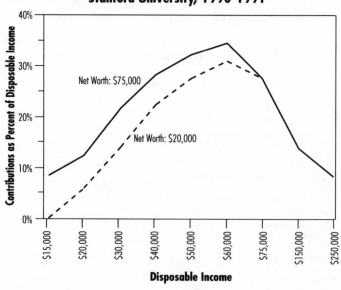

250

also paid 60.6% of the cost of a year at a public university in 1988–89, compared to 81.2% in 1980–81.

Some private colleges do provide their own aid for low income students. However, middle income families face a considerable burden. **Table 8.25** presents the expected family contributions towards tuition, room, and board at a typical private institution, Stanford University (see also **Figure 8G**). A family with a net worth of $75,000 and a disposable income of $40,000 would be expected to contribute $11,040, or 27.6% of its income, towards college costs. If the same family earned $50,000, it would be expected to pay $15,750, or 31.5% of income. On the other hand, college costs amount to only 8.1% of the income of a family that earns $250,000.

Minority Education: Uneven Results

Minorities have been doing better by some measures. As **Table 8.26** shows, although S.A.T. scores of whites have declined slightly, the scores of minorities have improved since 1976. The gains of minorities are greater in mathematics: average scores of black students on mathematics improved by 32 points between 1976 and 1989, and Mexican

A family with a net worth of $75,000 and a disposable income of $40,000 would be expected to contribute $11,040, or 27.6% of its income, towards college costs.

TABLE 8.26

Scholastic Aptitude Test Scores By Race/Ethnic Group, 1976–1989

	1976	1979	1985	1989	Change 1976–89
Verbal					
American Indian	388	386	392	384	−4
Black	332	330	346	351	+19
Mexican American	371	370	382	381	+10
Puerto Rican	364	345	368	360	−4
White	451	444	449	446	−5
Math					
American Indian	420	421	428	428	+8
Black	354	358	376	386	+32
Mexican American	410	410	426	430	+20
Puerto Rican	401	388	409	406	+5
White	493	483	490	491	−2

251

TABLE 8.27

Educational Attainment of 18- to 24-Year-Olds
By Race/Ethnic Group, 1967–1988

(Period Averages)

Period	High School Completion Rate			College Enrollment Rate*		
	White	Black	Hispanic	White	Black	Hispanic
1967–73	80.7%	61.1%	53.5%	27.0%	15.9%	14.7%
1974–79	82.5	67.0	55.8	26.2	20.4	17.9
1980–88	82.6	73.4	57.9	28.2	20.5	17.1

*Number enrolled as percent of number aged 18–24.

TABLE 8.28

Post-secondary Enrollment and Degree Attainment
By Race/Ethnic Group, School Year 1986–87
(U.S. Residents Only)

Group	Undergraduate Enrollment (Fall 1986)	Bachelor's Degree	Master's Degrees	Doctorates*
White, Non-Hispanic	80.8%	87.5%	88.2%	89.0%
Black, Non-Hispanic	9.4	5.9	5.3	3.9
Hispanic	5.3	2.8	2.7	2.7
American Indian/Alaskan Native	0.8	0.4	0.4	0.4
Asian/Pacific Islander	3.7	3.4	3.3	4.0
TOTAL	100.0	100.0	100.0	100.0

*Ph.D., Ed.D., and comparable degrees. Excludes first professional degrees, such as J.D. and M.D., but includes further professional degrees.

Americans' scores improved by 20 points. Puerto Ricans and American Indians saw smaller gains.

Even given these improvements, minorities still suffer significant disadvantages. Their S.A.T. scores remain lower than those of whites, for instance. Moreover, although high school graduation rates have been steadily improving among minorities, college enrollment rates have stagnated in the 1980s.

Table 8.27 gives high school completion rates and college enrollment rates of persons aged 18–24. We use the average rate during a given period, since annual rates are too volatile to show trends clearly. High school completion rates have improved for blacks: an average of 73.4% of blacks completed high school in the 1980–88 period, compared to 61.1% and 67.0% in the 1967–73 and 1974–79 periods, respectively. Rates among Hispanics have also improved, though by lesser amounts. The high school completion rate of whites has seen less improvement. The rate improved from 80.7% in the 1967–73 period to 82.5% in the 1974–79 period, but then remained nearly unchanged in the 1980–88 period, at 82.6%.

College enrollment rates show a markedly different pattern: rates among whites improved, while rates among minorities stagnated. After declining from 27.0% in the 1967–73 period to 26.2% in 1974–79, college enrollment among whites increased to 28.2% in 1980–88. In contrast, the enrollment rate for blacks was 20.5% in 1980–88, virtually unchanged from 20.4% in 1974–79. Enrollment among Hispanics actually fell, from 17.9% in 1974–79 to 17.1% in 1980–88.

Although high school graduation rates have been steadily improving among minorities, college enrollment rates have stagnated in the 1980s.

Few Minorities With Higher Degrees

In addition, fewer minority college graduates continue on to obtain advanced degrees. In the 1986–87 school year, non-Hispanic whites made up 80.8% of all undergraduates, but received 87.5% of bachelor's degrees, 88.2% of master's degrees, and 89.0% of doctorates (**Table 8.28**). On the other hand, non-Hispanic blacks accounted for 9.4% of all undergraduates, but received only 5.9% of bachelor's degrees, 5.3% of master's degrees, and 3.9% of doctorates. There are similar patterns for Hispanics and American Indians/Alaskan natives. Clearly, there is much progress yet to be achieved on the path to equal opportunity.

253

CHAPTER 9

TABLE 9.1

Per Capita GDP Growth in 10 Countries, 1979–1988
Broken Down into Growth of Employment and Productivity

Country	Annual Growth Rate of Real Per Capita GDP, 1979–1988	Percent of Growth Due to:		
		More Workers	Higher Productivity	Total
Australia	1.73%	38.9%	61.1%	100.0%
Canada	2.14	39.3	60.7	100.0
France	1.41	-39.0	139.0	100.0
West Germany	1.65	32.4	67.6	100.0
Italy	2.15	13.3	86.7	100.0
Japan	3.33	12.2	87.8	100.0
Netherlands	0.72	75.9	24.1	100.0
Sweden	1.89	28.6	71.4	100.0
United Kingdom	1.99	10.0	90.0	100.0
United States	**1.77**	**38.3**	**61.7**	**100.0**
Weighted Average*	2.06	21.2	78.8	100.0

*Weighted by each country's population, which is taken to be the average of the populations of 1979 and 1988.

INTERNATIONAL COMPARISONS: U.S. WORKERS SLIPPING

*I*n this chapter we focus on how American workers have fared in comparison to workers in other industrial countries. We find, first, that U.S. per capita income growth has been relatively sluggish and driven more by a greater proportion of the population's working than by higher productivity. Despite slower growth, U.S. per capita income still leads the industrial world when measured in terms of purchasing power, i.e., in terms of what incomes buy in each country. However, income is much more concentrated among the rich in the U.S. than in other industrial countries. In addition, the U.S. also has substantially higher levels of poverty, in terms of purchasing power, than most other industrialized countries.

Wages in the U.S. have been virtually stagnant since 1979, while wages in other countries have grown strongly. By some measures, other countries' wages are already considerably higher than ours. Job growth has been strong in the U.S. in the last decade, but so has population growth. Correcting for population growth, job growth in the U.S. has not been much greater than that of most other countries. Finally, U.S. public spending on job training and placement programs is among the lowest in the industrial West. Such neglect is likely to have a negative effect on future productivity, resulting in continued wage stagnation.

Wages in the U.S. have been virtually stagnant since 1979, while wages in other countries have grown strongly.

Incomes and Productivity

Per capita income growth comes from two sources: greater output per worker—also known as productivity—and more workers relative to the nonworking population. In general, if productivity growth is strong and wages rise accordingly, families can live better without sending more workers into the workforce; if it is weak, living standards can rise only if more people work.

Table 9.1 shows the 1979–88 growth rates of per capita income (GDP per person), in a selection of countries that includes the major 7 industrialized nations and some others. The U.S. annual growth rate, 1.77%, is just below the average rate for these countries, 2.06%. However, a large component of U.S. income growth has come from an increase in the proportion of the population who work. Columns 2 and 3 of Table 9.1 show how much of per capita income growth is due to more workers in the population, and how much is

255

TABLE 9.2

Growth of Per Capita GDP and of Productivity, 1979–1988

Country	Indices of 1979–1988 Growth Rates (Weighted Average = 100)	
	Real Per Capita GDP	Productivity (GDP/Worker)
Australia	84	65
Canada	104	80
France	68	121
West Germany	80	69
Italy	105	115
Japan	162	180
Netherlands	35	11
Sweden	92	83
United Kingdom	97	110
United States	**86**	**67**
Weighted Average*	100	100

*Weighted by each country's population, which is taken to be the average of the populations of 1979 and 1988.

TABLE 9.3

Annual Productivity Growth Rates, 1960–1988

Country	1960–67	1967–73	1973–79	1979–88	Cumulative 1960–88*
Australia	N/A	2.83%	1.62%	1.06%	1.72%
Canada	2.74%	2.56	1.25	1.30	1.82
France	5.05	4.15	2.40	1.96	3.12
West Germany	4.62	4.25	2.86	1.12	2.87
Italy	7.14	4.99	2.71	1.87	3.78
Japan	9.14	7.74	2.86	2.93	5.17
Netherlands	N/A	N/A	0.01	0.17	0.11
Sweden	4.71	2.84	0.52	1.35	2.16
United Kingdom	2.70	3.34	1.25	1.79	2.14
United States	**3.08**	**1.03**	**- 0.12**	**1.09**	**1.21**

*Netherlands: 1973–1988; Australia: 1967–1988.

due to greater productivity. A relatively large component, 38.9%, of U.S. per capita income growth since 1979 was due to greater workforce participation.

Another reflection of our slow productivity growth is that U.S. per capita income grew at 86% of the average rate, but U.S. productivity grew at a rate only 67% of the average (**Table 9.2**). Japan, on the other hand, saw its per capita income grow at 162% of the average rate, fueled by productivity growth that was 180% of the average.

U.S. productivity growth has been among the slowest since 1960 (**Table 9.3**). U.S. productivity grew 3.08%, 1.03%, –0.12%, and 1.09% per year in each of the four periods between 1960 and 1988. In the same periods, Japanese productivity grew 9.14%, 7.74%, 2.86%, and 2.93%, respectively. West German growth, at 4.62%, 4.25%, 2.86%, and 1.12%, also consistently exceeded U.S. growth. The poor performance of the U.S. adds up to a cumulative growth rate of productivity of only 1.21% (Table 9.3, **Figure 9A**). Japan, on the other hand, had a cumulative growth rate of 5.17%, and West Germany, 2.87%.

U.S. productivity growth has been among the slowest since 1960.

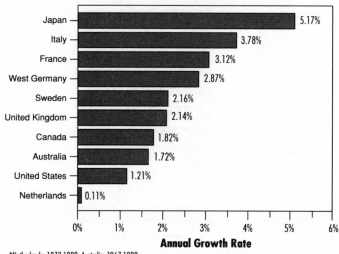

FIGURE 9A

Productivity Growth, 1960-1988*

Country	Annual Growth Rate
Japan	5.17%
Italy	3.78%
France	3.12%
West Germany	2.87%
Sweden	2.16%
United Kingdom	2.14%
Canada	1.82%
Australia	1.72%
United States	1.21%
Netherlands	0.11%

Annual Growth Rate

*Netherlands: 1973-1988; Australia: 1967-1988.

TABLE 9.4

Hourly Manufacturing Compensation Growth Compared, 1978–1988

| Country | Annual Growth Rate of Hourly Compensation in Manufacturing, 1979–1988 | |
	All Employees	Production Workers
Canada	0.81%	0.58%
Denmark	0.09	0.40
France	2.10	2.15
West Germany	2.37	1.89
Italy	0.99	0.41
Japan	2.08	0.92
Netherlands	1.35	0.81
Sweden	0.74	0.63
United Kingdom	2.17	1.86
United States	**0.32**	**– 0.41**

FIGURE 9B

Hourly Manufacturing Compensation Growth, 1979–1988

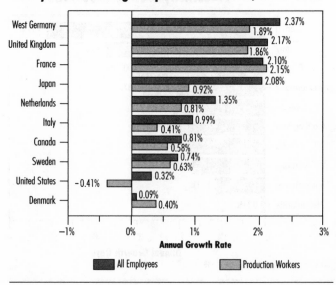

258

Wages

Productivity growth sets bounds on real wage growth. Parallel to the poor U.S. record on productivity, wage growth has also been slower than in most other industrial countries. **Table 9.4** and **Figure 9B** show annual growth rates for hourly compensation in manufacturing (the only comparison available) between 1979 and 1988. In the U.S., hourly compensation grew a mere 0.32% per year, which is next to last.

In fact, the only reason that growth was positive at all is that compensation growth among supervisors and managers was strong; the hourly compensation of production and nonsupervisory workers in manufacturing actually *fell* –0.41% per year during this period (Table 9.4, Figure 9B). No other country's production workers experienced declines in wages in this period; in fact, production workers in France and West Germany saw their wages grow by 2.15% and 1.89% per year, respectively, and the annual rate in the U.K. was 1.86% per year.

Equality

Although other countries are gaining on us rapidly, by one measure our per capita income is still the highest in the world. **Table 9.5** adjusts per capita income by what are known as Purchasing Power Parities (PPPs): special ex-

. . . wage growth has also been slower than in most other industrial countries.

TABLE 9.5
Per Capita Income Compared, 1973–1988

Country	Per Capita Income Adjusted for Purchasing Power (U.S. = 100)		
	1973	1979	1988
Australia	69	70	69
Canada	83	91	94
Denmark	70	71	69
France	68	72	70
West Germany	69	73	72
Italy	58	64	66
Japan	59	63	73
Netherlands	70	72	66
Norway	63	76	83
Sweden	74	75	76
Switzerland	95	87	85
United Kingdom	67	67	69
United States	**100**	**100**	**100**

259

TABLE 9.6

Inequality Measures For Disposable Income, 1979-1983 Period

Country	Atkinson 0.5		Gini		Theil	
			Inequality Indices			
Australia (1981)	87	(2)	314	(2)	165	(2)
Canada (1981)	83	(3)	306	(3)	157	(4)
West Germany (1981)	66	(8)	280	(8)	134	(8)
Israel (1979)	71	(7)	292	(6)	142	(7)
Netherlands (1983)	82	(4)	303	(4)	159	(3)
Norway (1979)	60	(9)	255	(10)	114	(9)
Sweden (1981)	60	(9)	264	(9)	114	(9)
Switzerland (1982)	79	(5)	292	(6)	154	(5)
United States (1979)	**99**	**(1)**	**330**	**(1)**	**182**	**(1)**
United Kingdom (1979)	78	(6)	303	(4)	153	(6)

Note: The rank order is shown in the parentheses.

TABLE 9.7

Relative and Absolute Poverty Among Children, Adults, and the Elderly, 1979-1982

Relative Poverty	Children	Adults	Elderly	Overall
		Poverty Rates		
Relative Poverty				
Australia (1981)	15.9%	9.9%	15.7%	12.2%
Canada (1981)	15.5	10.7	17.2	12.6
West Germany (1981)	4.9	4.5	11.1	5.6
Norway (1979)	4.8	5.4	5.6	5.2
Sweden (1981)	5.0	6.7	0.8	5.3
Switzerland (1982)	7.8	8.1	11.4	8.5
United Kingdom (1979)	9.3	5.7	29.2	9.7
United States (1979)	**22.4**	**13.4**	**23.9**	**17.1**
Absolute Poverty				
Australia (1981)	16.9%	10.5%	19.2%	13.2%
Canada (1981)	9.6	7.5	4.8	7.4
West Germany (1981)	8.2	6.5	15.4	8.3
Norway (1979)	7.6	7.1	18.7	8.6
Sweden (1981)	5.1	6.7	2.1	5.6
Switzerland (1982)	5.1	6.2	6.0	5.8
United Kingdom (1979)	10.7	6.9	37.0	11.8
United States (1979)	**17.1**	**10.1**	**16.1**	**12.7**

change rates that are designed to equate the purchasing power of different currencies. In other words, the indices in Table 9.5 show how much the average income in a given country can buy in that country. The U.S. remains in front, despite the recent gains of other countries.

On the other hand, income is also distributed more unequally in the U.S. than in most other industrial countries. **Table 9.6** gives three different indices of the inequality of disposable family income in a selection of countries for which data is available. The rank order is given in parentheses. The U.S. is ranked highest in income inequality by each measure. Australia ranks second by each measure; the two countries with the least inequality are Norway and Sweden. These figures imply that rich families in the United States received a higher proportion of national disposable income in the 1979–83 period than rich families in any of the other industrial countries listed.

The United States also leads most other industrial countries in rates of poverty.

Poverty

The United States also leads most other industrial countries in rates of poverty. **Table 9.7** compares poverty rates in the 1979–81 period, using two concepts of poverty. Absolute poverty uses the U.S. definition of poverty and adjusts incomes in other countries according to differences in purchasing power. Relative poverty, the other concept, is defined as having disposable family incomes below one-half of the national median.

As Table 9.7 shows, relative poverty in the U.S. is higher than in any of the other countries, except among the elderly, who have a higher relative poverty rate in the United Kingdom. Fully 17.1% of persons are relatively poor in the U.S.; the closest other country is Canada, with 12.6% relatively poor. The U.S. also leads in relative poverty among children, with a rate of 22.4%. In Australia, the next highest country, 15.9% of children are in relative poverty. Some countries have relative poverty rates that are dramatically low by American standards: only 5.2% of Norwegians, 5.3% of Swedes, and 5.6% of West Germans are relatively poor, and relative poverty rates among children are even lower in these countries.

These are relative rates of poverty. As we have seen, U.S. per capita income, in terms of purchasing power, is the highest in the world. At this point in the analysis it still

261

TABLE 9.8

Sensitivity of Child Poverty Rates to the Level of the Absolute Poverty Line

Country	Percent of Children Below:		
	75% of Poverty Line	Absolute Poverty	125% of Poverty Line
Australia	7.3%	16.9%	26.2%
Canada	4.4	9.6	15.2
West Germany	2.5	8.2	21.5
Norway	2.7	7.6	17.2
Sweden	2.2	5.1	9.7
Switzerland	2.0	5.1	9.3
United Kingdom	3.8	10.7	22.7
United States	**9.8**	**17.1**	**24.2**

TABLE 9.9

Poverty Among Children by Family Type

Country	Family Type			
	One-Parent	Two-Parent	Other	Total
Percentage of Children By Family Type:				
Australia	9.1%	75.3%	15.6%	100.0%
Canada	9.6	71.1	19.3	100.0
West Germany	5.5	72.2	22.3	100.0
Norway	15.7	78.1	6.2	100.0
Sweden	14.8	84.8	0.4	100.0
Switzerland	11.6	87.3	1.1	100.0
United Kingdom	8.0	76.7	15.3	100.0
United States	**14.7**	**61.9**	**23.4**	**100.0**
Poverty Rates of Children By Family Type:				
Australia	65.0%	12.4%	10.6%	16.9%
Canada	38.7	6.8	5.5	9.6
West Germany	35.1	4.9	12.1	8.2
Norway	21.6	4.4	12.7	7.6
Sweden	8.6	4.5	0.5	5.1
Switzerland	12.9	4.1	3.8	5.1
United Kingdom	38.6	9.5	2.5	10.7
United States	**51.0**	**9.4**	**16.2**	**17.1**

could be that, despite our relative inequalities, we still have fewer people who are *absolutely* poor, in the sense of having an absolute level of purchasing power below the American poverty line. But in fact, the reverse is true. The proportion of Americans in absolute poverty, 12.7%, is greater than in all the other countries except Australia, where 13.2% are absolutely poor (Table 9.7). America does rank slightly better in its elderly poverty rate: 16.1%, which is exceeded in Australia, Norway, and the United Kingdom. However, absolute poverty among American children, at 17.1%, is the very highest of the 8 countries; compare child poverty of 5.1% in both Sweden and Switzerland. Absolute poverty among American adults, 10.1%, is second only to Australia's 10.5%.

The absolute poverty rates in Table 9.7 and the per capita incomes in Table 9.5 were compared using the same technique of purchasing power adjustment. In other words, although the average U.S. income has the greatest purchasing power in the industrial world, the proportion of persons who cannot afford the basic necessities, by U.S. standards, is higher in the U.S. than in most other industrial countries.

The finding of high absolute child poverty in the richest country in the world may be surprising, so it makes sense to question whether it is a spurious result of the methods used—the poverty level, for example, or the prevalence of single motherhood in the United States. **Table 9.8** shows that the high rate is not due to the poverty line used: child poverty comes out highest or second highest in the U.S. using a variety of poverty thresholds.

Table 9.9 examines whether the higher level of child poverty is due to having fewer two-parent families, which are much less likely to be poor than other families. The first part of the table shows that the U.S. does indeed have fewer children living in two-parent families than any other of the countries listed. However, the second part of the table shows that absolute child poverty is among the highest in the U.S. within each family type. Fully 51% of American children in single-parent families are absolutely poor, which is exceeded only by Australia's 65%. In the other countries listed, child poverty in one-parent families ranges from 8.6%, in Sweden, to 38.6%, in the U.K. Among two-parent families, 9.4% of American children are absolutely poor,

Absolute poverty among American children, at 17.1%, is the very highest among 8 countries surveyed.

263

TABLE 9.10

Manufacturing Compensation Compared, 1988
(Using Purchasing Power Parity Exchange Rates)

| Country | Hourly Compensation (U.S. = 100) | |
	All Employees	Production Workers
Canada	91	96
Denmark	60	74
France	86	75
West Germany	81	94
Italy	72	83
Japan	55	56
Netherlands	96	97
Sweden	79	83
United Kingdom	65	70
United States	**100**	**100**

FIGURE 9C

Manufacturing Compensation Compared, 1988
(Using Purchasing Power Parity Exchange Rates)

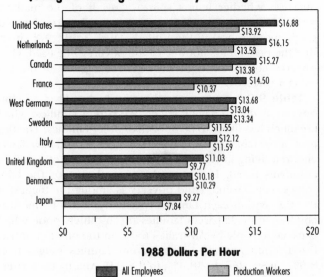

1988 Dollars Per Hour

All Employees   Production Workers

which is exceeded only by Australia and the U.K.; the other countries range from 4.1% to 6.8%. Absolute child poverty in other types of families is highest in the U.S. These figures confirm that different family structures play at best a small part in the higher absolute poverty of American children.

Becoming a Low-Wage, Low-Productivity Country

As in the case of per capita incomes, **Table 9.10** and **Figure 9C** show that compensation (wages plus fringe benefits) in manufacturing is also still the highest in the U.S., using Purchasing Power Parity exchange rates. Other countries are close behind: production workers in West Germany, Canada, and the Netherlands can buy 94%, 96%, and 97%, respectively, of what American production workers can buy with their wages.

On the other hand, if actual market exchange rates are used, American workers no longer lead the pack. The average manufacturing employee in the Netherlands and Sweden earns 115% of what the average American employee earns (**Table 9.11**, **Figure 9D**). Among production workers, Germans and Swedes earn 130% and 121% of Americans, respectively. These market exchange rate wage comparisons reflect the relative attractiveness of U.S. products in international markets and suggest that the United States is becoming a low-wage country.

Among production workers, Germans and Swedes earn 130% and 121% of Americans, respectively.

TABLE 9.11
Manufacturing Compensation Compared, 1988
(Using Market Exchange Rates)

Country	Hourly Compensation (U.S.=100)	
	All Employees	Production Workers
Canada	92	98
Denmark	93	114
France	107	93
West Germany	112	130
Italy	80	92
Japan	89	91
Netherlands	115	117
Sweden	115	121
United Kingdom	70	75
United States	**100**	**100**

FIGURE 9D

Manufacturing Compensation Compared, 1988
(Using Market Exchange Rates)

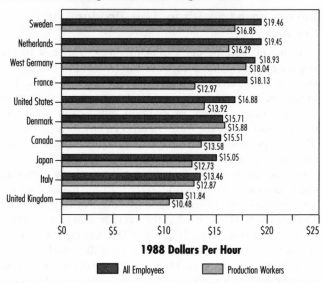

1988 Dollars Per Hour

■ All Employees　▨ Production Workers

Country	All Employees	Production Workers
Sweden	$19.46	$16.85
Netherlands	$19.45	$16.29
West Germany	$18.93	$18.04
France	$18.13	$12.97
United States	$16.88	$13.92
Denmark	$15.71	$15.88
Canada	$15.51	$13.58
Japan	$15.05	$12.73
Italy	$13.46	$12.87
United Kingdom	$11.84	$10.48

TABLE 9.12

Jobs Created in 10 Countries, 1979–1988

Country	Total Created 1979–1988 (000)	New Jobs As Percent of 1979 Employment
Australia	1,287	21.1%
Canada	1,849	17.8
France	(170)	–0.8
West Germany	1,260	4.9
Italy	940	4.7
Japan	5,270	9.8
Netherlands	560	10.5
Sweden	284	6.8
United Kingdom	840	3.4
United States	**16,144**	**16.3**

266

Job Growth

As **Table 9.12** shows, the U.S. has created more jobs than the other countries over the recent decade. The absolute number of jobs created, however, is a misleading indicator of labor market performance. For instance, the U.S. is the largest country by far, so it should not come as a surprise that we created the most new jobs. As can be seen in Table 9.12, the U.S. had a *rate* of job creation less than that of Australia and Canada. U.S. employment in 1988 was 16.3% greater than in 1979, compared to increases of 21.1% in Australia and 17.8% in Canada during the same period.

Another reason that simple job counts are misleading is that they do not take account of population growth, a factor that limits both the number of jobs created and job creation rates. This matters because some countries (e.g., West Germany) have had no population growth while most others have had far less population growth than the United States. Without population growth the only manner in which additional job growth can be achieved is by raising the percentage of the population with employment, which is always a slow process. On the other hand, countries with fast growing populations have the possibility of creating substantial growth in employment.

To address this issue, **Table 9.13** breaks down the growth

The U.S. had a rate of job creation less than that of Australia and Canada.

TABLE 9.13

Contributions to Employment Growth in 10 Countries, 1979–1988

| Country | Annual Employment Growth Rate, 1979–88 | Breakdown of Employment Growth Rate into Sum of: | |
		Population Growth Rate, 1979–88	Employment/Population Ratio Growth Rate, 1979–88
Australia	2.12%	1.45%	0.67%
Canada	1.82	0.98	0.84
France	-0.09	0.46	-0.55
West Germany	0.54	0.00	0.53
Italy	0.51	0.22	0.29
Japan	1.03	0.63	0.41
Netherlands	1.11	0.56	0.55
Sweden	0.73	0.19	0.54
United Kingdom	0.37	0.17	0.20
United States	**1.68**	**1.00**	**0.68**

TABLE 9.14
Unemployment in OECD Countries, 1973–1988

Country	Unemployment Rate		
	1973	1979	1988
Canada	5.5%	7.4%	7.7%
France	2.7	5.9	10.0
West Germany	0.8	3.2	6.1
Italy	6.2	7.6	11.3
Japan	1.3	2.1	2.5
United States	**4.8**	**5.8**	**5.4**
United Kingdom	3.0	5.0	8.3
Major Seven Countries	3.4	4.9	6.1
Smaller Countries			
Australia	2.3%	6.2%	7.2%
Belgium	2.7	8.2	9.9
Finland	2.3	5.9	4.5
Netherlands	2.2	5.4	9.5
Norway	1.5	2	3.2
Spain	2.5	8.5	19.1
Sweden	2.5	2.1	1.6
Total OECD	3.3	5.1	6.7

TABLE 9.15
Public Spending on Active Labor Market Programs
as Percent of GDP, 1988

Country	Training and Placement	Direct Job Creation	Total
Australia	0.24%	0.06%	0.30%
Belgium	0.52	0.68	1.20
Canada	0.50	0.02	0.52
Finland	0.49	0.41	0.90
France*	0.77	0.04	0.81
West Germany	0.83	0.22	1.05
Italy	0.90	0.00	0.90
Japan	0.07	0.13	0.20
Netherlands	1.07	0.06	1.13
Norway	0.40	0.02	0.42
Spain	0.38	0.40	0.78
Sweden	1.59	0.20	1.79
United Kingdom	0.57	0.20	0.77
United States	**0.24**	**0.01**	**0.25**

*1987

in employment into growth of population, on the one hand, and of the employment/population ratio on the other. The U.S. annual employment growth rate (1.68%) turns out to be due more to population growth (1.00%) than to a rising employment/population ratio (0.68%). By a more appropriate standard, the employment/population ratio, the U.S. has still done well in creating employment, but not orders of magnitude better than the others. And as shown above, we have accomplished this at the expense of wage growth.

Adjusting to Job Loss

Another measure of labor market performance, the unemployment rate, captures (only in broad strokes as we have seen in Chapter 4) the degree to which countries are able to supply employment to those looking for work. In the 1970s the U.S. had an above average unemployment rate (**Table 9.14**). Although the unemployment rate did not markedly improve in the U.S. in the 1980s, unemployment worsened considerably abroad. Still, several other countries had lower unemployment rates in 1988 (Japan and the Scandinavian countries).

Other countries also spend considerably more on training and placement programs, which help reduce the time spent unemployed and facilitate the transition back into an equally well-paid job. These programs are particularly important given the recent shifts in employment from manufacturing to services. The U.S. spends only 0.24% of GDP on such programs, compared to considerably higher levels in other countries, such as Sweden, which spends 1.59% of GDP while maintaining a lower unemployment rate (**Table 9.15**).

Other countries also spend considerably more on training and placement programs.

TABLE NOTES:

Frequently Cited Sources

The following abbreviations are used throughout the sources listing.

ERP: President of the United States. *Economic Report of the President*, various dates.

Green Book: U.S. House of Representatives, 1989 and 1990.

P-60 Series: U.S. Department of Commerce, Bureau of the Census, Series P-60, various dates.

SCB: U.S. Department of Commerce, *Survey of Current Business*, monthly.

Employment and Earnings: U.S. Department of Labor, *Employment and Earnings*, monthly and historical supplements.

NIPA: U.S. Department of Commerce, *National Income and Product Accounts*, from U.S. Department of Commerce, 1986b and subsequent July issues of the *Survey of Current Business*. Data for 1989 are from the May 1990 *Survey of Current Business*, unless otherwise noted.

Chapter 1

1.1   *Median Family Income. P-60 Series*, #97, p. 30; *P-60 Series*, #166, p. 11; *P-60 Series*, #168, p. 31.

1.2   *Annual Growth of Median Family Income.* Yearly dollar change is average of real yearly changes in period. Size-adjusted median family income is weighted by families and adjusted for family size using the poverty equivalence scale. This is actually the average income in the middle fifth, not the median. See note to Table 1.1, together with *Green Book* (1990, p. 1072, panel B).

1.3   *Growth of Median Family Income by Age of Household Head.* 1989 from *P-60 Series*, #168, p. 32; 1979 from *P-60 Series*, #129, p. 32; 1973 from *P-60 Series*,

#97, pp. 49-51; 1967 from *P-60 Series*, #59, pp. 32-34 (through telephone conversation with Ed Welniak on 6/15/90).

1.4 *Growth of Median Family Income By Race/Ethnic Group.* 1989 from *P-60 Series*, #166, pp. 32-34; 1979 from Fisher 1986, Table 1B; 1947-1973 from *P-60 Series*, #129, pp. 42-43.

1.5 *Income Growth By Type of Family.* These data are drawn from the Congressional Budget Office analysis of family income trends prepared by Roberton Williams for the House Ways and Means Committee 1990 *Green Book.* The data have been rescaled to be in PCE deflated dollars. The distribution of population by family type is from Table 56 (p. 1133, drawn from the March 1988 CPS). Since median family income measures were not available, the income growth for each family type is the mean income growth of the middle quintile from Table 33 (pp. 1078-80). These data are family size adjusted and weighted by persons.

1.6 *Average Income of the Top 5% Compared to the Bottom 80%.* 1989 from *P-60 Series,* #168, p. 30; 1979 from *P-60 Series*, #129, p. 31; 1947-1973 from *P-60 Series*, #97, p. 43. Average family income in an income class is derived using the shares of incomes by income class, the number of families, and aggregate income.

1.7 *Shares of Family Income Going to Various Fifths, and to Top 5%.* See note to Table 1.6.

1.8 *The Effects of Shifts in Family Income Inequality.* See note to Table 1.6.

1.9 *Income Growth By Fifth and Family Type. Green Book*, 1990, Table 33, pp. 1078-80.

1.10 *Income Growth Among Top Fifth and by Fifth.* 1990 from *Green Book*, 1990, p. 46; 1977, 1980 from Congressional Budget Office, 1990. Used numbers of families and average income in each decile to get average by fifths. Nominal figures were adjusted using projected 1990 PCE (projected using annual 1980-89 inflation rate).

Persons are placed into fifths and percentiles based on adjusted family income; the numbers in the table, however, are average *unadjusted* family incomes for the families in each group. The numbers of persons in each fifth are the same, although the numbers of families differ. Averages are weighted by families, not by persons. "All" includes families with zero or negative incomes, but the bottom fifth excludes these families.

1.11   *Changes in Family Income Shares.* See note to Table 1.10. Shares for groups add up to slightly more than 100% because families with negative incomes are excluded from the lowest fifth but included in "All."

1.12   *Distribution of Aggregate Income Gains.* See note to Table 1.10. The bottom fifth gained some aggregate income despite losing average income because the number of families increased. Shares for groups add up to slightly more than 100% because families with negative incomes are excluded from the lowest fifth but included in "All."

1.13   *Sources of Family Income for Each Fifth of Families.* Congressional Budget Office, 1987, Table A-4, p. 67. Corporate income allocated to capital income. Data are estimates. Unlike Tables 1.10-1.12, there is an *equal* number of families in each fifth in Table 1.13.

1.14   *Real Income Growth By Type of Income. NIPA*, Table 2.1. 1989 data are from a prerelease, on disks, of the July 1990 *NIPA* figures.

1.15   *Shares of Market-Based Income By Type. NIPA*, Table 2.1. 1989 data are from a prerelease, on disks, of the July 1990 *NIPA* figures.

1.16   *Change in Adjusted Family Income By Source of Income. Green Book* (1990) By Quintile, Table 49, pp. 1120-21; Families with Children, Table 64, p. 1141; Married Couples with Children, Table 65, p. 1142; Single Mothers, Table 66, p. 1143; Nonelderly Childless Units, Table 67, p. 1145. Data drawn from columns for family earnings, investment income and total transfer income. Total income based on sum of earnings, private income and transfer income.

1.17 *Sources of Income of High-Income Families. Green Book,* 1990, p. 1167. Readjusted using PCE index from *NIPA.*

1.18 *Growth Rates of Real Per Capita Income and Consumption. NIPA.* 1989 data are from a prerelease, on disks, of the July 1990 *NIPA* figures. Personal consumption expenditure growth based on *NIPA* (Table 2.4, line 1). Personal income is from *NIPA* Table 2.1, line 1; disposable personal income is from *NIPA* Table 2.1, line 25.

1.19 *Consumption Growth By Income Fifth.* Blecker, forthcoming, Table 2.

1.20 *Growth in Number of Earners Per Family. Green Book,* 1990, Table 58, p. 1135 and Table 60, p. 1137.

1.21 *Earnings Growth in Married Couple Families By Member and Fifth. Green Book,* 1990, Table 65, p. 1142. Earnings growth of "other earners" is included in total earnings growth but not shown separately.

1.22 *Effect of Adult Female Earnings Growth on Married Couple Family Income. Green Book,* 1990, Table 65, p. 1142. Total includes noncash transfers. The "change in family income without increased adult female earnings" is the absolute change in size adjusted family income between 1979 and 1987 less the change in earnings of the highest paid adult female earner expressed as a percentage of 1979 size adjusted family income. The "difference" is simply the first column minus the second column.

1.23 *Factors Explaining Wives' Increased Earnings.* Unpublished tabulations from Chris Tilly of earnings by family, head, wife, and others from the data developed for Albelda and Tilly (1989). These data are family size adjusted. Because the wage data provided was rounded to three decimals (i.e., weekly wage is .029, or 2.9% of poverty threshold), the weekly earnings were derived from annual earnings and weeks worked. As a result, the covariance between family size and weeks worked and weekly wages is embedded in our derived weekly wage change. Any difference in results from using the derived weekly wage is likely to be small, given our experience with the data in Chapter 7 where the results for actual and derived wage data for young families could be compared.

1.24 *Relative Importance of Factors Explaining Wives' Increased Earnings.* Computations based on data in Table 1.23.

1.25 *Effect of Second Earner on Household Expenditures.* Democratic Study Group, 1990, Table 1, pp. 8-9.

1.26 *Child Care Expenditures and Family Income for Employed Women With Children.* Democratic Study Group, 1990, Table 3.

1.27 *Trends in Paid and Unpaid Work.* Schor and Leete-Guy, forthcoming.

1.28 *Per Capita and Per Adult Income Growth.* Mishel and Teixeira, 1990, Table 11.

Chapter 2

2.1 *Total U.S. Tax Burden. NIPA,* Tables 1.1, 3.2, 3.3; 1989 data from *SCB,* March 1990.

2.2 *Tax Revenues in OECD Countries.* OECD, 1989b.

2.3 *Shares of After-Tax Income for All Families.* U.S. House of Representatives, 1990b, pp. 49-51.

2.4 *Effects of Federal Tax Changes on Shares of After-Tax Income.* 1977 and 1990 actual effective rates (Congressional Budget Office, 1990a) were applied to 1990 average before-tax incomes (U.S. House of Representatives, 1990b, p. 24). The resulting average after-tax incomes were multiplied by the number of families in each group to get total after-tax incomes per group. Then these were converted to shares by dividing each group's total by the sum over the groups. Shares in the second column differ somewhat from corresponding shares in Table 2.3 because of rounding error in Congressional Budget Office (1990a) tables—particularly for the number of families in the top 1%—and because total income for all families in Table 2.4 necessarily excludes families with zero or negative incomes, while in Table 2.3 such families are included.

2.5 *Effective Federal Taxes in 1977 and 1990.* U.S. House of Representatives, 1990b, pp. 15-16. Breakdown of top quintile is from Congressional Budget Office, 1990a. Figures for the lowest quintile exclude families with zero or negative incomes; figures for all families include these families.

2.6 *Changes in Federal Taxes in Selected Periods.* See note to Table 2.5.

2.7 *Effect of Federal Tax Changes on Family Ater-Tax Income, 1977–1990.* See note to Table 2.5. U.S. House of Representatives (1990b, p. 24) was also consulted.

2.8 *Effective Tax Rates for Specific Federal Taxes.* See note to Table 2.5.

2.9 *Changes in Specific Federal Taxes.* See note to Table 2.5.

2.10 *Taxed and Untaxed Corporate Profits.* Figures are from *NIPA*, Tables 1.1 and 1.16. Taxes include federal, state, and local combined. Actual profits are taxed profits plus net interest (interest paid minus interest received) and the difference between the allowance for inventory investment and capital depreciation allowed in the tax code, on the one hand, and actual inventory investment and capital depreciation, on the other. The idea for this analysis is based on an unpublished paper of Thomas Karier. Only nonfinancial corporations are included because banks don't pay net interest—they *receive* net interest.

2.11 *Corporate Profits Tax Rates. NIPA*, Tables 1.1 and 1.16.

2.12 *Expenditures on Tobacco, Alcoholic Beverages, and Motor Fuels as Percentages of After-Tax Family Income.* Congressional Budget Office, 1990c.

2.13 *Federal vs. State and Local Tax Burdens. NIPA*, Tables 1.1, 3.2, 3.3.

2.14 *Regressive State and Local Taxes and Nontax Revenues.* Tax Foundation, 1989, p. 42. Burden of property taxes assumes that the incidence of property taxes is 50% on landlords and 50% on tenants (100% on homeowners). The progressivity index is the ratio of the effective rate on the top income group to the rate on the bottom. Other taxes include vehicle licenses, severance taxes, etc., and the Tax Foundation report indicates that these are approximately as regressive as sales taxes. Nontax revenues include fines, certain fees, rents, royalties, hospital charges, etc.

2.15 *Federal vs. State and Local Taxes, 1989, as Percent of Revenue at Each Level.* NIPA, Tables 3.2, 3.3. See note to Table 2.14 on other taxes and nontax revenues.

2.16 *Federal vs. State and Local Personal Income Taxes.* Tax Foundation, 1989, p. 42. State and local income tax incidence is on a national basis—i.e., it is weighted by state populations.

2.17 *The Composition of Taxes.* NIPA, Tables 1.1, 3.2, 3.3. Progressive taxes include personal and corporate income taxes, and estate and gift taxes. Regressive taxes include customs, excise, sales, and property taxes, contributions for social insurance, and other taxes such as vehicle licenses, severance taxes, etc. Nontaxes include fines, certain fees, rents, royalties, tuition, hospital fees, etc.

Chapter 3

3.1 *Trends in Average Wages and Average Hours.* Murphy and Welch, 1989; hours data from Table 3 and earnings data from Table 2. The earnings data were scaled to PCE deflated dollars from GNP implicit price deflated dollars and rebased to 1982 = 100. Productivity data are from *ERP* (1990, Table C-46, p. 346) for the nonfarm business sector.

3.2 *Change in Hourly Compensation, Wages, and Benefits.* Based on the data underlying the BLS Employment Cost Index (ECI). Data for 1980 are from unpublished tabulation of compensation cost levels for March 1980 using 1970 Census weights. Data for 1989 are the compensation levels for March 1989 from U.S. Department of Labor (1989d, Tables 1 and 2), which are based on March 1989 weights. The switch from 1970 to 1980 weights occurred in the June 1986 ECI numbers with no remarkable effect, suggesting that structural change between 1970 and 1980 was slight. Thus, these data accurately reflect 1980 to 1989 changes. The data were deflated by the PCE index for the first quarter of each year.

3.3 *Hourly and Weekly Earnings of Production and Nonsupervisory Workers. ERP*, 1990, Table C-44, p. 344.

3.4 *Hourly Wages and Benefits By Occupational Groups.* See note to Table 3.2.

3.5 *Wages for All Workers By Wage Percentile.* Karoly, 1990, Appendix Table B.2, a. All Wage and Salary Workers.

3.6 *Wages for Male Workers By Wage Percentile.* Karoly, 1990, Appendix Table B.2, b. Male Wage and Salary Workers.

3.7 *Wages for Women Workers By Wage Percentile.* Karoly, 1990, Appendix Table B.2, c. Female Wage and Salary Workers.

3.8 *Changes in the Gender Wage Differential.* Based on wage data in Tables 3.6 and 3.7.

3.9 *Shares of Workers By Wage Level and Gender.* Harrison and Gorham, 1990, Appendix Tables 1 and 3. These wage data are deflated by the CPI-U-X1. If the PCE index had been used the shift towards low-wage employment would be larger.

3.10 *Shares of Workers By Wage Level and Race/Ethnic Group.* Harrison and Gorham, 1990, Appendix Table 4, with Hispanic data obtained in phone conversation with Lucy Gorham. These wage data are deflated by the CPI-U-X1. If the PCE index had been used the shift towards low-wage employment would be larger.

3.11   *Hourly Benefit Costs By Type.* Employment Cost Index data as described for Table 3.2. The data are deflated by PCE index except health insurance which is also deflated by the PCE index for health insurance in the first quarter of each year from *NIPA* (Table 7.10, line 71).

3.12   *Health Insurance Coverage By Wage Fourth.* From unpublished tabulations of CPS data for 1979 and 1987 provided by Lynn Karoly. The data were aggregated into fourths by computing weighted averages of the bottom 10% and next 15% for the lowest fourth and the top 10% and next 15% for the highest fourth.

3.13   *Pension Coverage By Wage Fourth.* See note to Table 3.12.

3.14   *Trends in Days Off With Pay.* Based on unpublished Bureau of Labor Statistics data on the ratio of hours at work to hours paid for production and nonsupervisory workers in nonagricultural business (limited to 1981-1988) and in manufacturing (1947-1988). The days off of paid leave is computed from one less the ratio of hours at work to hours paid times 260 days (assumes a 5-day week for 52 weeks).

3.15   *Change in Days Off With Pay.* Data on pay for time off are from ECI data described in note to Table 3.2. Days off with pay are calculated from data on hourly cost of paid leave and the straight-time hourly wage. The ratio of the hourly cost of paid leave to the sum of the hourly wage and paid leave cost (exclusive of any premium or supplemental pay) represents the percentage of total paid hours that are paid hours on leave (assuming days off are paid at straight-time rates). This ratio times 260 days gives our estimate of paid days off. This estimation method reverses the process that BLS goes through to convert the number of paid days off into an hourly cost.

3.16   *International Comparison of Manufacturing Workers' Hours.* Japan Economic Institute, 1990, Table 2.

3.17   *Real Wage Trends By Education Level.* Based on unpublished tabulations from Larry Katz of the data used in Katz and Murphy (unpublished). The data are deflated by the implicit, rather than fixed, PCE index as in the Katz and Murphy paper. The underlying data are the mean weekly wages of full-time wage and salary workers in 320 gender-education-experience cells (with 4 education and 40 experience categories). All aggregate changes are based on a fixed weight scheme with the weights being average population weights for the entire time period. Relative supply changes are the log changes in each group's share to total labor supply measured in efficiency units (annual hours times the average relative wage) from Katz and Murphy (1990, Table 2).

3.26 *Industry Pay Differentials.* Employment Cost Index pay levels in U.S. Department of Labor (1989d, Table 1).

3.27 *Distribution of Hours Worked By Men By Sector and Education.* Unpublished tabulations of CPS data for 1979, 1980, and 1981 from Larry Katz, based on data developed for Katz and Murphy (1990, Table 5). Education breakdown from *P-60 Series* (#132, Table 52, pp. 179-80).

3.28 *Distribution of Hours Worked By Women By Sector and Education.* See note to Table 3.27.

3.29 *Pay in Expanding and Shrinking Industries.* Costrell, 1988, Tables A4 and A5.

3.30 *Effect of Industry Employment Shifts on Pay.* Based on Costrell (1988) as shown in Mishel (1989, Table 3).

3.31 *Industry Employment Shifts and Production Worker Weekly Wages.* Based on Costrell (1988) as shown in Mishel (1989, Table 4).

3.32 *Industry Shift Effect on Wage Growth By Region.* Costrell, unpublished, Table 6.

3.33 *Full-Time Weekly Wages, Union and Nonunion. Employment and Earnings*, January 1990, Table 59, p. 233. The union wage is for workers represented by unions.

3.34 *Comparison of Union and Nonunion Wages and Benefits.* Employment Cost Index pay level data in U.S. Department of Labor (1989d, Table 10).

3.35 *Union Wage Advantage By Race/Ethnic Group and Sex.* Based on data from an analysis of 1984 SIPP data by Heidi Hartmann and colleagues at the Institute for Women's Policy Research as presented in Public Employee Department (1990), converted from 1984 to 1989 dollars.

3.36 *Value of Minimum Wage.* Historic values of minimum wage from Shapiro (1987, p. 19). Wages for 1990 and 1991 are based on legislated increases to $3.80 on 4/1/90 and to $4.25 on 4/1/91. PCE is projected to 1990-91 using inflation projections from Congressional Budget Office (January 1990b).

3.37 *Amount By Which Earnings of a Full-Time, Full-Year Minimum Wage Worker Are Above (Below) the Poverty Line.* See note to Table 3.36 for source of minimum wage, projections of PCE. Annual earnings are based on 2,080 paid hours of work, and assuming no additional income. Poverty lines are from *P-60 Series* (#166, p. 88). This source gives poverty lines adjusted by the CPI-U, which is the official method. We convert these poverty lines back to actual (nominal) poverty lines for each year using the CPI-U, take the difference between these lines and the actual annual salary of a minimum wage worker, and adjust this "gap" for inflation using the PCE index.

3.38 *Hourly Workers Who Earn Minimum Wage or Less.* U.S. Department of Labor, Bureau of Labor Statistics, unpublished data.

3.39 *Distribution of Low Paid Wage and Salary Workers By Family Relationship.* Computed from Klein and Rones (1989, p. 22).

3.40 *Executive Pay Levels, 1979 and 1989. The Economist* (December 23, 1989), using data on gross and net income in dollars.

3.41 *Real Growth in Executive Pay.* Based on data in Table 3.40, converted from dollars to national currency using exchange rates from *ERP* (1990, Table C-109, p. 418) and then converting to constant currency values using an index for domestic consumer prices from International Monetary Fund, *International Financial Statistics*, except the PCE index was used for the U.S.

3.42 *Comparative Pay Levels of Workers and CEOs.* Towers, Perrin and Company, October 1988, Exhibits 8 and 9, pp. 18-19.

3.43 *The Pay Gap Between Executives and Production Workers.* Hourly compensation of production workers from U.S. Department of Labor (1989b). CEO pay from Towers, Perrin and Company (October 1988).

3.44 *Effect of Industry and Occupation Employment Shifts on Compensation and Education Requirements.* Mishel and Teixeira, 1990, Table 2.

3.45 *Effect of Occupation Employment Shifts on Skill and Education Requirements.* Mishel and Teixeira, 1990, Table 7.

Chapter 4

4.1 *Unemployment Rates. Employment and Earnings,* January 1990, Table 3, pp.162-64; Table 39, p.206.

4.2 *Rates of Underemployment.* For 1973 and 1979, U.S. Department of Labor (1985, p. 6, Table 1, p. 14, Table 4, p. 58). For 1989, *Employment and Earnings* (January 1990: Table 1, p. 160; Table 31, p. 199; Table 35, p. 202).

4.3 *Proportion of the Unemployed Who Receive Some Unemployment Insurance Payment. ERP,* 1990, Table C-42, p. 295 and Table C-41, p. 341.

4.4 *Employment Growth.* For full-time equivalent, *NIPA* (Tables 6.7A and 6.7B). For hours, *NIPA* (Table 6.11, earliest year is 1948 so growth rate for earliest period adjusted accordingly). For Labor Force Participation, Working Age Population, and Civilian Employment, *Employment and Earnings* (January 1990, Table 1, p. 160). Note the slowdown in labor force participation is even greater when the measure is decline in non-participation.

4.5 *Composition of Non-Agricultural Employment.* U.S. Department of Labor, 1989a, Table 23, p. 121.

4.6 *Rate of Part-Time Employment for Various Workforce Groups.* Tilly, 1990, Table 1, p. 6.

4.7 *Age and Gender Composition of the Labor Force and Rate of Part-Time Employment.* Tilly, 1990, Table 2, p. 14.

4.8 *Rate of Involuntary, Voluntary, and Total Part-Time Work By Industry.* Tilly, 1990, Table 4, p. 17. The difference in the total rate of part-time work between this table and Table 4.7 is due to the exclusion of agricultural workers and the self-employed from this table (due to limitations of published BLS data).

283

4.21   *Self-Employment and Paid Employment Earnings.*
Haber et al., 1987, Table 4, p. 20.

Chapter 5

5.1   *Median Net Worth by Family Income.* Avery et al.,
1984, Table 7. The Survey of Consumer Finances
include as assets all financial assets, together with
equity in homes and other real property. Debts include all financial liabilities such as consumer credit
and other debt. However, assets do not include consumer durables such as automobiles and home furnishings, the cash value of life insurance, equity in
small businesses and farms, and the present value of
expected future benefits from pensions and social
security.

5.2   *Percent Distribution of Wealth and Income.* Avery
et al., 1984, pp. 863-64.

5.3   *Selected Holdings of American Families.* U.S. Congress, 1986, Table 2, p. 24. Based on an analysis of
James D. Smith. It has been alleged that an error was
made in the underlying survey; to correct for this,
the data were revised by subtracting $990 billion of
net business assets for the top 0.5%.

5.4   *Median Net Worth by Race and Monthly Household
Income.* U.S. Department of Commerce, 1986, Table
G, p. 5. The data on net worth are from a special
supplement to the Survey of Income and Program
Participation (SIPP). Net worth is defined as the value
of assets covered in the survey minus liabilities. Assets include interest earning assets, stocks and mutual
fund shares, real estate, own businesses or professions, mortgages held by sellers, and automobiles.
Liabilities include all debts, secured and unsecured.
The survey did not cover equities in pension plans,
cash surrender value of life insurance, or the value of
jewelry and home furnishings.

5.5   *Median Net Worth by Type of Household.* U.S. Department of Commerce, 1986, Table G, p. 5.

5.6 *Growth of Household Wealth.* Nonprofit organizations, a small component judging from the breakout on tangible assets, were included because Federal Reserve System (1990) does not give breakout for financial assets. Authors' calculations using asset and liabilities data from Federal Reserve System (1990, pp. 19-24), Personal Consumption Expenditures price index from *NIPA*, and number of adults from *ERP* (1989, Table B-31), and from telephone conversation with Census Bureau's Population Estimates Department (Fred Holman's staff, 763-7950).

5.7 *Growth of Tangible Asset Values.* See note to Table 5.6. Nonprofit organizations excluded. In the first two lines, growth is deflated by increases in the overall price level, as measured by the PCE index. In other words, growth in housing, for example, may be due to more and better housing, or to housing that appreciates faster than the general price level. In the second two lines, owner-occupied housing was deflated by the price index for private residential structures (*NIPA*, Table 7.12, line 22), and consumer durables were deflated by the price index for consumer durables (*NIPA*, Table 7.10, line 2). These growth rates control for booms and busts in the housing market and the different growth rates of consumer durable prices, unlike the PCE. In other words, these rates refer to growth in the actual quality and quantity of housing and durables per adult.

5.8 *Household Debt Burden.* Debt and assets from Federal Reserve System (1990, pp. 19-24). Personal income from *NIPA* (Table 2.1, line 1).

5.9 *Annual Household Debt Servicing Burdens as Percents of Household Incomes.* Pollin, forthcoming. Sources are the Surveys of Consumer Finances of 1970 and 1983. Surveys were also carried out in 1977 and 1986; however, the 1977 survey results did not incorporate imputed values for missing items as the other surveys did, and the 1986 survey was based on a follow-up to the 1983 survey rather than a new random sample. Pollin regards the 1970 and 1983 surveys as the most reliable. Moreover, they both

286

come from similar points in business cycles: times when the economy was just beginning to recover from recessions (debt/asset ratios tend to rise in recoveries and fall in recessions).

5.10 *The Changing Distribution of Wealth.* 1983 data from U.S. Congress (1986) were used to determine the share of each asset and debt possessed by the families in each wealth class. It was assumed that the asset/debt shares of each class in 1979 and 1989 were equal to the shares in 1983 (e.g., the super rich were assumed to hold 46.5% of corporate stock in 1979 and 1989, as well as in 1983). Then the asset/debt *totals* were scaled to the totals for each year in Federal Reserve System (1990, pp. 19-24), for households, trusts, and nonprofit organizations.

In nearly every case, U.S. Congress (1986) totals in 1983 were less than Federal Reserve System (1990) totals, which may indicate underreporting, or the different treatment of trusts in the two sources. Nearly all financial assets were underreported except tax-exempt bonds. However, the Federal Reserve System (1990) aggregate housing estimate for 1983, $3,062.6, was actually much lower than the aggregate in U.S. Congress (1986), $5,362.3.

Since trusts were included as an asset category in U.S. Congress (1986) but are combined with households in Federal Reserve System (1990) information on the distribution of trusts was not used. Instead, it was implicitly assumed that the assets of trusts are distributed in the same way as all other assets and debts are. Since the top 0.5% of families actually own 77% of trusts, this approach would tend to understate the concentration of wealth.

The amount of wealth a household has in a kind of asset, such housing or shares of corporate stock, can change for two different reasons. The value of the asset may simply appreciate or depreciate, because of a market boom or slump, for instance. If this were all that happened, then our projection of the distribution of wealth would be accurate. However, a household can also buy more of an asset, or sell some of it. To the extent that this is an important factor, our projection may be somewhat inaccurate. For example, if the wealthy added to their net worth more quickly than the rest of the population between 1979 and 1989, wealth inequality would have become greater than our projection indicates. Since the distribution of income became much more unequal in the 1980s, this is a more likely scenario than the opposite, in which the bottom 90% were able to add to their net worth faster than the wealthier households. Thus, the assumptions of Table 5.10 probably understate the increased concentration of wealth to some extent.

5.11   *Distribution of Wealth by Age.* Greenwood and Wolff, 1988, Table 6.1. The authors report (p. 127) that price levels were converted using the CPI-U deflator. We deflated back to nominal dollars for 1983, 1973, and 1962 using the 1967-based CPI-U index in *ERP* (1987, p. 307). Then we used the PCE (1982 weights) from *NIPA* (Table 7.9/10) to reflate to 1989 dollars.

5.12   *Growth of National Wealth.* Authors' calculations using net worth data from Federal Reserve System (1990, pp. 1-6), together with the PCE price index and number of adults from sources given for Table 5.6.

The main difference between household net worth, on the one hand, and combined business and household net worth, on the other, is the treatment of corporate stock. Household net worth includes the market value of stock shares owned by households in its asset totals. Combined business and household net worth ignores these shares of stock and instead counts assets owned by businesses. Household net worth may have grown faster in the 1979-89 period because the stock market boom exceeded the growth in business assets.

Chapter 6

6.1   *Percent in Poverty.* 1959-79 rates from *Green Book* 1989, pp. 944-45. 1989 rate from *P-60 Series*, #168, p. 57.

6.2   *Poverty Rates when Noncash Benefits Are Included.* U.S. Department of Commerce, 1988, p. 11.

6.3 *The Market Value of Medicare in the Six Largest States.* U.S. Department of Commerce, 1988, p. 8.

6.4 *Poverty Income Deficits.* 1988 deficits from *P-60 Series*, #166, p. 78; 1979 deficits from *P-60 Series*, #130, p. 175; 1973 deficits from *P-60 Series*, #98, p. 138. CPI-U from *ERP*, 1990, p. 359.

6.5 *Poverty by Age and Race/Ethnic Group. P-60 Series*, #166, p. 66.

6.6 *Poverty by Age and Sex. P-60 Series*, #166, p. 66.

6.7 *Poverty Rates by Race/Ethnic Group.* Barancik, 1989, p. 1.

6.8 *Poverty by Sex.* 1973 data from *P-60 Series*, #98, p. 35; 1979 data from *P-60 Series*, #130, p. 48; 1988 data from *P-60 Series*, #166, p. 66.

6.9 *Poverty Among the Elderly and All Persons Before and After Cash Transfers.* Slotsve and Donley, 1990, Tables 2 and 3.

6.10 *The Poor and the Near-Poor.* 1969-88 poverty rates from Barancik, 1989, pp. 1, 18 and *P-60 Series*, #168, p. 63. Near poor rates: 1973 from *P-60 Series*, #98, p. 144; 1979 from *P-60 Series*, #130, p. 16; 1989, from *P-60 Series*, #168, p. 66.

6.11 *Annual Poverty Rates in 1986 under Alternative Poverty Thresholds for the Elderly.* Ruggles, 1990.

6.12 *Poverty Rates of Children under Age 18.* Barancik, 1989, p. 15, and *P-60 Series*, #168, p. 65.

6.13 *Poverty Rates for Children under 18 in Female-Headed Families.* Center on Budget and Policy and Priorities (1987), except the 1989 figure, which is from *P-60 Series*, #168, p. 72.

6.14 *Effects of Transfers and Taxes on Poverty. Green Book* 1990, pp. 1041, 1045, 1047. The percent removed from poverty by means-tested benefits and taxes includes only those not already removed by social insurance.

6.15 *Poverty Rates Using Different Income Definitions. Green Book* 1990, pp. 1042, 1046, 1048. Final column is difference between column 1, the pretransfer/ pretax poverty rate, and column 5, the posttransfer/ posttax poverty rate. In each group, row 3 of final column is the *change* in the effect of taxes and transfers on the poverty rate.

6.16 *Contributions to Increase in Poverty.* Summary of Table 6.15. For each type of person (all persons and persons in each type of family) the decomposition of the increase in the poverty rate is derived from Table 6.15 as follows. The increase in the poverty rate due to labor market and demographics for each type of person is just the third row of column one of the corresponding group in Table 6.15, which gives the change in the poverty rate as measured using only cash income before transfers. The increase in the poverty rate due to government comes from the third row of column six of Table 6.15, which gives the change in poverty rate reduction due to taxes and benefits. Finally, the increase in the poverty rate for all persons in Table 6.16 comes from the third row of column five of Table 6.15, which gives the increase in the poverty rate after all taxes and benefits.

6.17 *Work Experience of the Poor. P-60 Series*, #168, p. 65. Employable poor are those who are neither retired, ill, disabled, nor in school. Those who are keeping house are employable. Year-Round means at least 50 weeks.

6.18 *Changing Family Structure and Poverty. P-60 Series*, #168, p. 57. Married-couple and male-headed families includes unrelated subfamilies since 1979. Number of persons in female-headed families is deduced from the number of poor in such families, together with the poverty rate among such families.

6.19 *Contributions of Changes in Family Structure to Changes in the Poverty Rate. P-60 Series*, #168, p. 57. Predicted change due to family structure is the effect on the overall poverty rate of changes in proportions of persons in female-headed families, married-couple and male-headed families, and not in families. Difference (column 3) is the change attributable to changing poverty rates within each family type.

290

6.20 *Poverty Rates for Female-Headed Families.* Barancik, 1989, p. 3; *P-60 Series*, #168, pp. 61-64.

6.21 *Increase in Poverty in Female-Headed Families.* Computed from Barancik (1989, p. 3); and *P-60 Series*, #168, pp. 61-64.

6.22 *Family Relationships of Poor Persons by Race/ Ethnic Group.* Computed from *P-60 Series*, #168, pp. 57-60.

6.23 *The Reasons for Poverty in Married-Couple Families.* Bane and Ellwood, 1989.

6.24 *Role of Part-Time Spousal Earnings in Poverty Avoidance.* Levitan and Conway, 1988, p. 17.

6.25 *Percent of Poor Married-Couple Families without Benefits and Medical Protection.* From Current Population Survey, March 1985 supplement, tabulated in Ellwood (1988, Tables 4.3 and 4.4).

6.26 *Work Status of Poor Female Heads of Families.* *P-60 Series*, #168, p. 74. Suggested by Table 6.3 in Ellwood (1988).

6.27 *Comparison of Selected Characteristics of All Healthy Female Family Heads (Poor and Non-Poor) By Level of Work.* From Current Population Survey, March 1985 supplement, tabulated in Ellwood (1988, Table 5.4).

6.28 *Receipt of Child Support by Single Mothers.* U.S. Department of Commerce, 1990.

6.29 *Effect of Wages on AFDC, Food Stamps, and Medicaid for a Mother of Two Children.* AFDC levels from *Green Book* (1989, p. 888). Medicaid coverage requirement comes from Children's Defense Fund (1989, p. 73). According to *Green Book* (1989, p. 1129), on 4/1/90 the U.S. government began to require that states phase out Medicaid coverage over 12 months for families that cease to qualify because of earnings.

6.30 *AFDC Levels and Single Motherhood.* AFDC and Food Stamp levels from *Green Book* (1989, pp. 880-81). This is a weighted average among the 48 contiguous states, plus the District of Columbia. Percent of families that are female-headed comes from U.S. Department of Commerce (*P-20 Series*, #441, 1989). Data are from March of the given year (family relationship questions relate to March of the survey year, unlike other questions which relate to the previous year).

6.31   *Marital Status of Female Family Heads.* Women without dependents are not included. 1973, 1979 are for women aged 14 and over, while 1989 is restricted to women aged 15 and over. 1973 numbers are from U.S. Department of Commerce, *P-20 series*, #255, pp. 25-26; 1979 data come from U.S. Department of Commerce, *P-20 series*, #349, pp. 31-32; 1989 data are from Saluter, 1989, p. 55.

6.32   *Percent in Poverty Using Standard and Experimental Deflators.* P-60 Series, #168, p. 15.

6.33   *Poverty Rates under Alternative Thresholds.* From unrevised Current Population Survey, March 1988 supplement, reproduced from Ruggles (1990, p. 55).

Chapter 7

7.1   *Median Income of Young Families By Race.* 1973 from *P-60 Series*, #97, pp. 49-56; 1979 from *P-60 Series*, #129, pp. 81-92 (unpublished Hispanic data by phone); 1989 from *P-60 Series*, #168, pp. 32-34.

7.2   *Median Family Income of Young Families By Educational Attainment and Race.* Based on unpublished Census data. The latest year for which data are available with the appropriate age range (25-34 years old) and education detail (separating high school graduates from 1-3 years of college) is 1987.

7.3   *Young Family Income Growth, By Type of Family.* These data on the income of young families by type are based on special tabulations prepared by Chris Tilly using the data base prepared for Albelda and Tilly (1990). Their definition of families includes what Census calls households, e.g., single men. Their data has been converted to PCE deflated dollars from CPI-U-X1 deflated dollars.

7.4   *Composition of Young Families By Family Type.*
        Unpublished tabulations from Albelda and Tilly (see
        note to Table 7.3). Family composition based on
        counts of families by family type. The shift share
        analysis uses 1987 relative incomes by family type
        and computes the average income with the distribu-
        tions of families as of 1973, 1979, and 1987.

7.5   *Sources of Income for Young Families.* From un-
        published Albelda and Tilly data (see note to Table
        7.3). Earnings includes wage and salary and self-
        employment income. Capital income includes inter-
        est, dividends, rental income, royalties, and pen-
        sions. Government transfers includes cash transfers
        such as social security benefits, railroad retirement,
        supplemental security income, welfare, veteran's
        payments, unemployment insurance, temporary dis-
        ability benefits, and worker's compensation. Other
        income is alimony and child support.

7.6   *Young Family Income Growth, By Type of Income.*
        From unpublished Albelda and Tilly data (see note to
        Table 7.3).

7.7   *Earnings Growth in Families With Children, By
        Family Type and Earner.* From unpublished Albelda
        and Tilly data (see note to Table 7.3). We recoded
        their data so that adult earners are noted by gender
        (men, women) rather than householder status (head,
        spouse).

7.8   *Earnings Growth in Families Without Children, By
        Family Type and Earner.* See note to Table 7.7.

7.9   *Effect of Young Wives' Earnings Growth on Married
        Couple Earnings.* From unpublished Albelda and
        Tilly data (see note to Table 7.3). Change in family
        income "not including increased earnings of wives"
        is based on the change from the beginning year to the
        end year where the end year income is the hypotheti-
        cal income that would have prevailed if the earnings
        of wives had stayed at the beginning year level. Col-
        umn three is the difference between columns one
        and two.

7.10 *Factors Explaining Young Wives' Increased Annual Earnings.* From unpublished Albelda and Tilly data (see note to Table 7.3).

7.11 *Contribution of Increased Weekly Wages and Weeks Worked to Annual Earnings Growth of Young Wives.* Based on a log decomposition of annual earnings growth into that due to annual growth in weeks employed and weekly wages. The underlying data are those from Table 7.7. Because of the family size adjustment (the correlations between family size and weeks and weekly wages) the growth in weeks and weekly wages do not sum to the growth in annual earnings. The residual (representing less than 5% of the growth) was equally apportioned to each factor. The computations were done to two decimal places although only one decimal place is shown in the table.

7.12 *Wage Growth of Young Workers.* Harrison and Gorham, 1990, Tables 2 and 5. In order to match Tables 7.13, 7.14, and 7.15, these data have *not* been converted from CPI-U-X1 deflated to PCE deflated dollars. The declines would be somewhat larger in PCE deflated dollars.

7.13 *Shares of Young Workers By Wage Level By Age.* Harrison and Gorham, 1990, Tables 1 and 2. Their underlying wage data are CPI-U-X1 deflated. The expansion of low-wage employment would be greater with PCE deflated wage data.

7.14 *Shares of Workers By Wage Level, Aged 16-24, 1979-1987.* Harrison and Gorham, 1990, Table 5. Their underlying wage data are CPI-U-X1 deflated. The expansion of low-wage employment would be greater with PCE deflated wage data.

7.15 *Shares of Workers By Wage Level, Aged 25-34, 1979-1987.* Harrison and Gorham, 1990, Table 5. Their underlying wage data are CPI-U-X1 deflated. The expansion of low-wage employment would be greater with PCE deflated wage data.

7.16 *Education Wage Gaps Among White Male Full-Time, Full-Year Workers, Aged 25-34.* Blackburn et al., 1990, Tables 1, 3, and 6.

7.17 *Effect of Industry Employment Shift on Education Differentials.* Blackburn et al. (1990, Tables 4 and 5), with half of interaction effect in Table 4 attributed to each factor.

7.18 *Effect of Deunionization on Average Earnings By Education, White Male Workers Aged 25-34.* Blackburn et al., 1990, Table 10.

7.19 *Explanation for Increased College/High School Wage Gap Among White Male Workers Aged 25-34.* Blackburn et al., 1990, Table 11.

Chapter 8

8.1 *Home Ownership Rates by Age of Household Head.* Tabulated in Apgar et al., 1990, p. 16. Drawn from American Housing Survey, 1973-80; Current Population Survey, 1989.

8.2 *Burdens of Buying Homes and Renting.* Tabulated in Apgar et al., 1990, p. 26. Incomes: 1970 is from the 1970 Census of Population; 1967-69 are from the Panel Survey of Income Dynamics (PSID); 1971-72 are interpolated from the PSID and 1970 Census of Population; 1973-83 are from the American Housing Survey (AHS); 1983-89 are from the AHS, adjusted by the Current Population Survey. Prime first-time home buyers are married-couple renters aged 25 to 29. House prices are the AHS median values of houses purchased by first-time home buyers aged 25 to 29 in 1977, indexed by Census Department's Construction Reports C-27 Constant Quality Home Price Index. Mortgage rates equal Federal Home Loan Bank Board contract mortgage rate. Yearly payments are calculated based on a 30-year mortgage with a 20% downpayment. Also included in yearly home costs are property taxes, insurance, fuel and utilities, and maintenance. The tax benefits are deducted. Rent is median 1977 contract rent from AHS, indexed by the CPI residential rent index, with depreciation adjustments. Also included in rental costs are fuel and utilities, property taxes, and insurance.

295

8.3   *Median Incomes of Renters and Owners.* Incomes from Apgar et al., 1990, p. 26 (see note to Table 8.2). They are redeflated using the PCE price index. To redeflate we first had to convert from CPI-U-X1 adjusted dollars to nominal dollars; we used the CPI-U-X1 series in *P-60 Series* (#166, p. 11) to do this.

8.4   *Households Paying Over 25% of Income for Housing, by Household Size.* Stone, 1990. Averages are computed using fixed 1979 weights for the number of households in each size category.

8.5   *Shelter Poverty, by Household Size.* See note to Table 8.4. A household is shelter poor if after housing expenses it does not have enough to pay for other necessities according to the Bureau of Labor Statistics' Lower Budget.

8.6   *OECD Spending on Health.* Data are from Schieber and Poullier (1989).

8.7   *Medical Service Fees.* Fees in other countries were multiplied by ratio of U.S. per capita GDP to other country per capita GDP, to get fees in "adjusted dollars." (Adjustment using Purchasing Power Parity exchange rates makes U.S. fees look relatively higher.) Prices in own currencies from OECD (1987, p. 74). When a choice of fees or plans was available in any country, the highest fee was selected. In particular, U.S. data come from Kings County (Manhattan), New York, where fees are almost double the U.S. average. However, even if U.S. fees are halved, most still considerably exceed the average of the other three countries. GDP from OECD (1990). Population from OECD (1989a).

8.8   *Health Indicators in U.S. and in Average OECD Country.* Health Care Financing Administration, 1989, pp. 177, 178, 185, 186. Turkey is excluded from OECD averages as it has the health statistics and living standards of a third world country and would skew the averages. Infant mortality is deaths of infants less than 1 year old, as a percent of all live births. Perinatal mortality is fetal deaths occurring after 28 weeks of pregnancy, plus infant deaths occurring prior to 7 days after birth. 1986 perinatal mortality for Belgium, France, Italy, and Spain are actually from 1984, and for Ireland, from 1985. Canadian life expectancies in 1960 and 1980 are actually from 1961 and 1981, respectively. Portuguese life expectancies in 1980 are also from 1981 instead. Some 1986 life expectancies came from U.S. Department of Health and Human Services (1990, pp. 117-18). This source was used for Belgium, Canada, Greece, Ireland, Italy, and Portugal. Spain came from the Health Care Financing Administration (1989), and is for 1985.

8.9 *Number and Percent of the Population Under Age 65 Without Health Insurance. Green Book* 1990, p. 293. Table prepared by Congressional Research Service based on data from the 3/80, 3/84, 3/85, 3/86, and 3/87 Current Population Surveys. Information for 1980 to 1982 is not presented due to errors on the computer tape for those years.

8.10 *Breaks in Health Insurance During a 28-Month Period.* Nelson and Short, 1990. Sample is those members of the Survey of Income and Program Participation 1985 panel (interviewed 2/85-8/87) for whom 28 months of continuous information was available.

8.11 *Workers Receiving Health Insurance from Own Job, by Job Status.* Data are from Current Population Survey, tabulated in *Green Book* (1989, p. 274). Full-time workers are those who worked 35 hours per week or more during most of the weeks they worked during the year. Full-year workers are those who worked in civilian jobs for 50 weeks or more during the year.

8.12 *Health Insurance Coverage of Workers, by Firm Size.* Data are from Current Population Survey, tabulated in *Green Book* (1990, p. 291).

8.13 *Health Insurance Coverage of Workers, by Industry.* Data are from Current Population Survey, tabulated in *Green Book* (1990, p. 292).

8.14 *Overall Inflation vs. Health Insurance Inflation. NIPA,* Table 7.10. Overall prices proxied by PCE,

297

1982 weights. Health insurance prices are from line 71.

8.15 *Employer vs. Employee Spending on Private Health Insurance Premiums.* Levit, Freeland, and Waldo, 1989.

8.16 *Medical Benefits for Full-Time Workers in Large Firms.* 1982 from U.S. Department of Labor, 1983; 1988 from U.S. Department of Labor, 1989e, p. 123. Figures exclude most of the service industries, such as health and education services, and include only establishments that employed at least 250 workers in the mining, construction, retail trade, and some manufacturing and transportation industries (U.S. Department of Labor, 1989e, p. 140). For 1982, wholly employer-financed family insurance excluded any employees with own insurance but without dependent coverage. In 1988, such an employee was instead included in the wholly financed category, if the employer paid for all of his/her *individual* policy. This was necessary because BLS methodology changed. However, the difference can only *mitigate* the decrease in employer financing of family coverage between 1982 and 1988, since some employees who would not be listed as having wholly employer-financed family coverage in 1982 would be reassigned to wholly employer-financed family coverage in 1988. Note also that BLS expanded the survey scope between 1982 and 1988, but published tables for 1988 that had the same scope as in 1982. It is these same-scope tables that were used.

8.17 *Public Health Coverage in OECD Countries.* Health Care Financing Administration, 1989, pp. 135-37.

8.18 *Science Test Scores for 14-Year-Olds.* U.S. Department of Education, 1989, p. 390.

8.19 *Mathematics Test Scores for 8th Graders.* U.S. Department of Education, 1989, p. 389.

8.20 *Effects of Family Background on Scores of 8th Graders.* U.S. Department of Education, 1989, p. 118. Family background, or "socioeconomic status," is based on a composite score of parental education and occupations, family income, and household characteristics. The "disadvantaged" group is the lowest fourth; the "average" is the middle one-half; the "advantaged" group is the top fourth.

8.21 *Country Education Expenditures.* Rasell and Mishel, 1990.

8.22 *Public School Expenditures Per Pupil.* American Federation of Teachers, 1989, pp. 22, 55-56. State cost of living indices computed by AFT Research Department. For details on methods, see Nelson (1989).

8.23 *Public and Private College Costs.* Prices deflated using PCE, from *NIPA* (Tables 7.9/10). Costs from U.S. Department of Education (1989).

8.24 *Federal Student Aid.* College Board, 1989. Some numbers computed by Michael Pons of the National Educational Association.

8.25 *Parental Contributions to College Costs at Stanford University.* Based on authors' calculations using the Congressional methodology for determining financial need, as set out in U.S. Department of Education (1990). Figures are for a family of 4, with the older parent aged 45, 1 child in college, no business or farm assets, one parent working, and no income or assets owned by the student. Contributions at other universities may differ if their fees are different or if they do not use the official guidelines.

8.26 *Scholastic Aptitude Test Scores by Race/Ethnic Group.* 1976 data from U.S. Department of Education, 1989, Table 109. Later years from Quality Education for Minorities Project (1990).

8.27 *Educational Attainment of 18- to 24-Year-Olds by Race/Ethnic Group.* Rates are numbers aged 18-24 and graduated/enrolled in college as percent of number aged 18-24. Rates given are arithmetic averages of the rates in the given period. Hispanic averages for 1967-1973 period are for 1972-1973 only. All data from U.S. Department of Commerce, Bureau of the Census, *P-20 Series*, various years. Data were tabulated by the following authors. 1976-1988 data from

Carter and Wilson (1989, pp. 20-21). 1967-1975 data from U.S. Department of Education (1989, p. 199).

8.28   *Post-secondary Enrollment and Degree Attainment by Race/Ethnic Group.* U.S. Department of Education, 1989, Tables 176, 214, 216, 218.

Chapter 9

9.1   *Per Capita GDP Growth in 10 Countries.* GDP stands for "Gross Domestic Product," and is essentially the total of all money received for goods and services produced in the economy in a single year. It is not exactly the same thing as Gross National Product, or GNP, which is total money received from all productive sources, because GNP also includes net investment income from abroad. However, the differences between GDP and GNP are usually very small, which is why GDP per capita is commonly used as an indicator of national living standards. Real GDP comes from OECD (1990); civilian employment comes from U.S. Department of Labor, *Monthly Labor Review* (July 1986, p. 96, and January 1990, p. 125); and total population comes from OECD, *Main Economic Indicators* (January 1987, p. 173, and January 1990, p. 178).

9.2   *Growth of Per Capita GDP and of Productivity.* Growth rates for real per capita GDP and for productivity (GDP per civilian worker) were computed, and a straightforward weighted average of these rates was computed. Then the growth rates were converted to indices, with the weighted average growth rates equal to 100. The weighted averages were weighted by the populations of the countries; a country's population was taken to be the arithmetic average of the populations in 1979 and 1988. These countries were selected because the Bureau of Labor Statistics regularly compiles information about their employment levels. Civilian employment levels come from U.S. Department of Labor, *Monthly Labor Review* (October 1989, p. 96) and U.S. Department of Labor (1989a, pp. 552-53). Real GDP comes from OECD (1990).

300

9.3 *Annual Productivity Growth Rates.* Civilian employment levels are from U.S. Department of Labor, *Monthly Labor Review* (October 1989, p. 96) and U.S. Department of Labor (1989a, pp. 552-53). Real GDP comes from OECD (1990).

9.4 *Hourly Manufacturing Compensation Growth Compared.* The consumer price index listed in International Monetary Fund (1989) was used to deflate hourly compensation in all countries except the U.S. We deflated U.S. compensation growth using the PCE. Data for all employees is from U.S. Department of Labor (1989c); data for production workers in manufacturing is from U.S. Department of Labor (1989b). U.S. PCE index came from *NIPA*.

9.5 *Per Capita Income Compared.* OECD, 1990.

9.6 *Inequality Measures for Disposable Income.* Coder, Rainwater and Smeeding, 1989, pp. 320-24.

9.7 *Relative and Absolute Poverty Among Children, Adults, and the Elderly.* Smeeding, Torrey, and Rein, 1988, p. 96.

9.8 *Sensitivity of Child Poverty Rates to the Level of the Absolute Poverty Line.* Smeeding, Torrey, and Rein, 1988, p. 9.

9.9 *Poverty Among Children by Family Type.* Smeeding, Torrey, and Rein, 1988, p. 102.

9.10 *Manufacturing Compensation Compared (Using Purchasing Power Parity Exchange Rates).* Purchasing Power Parity exchange rates from OECD (1990). Compensation from U.S. Department of Labor (1989b and 1989c).

9.11 *Manufacturing Compensation Compared (Using Market Exchange Rates).* Exchange rates from OECD (1990). Compensation from U.S. Department of Labor (1989b and 1989c).

9.12 *Jobs Created in 10 Countries.* Civilian employment from U.S. Department of Labor, *Monthly Labor Review* (July 1986, p. 96, and January 1990, p. 125).

9.13 *Contributions to Employment Growth in 10 Countries.* U.S. Department of Labor, *Monthly Labor Re-*

view, July 1986, p. 96, and January 1990, p. 125; OECD, *Main Economic Indicators*, January 1987, p. 173, and January 1990, p. 178.

9.14 *Unemployment in OECD Countries.* OECD, *Economic Outlook,* December 1989, p. 182. Uses a standardized definition of unemployment to permit comparisons.

9.15 *Public Spending on Active Labor Market Programs as Percent of GDP.* OECD, *Employment Outlook,* July 1989, pp. 206-07.

FIGURE NOTES

Figures:

1A   *Median Family Income.* See note to Table 1.1.

1B   *Annual Increase in Median Family Income.* See note to Table 1.2.

1C   *Changes in Family Incomes Due to Increased Inequality.* See note to Table 1.8.

1D   *Family Income Growth.* See note to Table 1.10.

1E   *Shares of Income Gains.* See note to Table 1.12.

1F   *Growth of Income by Type.* See note to Table 1.14.

1G   *Personal Consumption Expenditures Per Capita, Annual Growth Rates.* See note to Table 1.18.

1H   *Effect of Increased Female Earnings on Income of Married Couples with Children.* See note to Table 1.22.

2A   *Federal Tax Burden by Family Income Group.* See note to Table 2.5.

2B   *Personal Income Tax Burden by Family Income Group.* See note to Table 2.8.

2C   *Social Insurance Tax Burden by Family Income Group.* See note to Table 2.8.

2D   *Corporate Income Tax Burden by Family Income Group.* See note to Table 2.8.

2E   *Excise Tax Burden by Family Income Group.* See note to Table 2.8.

2F   *Corporate Profits Taxes.* See note to Table 2.10.

2G   *Excise Tax Burden.* See note to Table 2.11.

2H   *Federal Revenue Sources.* See note to Table 2.13.

2I   *State and Local Revenue Sources.* See note to Table 2.15.

3A   *Average Hourly Compensation, Wages, and Benefits, All Private Sector Workers.* See note to Table 3.2.

3B   *Earnings Growth for Production Workers.* See note to Table 3.3.

3C   *Growth of Hourly Wages by Wage Percentile, All Workers and Men Only.* See notes to Tables 3.5 and 3.6.

3D   *Percent of Workers Earning Poverty Wages.* See note to Table 3.9.

3E   *Hourly Benefits by Type.* See note to Table 3.11.

3F   *Health Benefits by Wage Fourth.* See note to Table 3.12.

ries, #168, p. 65. Note that the horizontal axis is age group, not year.

6C   *Poverty Rates by Race/Ethnic Group. Green Book*, 1989, pp. 944-5. 1988-89 data from *P-60 Series*, #168, pp. 57-8.

6D   *Poverty Rates Among Children and the Elderly. P-60 Series*, #168, p. 59.

6E   *Poverty Among the Elderly and All Persons, Before and After Cash Transfers.* Slotsve and Donley, 1990, Tables 2 and 3.

6F   *Poverty among Families with Children, Before and After Cash Transfers.* Slotsve and Donley, 1990, Tables 5 and 6. Rates are for persons in families with nonaged heads and with children under 18.

6G   *Poverty by Family Relationship. P-60 Series*, #168, p. 57. Unrelated subfamilies, a very small group, are allocated according to whether they are female-headed or not through 1978. However, because of a change in Census procedures starting in 1979, they are all allocated to married-couple and male-headed families in 1979 and after.

6H   *Unmarried Births and Benefit Levels by State, 1980.* D.C. is the box that is above the rest. Births to unmarried women as a percent of all births is from the Children's Defense Fund 1990, "Children 1990: A Report Card, Briefing Book, and Action Primer." Data come originally from National Center for Health Statistics, 1984, "Vital Statistics of the United States, 1980, v. I - Natality." Combined AFDC and Food Stamp benefit levels for a family of four with no income are expressed in 1988 dollars (using the CPI-U) and come from the *Green Book* (1989, pp. 880-1).

7A   *Median Income of Young Families by Education.* See note to Table 7.2.

7B   *Median Income of Young Families Headed by High School Graduates, by Race.* See note to Table 7.2.

7C   *Total Change in Weekly Earnings in Young Married Couples with Children.* See note to Table 7.7.

7D   *Effect of Wives' Earnings Growth on Incomes of Young Married Couples with Children.* See note to Table 7.9.

BIBLIOGRAPHY

Albelda, Randy, and Chris Tilly. "Resources, Opportunity, and Effort: Sources of Family Income 1973-87 and Implications for Poverty Policy." Paper presented at Allied Social Sciences Association meeting, Atlanta, Georgia, October 1989.

Albelda, Randy, and Chris Tilly. "All in the Family: Family Types, Access to Income, and Implications for Family Income Policies." Submitted to *Journal of Policy Analysis and Management*. Boston, MA: University of Massachusetts, 1990.

American Federation of Teachers. *Survey & Analysis of Salary Trends, 1989*. Washington, DC: AFT, 1989.

Apgar, Jr., William C., Denise DiPasquale, Jean Cummings and Nancy McArdle. "The State of the Nation's Housing 1990." Cambridge, MA: Joint Center for Housing Studies of Harvard University, 1990.

Avery, Robert B., Gregory E. Elliehausen, Glenn B. Canner and Thomas Gustafson. "Survey of Consumer Finances, 1983: A Second Report." *Federal Reserve Bulletin*, December 1984.

Bane, Mary Jo, and David T. Ellwood. "One Fifth of the Nation's Children: Why Are They Poor?" *Scientific American*, Vol. 245, September 8, 1989.

Barancik, Scott. *1988 Poverty Tables: Based on Data from the U.S. Bureau of the Census and Other Sources*. Washington, DC: Center on Budget and Policy Priorities, 1989.

Blackburn, McKinley L., David E. Bloom, and Richard B. Freeman. "The Declining Economic Position of Less Skilled American Men." In Gary Burtless, ed., *A Future of Lousy Jobs?* Washington, DC: The Brookings Institution, 1990.

Blank, Rebecca M. "Are Part-Time Jobs Bad Jobs?" In Burtless, ed., *A Future of Lousy Jobs?* Washington, DC: The Brookings Institution, 1990.

Blecker, Robert. "Low Saving Rates and the 'Twin Deficits': Confusing the Symptoms and Causes of Economic Decline." In Paul Davidson and Jan Kregel, eds., *Economic*

Problems of the 1990s. Brookfield, VT: Edward Elgar, forthcoming.

Carre, Francoise. *Contingent Workers*. Washington, DC: Economic Policy Institute, forthcoming.

Carter, Deborah J., and Reginald Wilson. *Eighth Annual Status Report on Minorities in Higher Education*. Washington, DC: American Council on Education, Office of Minority Concerns, 1989.

Center on Budget and Policy Priorities. "1986 Poverty Graphs and Tables." Washington, DC, 1987.

Children's Defense Fund. *The Health of America's Children: Maternal and Child Health Data Book*. Washington, DC: CDF, 1989.

Coder, John, Lee Rainwater, and Timothy Smeeding. "Inequality Among Children and Elderly in Ten Modern Nations: The United States in an International Context." *American Economic Review*, Vol. 79, No. 2, May 1989.

College Board. *Trends in Student Aid: 1980 to 1989*. August 1989.

Congressional Budget Office. "The Changing Distribution of Federal Taxes: 1975-1990." Washington, DC: U.S. Government Printing Office, 1987.

Congressional Budget Office. "Average Income and Effective Tax Rates in 1977, 1980, 1985 and 1990." Washington, DC, 1990a, unpublished.

Congressional Budget Office. "The Economic and Budget Outlook: Fiscal Years 1991-1995." Washington, DC: U.S. Government Printing Office, January 1990b.

Congressional Budget Office. *Federal Taxation of Tobacco, Alcoholic Beverages, and Motor Fuels*. Washington, DC: U.S. Government Printing Office, June 1990c.

Costrell, Robert M. "The Effects of Industrial and Regional Employment Shifts on Wage Growth, 1969-87," unpublished.

Costrell, Robert M. "The Effects of Industry Employment Shifts on Wage Growth: 1948-87." A study prepared for the Joint Economic Committee, August 1988.

Democratic Study Group. "They Didn't Come to the Party: A Tough Decade for Families in the Middle." Special Report, No. 101-32. Washington, DC: U.S. House of Representatives, 1990.

Economic Policy Institute. *Family Incomes in Trouble.* Briefing paper. Washington, DC: Economic Policy Institute, 1986.

The Economist, December 23, 1989.

Ellwood, David T. *Poor Support: Poverty in the American Family.* New York: Basic Books, 1988.

Federal Reserve System. "Balance Sheets for the U.S. Economy: 1945-1989." Washington, DC: Federal Reserve Board, April 1990.

Fisher, Gordon M. "Trends in Money Income and Poverty." U.S. Census Bureau, November 1986, unpublished.

Greenwood, Daphne T., and Edward N. Wolff. "Relative Wealth Holdings of Children and the Elderly in the United States, 1962-83". In Palmer, Smeeding, and Torrey, eds., *The Vulnerable.* Washington, DC: Urban Institute Press, 1988.

Haber, Sheldon E., Enrique L. Lamas, and Jules H. Lichtenstein. "On Their Own: The Self-employed and Others in Private Business." *Monthly Labor Review*, May 1987.

Harrison, Bennett, and Barry Bluestone. *The Great U-Turn.* New York: Basic Books, Inc., 1988.

Harrison, Bennett, and Lucy Gorham. "What Happened to Black Wages in the 1980s? Family Incomes, Individual Earnings, and the Growth of the African-American Middle Class," working paper. Economic Policy Institute, 1990.

Health Care Financing Administration. *Health Care Financing Review: 1989 Annual Supplement.* Washington, DC: U.S. Government Printing Office, December 1989.

International Monetary Fund. *International Financial Statistics Yearbook.* Washington, DC: IMF, monthly.

Japan Economic Institute Report. "The Long Workweek in Japan: Difficult to Reduce." March 16, 1990.

Katz, Lawrence F., and Kevin M. Murphy. "Changes in Relative Wages, 1963-1987: Supply and Demand Factors," unpublished.

Karoly, Lynn A. "The Trend in Inequality Among Families, Individuals, and Workers in the United States: A Twenty-Five Year Perspective." Paper prepared for the Population Association Meetings of America, and the Russell Sage Conference on "Caused of Increasing Inequality in the U.S.," 1990.

Klein, Bruce W., and Philip L. Rones. "A Profile of the Working Poor" (Bulletin 2345). Washington, DC: Division of Labor Force Statistics, Bureau of Labor Statistics, U.S. Department of Labor, December 1989.

Levit, Katharine R., Mark S. Freeland, and Daniel R. Waldo. "Health Spending and Ability to Pay: Business, Individuals, and Government." *Health Care Financing Review*, Vol. 10, No. 3, Spring 1989.

Levitan, S., and E. Conway. "Part-Time Employment: Living on Half Rations." Washington, DC: Graduate Institute for Policy Education and Research, George Washington University, 1988.

Mishel, Lawrence. *The Polarization of America: The Loss of Good Jobs, Falling Incomes and Rising Inequality*. Washington, DC: Industrial Union Department, AFL-CIO, October 1986.

Mishel, Lawrence, and Jacqueline Simon. *The State of Working America*. Washington, DC: Economic Policy Institute, 1988.

Mishel, Lawrence R. "The Late Great Debate on Deindustrialization." *Challenge*, January/February 1989.

Mishel, Lawrence, and Ruy Teixeira. *The Myth of the Coming Labor Shortage: Jobs, Skills, and Incomes of America's Workforce 2000*. Washington, DC: Economic Policy Institute, 1990.

Murphy, Kevin, and Finis Welch. "Recent Trends in Real Wages: Evidence From Household Data." Paper prepared for the Health Care Financing Administration of the U.S. Department of Health and Human Services, January 1989.

Nelson, Charles, and Kathleen Short. *Health Insurance Coverage: 1986-88*. Current Population Reports, Household Economic Studies, Series P-70, No. 17. Washington, DC: U.S. Government Printing Office, 1990.

Nelson, F. Howard, "An Interstate Cost-of-Living Index." Washington, DC: American Federation of Teachers, November 1989.

OECD. *Financing and Delivering Health Care: A Comparative Analysis of OECD Countries*. Paris: Organization for Economic Cooperation and Development, 1987

OECD. *Labor Force Statistics: 1967-1987*. Paris: Organization for Economic Cooperation and Development, 1989a.

OECD. *Revenue Statistics of OECD Member Countries, 1965-1988*. Paris: Organization for Economic Cooperation and Development, 1989b.

OECD, Department of Economics and Statistics. *National Accounts, Vol. 1 (Main Aggregates), 1960-1988*. Paris: Organization for Economic Cooperation and Development, 1990.

OECD. *Economic Outlook*. Paris: Organization for Economic Cooperation and Development, various dates.

OECD. *Employment Outlook*. Paris: Organization for Economic Cooperation and Development, various dates.

OECD, Department of Economics and Statistics. *Main Economic Indicators*. Paris: Organization for Economic Cooperation and Development, various dates.

Pollin, Robert. *Deeper in Debt: The Changing Financial Conditions of U.S. Households*. Washington, DC: Economic Policy Institute, forthcoming.

President of the United States. *Economic Report of the President*. Washington, DC: U.S. Government Printing Office, annual.

Public Employee Department, AFL-CIO. "Strategies to Help the Working Poor." Washington, DC: AFL-CIO, March 1990.

Quality Education for Minorities Project. *Education that Works: An Action Plan for the Education of Minorities*. Cambridge, MA: Massachusetts Institute of Technology, January 1990.

Rasell, M. Edith, and Lawrence Mishel. *Shortchanging Education: How U.S. Spending on Grades K-12 Lags Behind*

Other Industrial Nations. Washington, DC: Economic Policy Institute, 1990.

Ruggles, Patricia. *Drawing the Line: Alternative Poverty Measures and Their Implications for Public Policy.* Washington, DC: Urban Institute, 1990.

Saluter, Arlene F. "Marital Status and Living Arrangements: March 1989." U.S. Department of Commerce, Bureau of the Census, P-20 series, #445. Washington, DC: U.S. Government Printing Office, 1989.

Schieber, George J., and Jean-Pierre Poullier. "International Health Care Expenditure Trends: 1987." *Health Affairs,* Vol. 8, No. 3, Fall 1989.

Schor, Juliet, and Laura Leete-Guy. *Trends in Leisure Time.* Washington, DC: Economic Policy Institute, forthcoming.

Sekscenski, Edward S. "Women's Share of Moonlighting Nearly Doubles During 1969-79." *Monthly Labor Review* Vol. 103, No. 5, May 1980.

Shank, Susan. "Preferred Hours of Work and Corresponding Earnings." *Monthly Labor Review,* November 1986.

Shapiro, Isaac. "No Escape: The Minimum Wage and Poverty." Washington, DC: Center on Budget and Policy Priorities, June 1987.

Slotsve, George, and Thomas Donley. "A Supplement to the Trend in Poverty, 1967-1988: Tables from the Current Population Survey." Madison, WI: Institute for Research on Poverty, 1990.

Smeeding, Timothy, Barbara Boyle Torrey, and Martin Rein, "Patterns of Income and Poverty: The Economic Status of Children and the Elderly in Eight Countries." In Palmer, Smeeding, and Torrey, eds., *The Vulnerable.* Washington, DC: Urban Institute, 1988.

Stinson, Jr., John F. "Moonlighting by Women Jumped to Record Highs." *Monthly Labor Review,* Vol. 109, No. 11, November 1986.

Stone, Michael E. *One Third of a Nation: Reconsidering the Housing Affordability Problem.* Washington, DC: Economic Policy Institute, 1990.

Tax Foundation. *Tax Burden by Income Class: 1986-1987*. Washington, DC: Tax Foundation, 1989.

Tilly, Chris, and Randy Albelda. "Family Structure and Family Earnings: How Resources, Opportunity, and Effort Shape Earnings." Lowell, MA: University of Lowell, 1990.

Tilly, Chris, *Short Hours, Short Shrift*. Washington, DC: Economic Policy Institute, 1990.

Towers, Perrin and Company. "Worldwide Total Remuneration, 1988." October 1988.

U.S. Congress, Joint Economic Committee. *The Concentration of Wealth in the United States*. Washington, DC: U.S. Congress, 1986.

U.S. Department of Commerce, Bureau of the Census. *Household Wealth and Asset Ownership: 1984*. CPS P-70 series, No. 7. Washington, DC: U.S. Government Printing Office, July 1986.

U.S. Department of Commerce, Bureau of the Census. *Estimates of Poverty Including the Value of Noncash Benefits: 1987 (Technical Paper 58)*. Washington, DC: U.S. Government Printing Office, August 1988.

U.S. Department of Commerce, Bureau of Economic Analysis. *National Income and Product Accounts*. Washington, DC: U.S. Government Printing Office, 1989.

U.S. Department of Commerce, Bureau of the Census. *Child Support and Alimony: 1987*, Series P-23, No. 167, 1990.

U.S. Department of Commerce, Bureau of Economic Analysis. *Survey of Current Business*. Washington, DC: U.S. Government Printing Office, monthly.

U.S. Department of Commerce, Bureau of the Census. "Marital Status and Living Arrangements." *Current Population Reports: Series P-20*. Washington, DC: U.S. Government Printing Office, various dates.

U.S. Department of Commerce, Bureau of the Census. *Current Population Reports: Series P-60*. Washington, DC: U.S. Government Printing Office, various dates.

U.S. Department of Education, National Center for Educational Statistics. *Digest of Educational Statistics 1989*. Washington, DC: U.S. Government Printing Office, 1989.

U.S. Department of Education, Office of Student Financial Assistance. *The Congressional Methodology: 1990-91.* Washington, DC: U.S. Government Printing Office, 1990.

U.S. Department of Health and Human Services, National Center for Health Statistics. *Health, United States, 1989.* Hyattsville, MD: Public Health Services, 1990.

U.S. Department of Labor, Bureau of Labor Statistics. "Employee Benefits in Medium and Large Firms, 1982." U.S. Department of Labor publication #83-234, May 20, 1983.

U.S. Department of Labor, Bureau of Labor Statistics. *Handbook of Labor Statistics (Bulletin 2217).* Washington, DC: U.S. Government Printing Office, June 1985.

U.S. Department of Labor, Bureau of Labor Statistics. *Handbook of Labor Statistics (Bulletin 2340).* Washington, DC: U.S. Government Printing Office, August 1989a.

U.S. Department of Labor, Bureau of Labor Statistics, Office of Productivity and Technology. "Hourly Compensation Costs for Production Workers; 40 Manufacturing Industries; 34 Countries, 1957 and 1978-88." Washington, D.C: U.S. Government Printing Office, August 1989b.

U.S. Department of Labor, Bureau of Labor Statistics, Office of Productivity and Technology. "Underlying Data for Indexes of Output per Hour, Hourly Compensation, and Unit Labor Costs in Manufacturing, Twelve Industrial Countries, 1950-1988 and Unit Labor Costs in Korea and Taiwan, 1970-1988." Washington, DC: U.S. Government Printing Office, November 2, 1989c.

U.S. Department of Labor, Bureau of Labor Statistics. "Employer Costs for Employee Compensation—March 1989." USDL: 89-295, Washington, DC, June 15, 1989d.

U.S. Department of Labor, Bureau of Labor Statistics. *Employee Benefits in Medium and Large Firms, 1988.* August, 1989e.

U.S. Department of Labor, Bureau of Labor Statistics. "Multiple Jobholding Reached Record High in May 1989." USDL: 89-529, Washington, DC, November 6, 1989f.

U.S. Department of Labor. *Employment and Earnings.* U.S. Department of Labor, Bureau of Labor Statistics. Washington, DC: U.S. Government Printing Office, monthly.

314

U.S. Department of Labor. *Monthly Labor Review*. Washington, DC: U.S. Department of Labor, Bureau of Labor Statistics, monthly.

U.S. House of Representatives. Committee on Ways and Means, *Background Material and Data on Programs within the Jurisdiction of the Committee on Ways and Means*. Washington, DC: U.S. Government Printing Office, 1989.

U.S. House of Representatives. Committee on Ways and Means. *Background Material and Data on Programs within the Jurisdiction of the Committee on Ways and Means*. Washington, DC: U.S. Government Printing Office, 1990a.

U.S. House of Representatives Committee on Ways and Means. *Tax Progressivity and Income Distribution*, Washington, DC: U.S. Government Printing Office, March 23, 1990b.

Lawrence Mishel is the Research Director of the Economic Policy Institute and the author of various EPI publications, including *Manufacturing Numbers*, *The State of Working America* (with Jacqueline Simon), *Shortchanging Education* (with M. Edith Rasell), and *The Myth of the Coming Labor Shortage* (with Ruy Teixeira). He holds a Ph.D. in economics from the University of Wisconsin and has published in a variety of academic and non-academic journals.

David M. Frankel received an A.B. in mathematics from Harvard University and an M.Sc. in sociology from St. Catherine's College, Oxford. He is currently studying economics at the Massachusetts Institute of Technology.

The Economic Policy Institute was founded in 1986 to widen the debate about policies to achieve healthy economic growth, prosperity and opportunity in the difficult new era America has entered.

Central to the Economic Policy Institute's search for solutions is the exploration of the economics of teamwork—economic policies that encourage every segment of the American economy (business, labor, government, universities, voluntary organizations, etc.) to work cooperatively to raise productivity and living standards for all Americans. Such an undertaking involves a challenge to conventional views of market behavior and a revival of a cooperative relationship between the public and private sector.

With the support of leaders from labor, business, and the foundation world, the Institute has sponsored research and public discussion of a wide variety of topics: trade and fiscal policies; trends in wages, incomes, and prices; the causes of the productivity slowdown; labor market problems; U.S. and Third World Debt; rural and urban policies; inflation; state-level economic development strategies; comparative international economic performance; and studies of the overall health of the U.S. manufacturing sector and of specific key industries.

The Institute works with a growing network of innovative economists and other social science researchers in universities and research centers all over the country who are willing to go beyond the conventional wisdom in considering strategies for public policy.

The research committee of the Institute includes:

Jeff Faux, EPI President;

Lester Thurow, Dean of MIT's Sloan School of Management;

Ray Marshall, former U.S. Secretary of Labor now a Professor at the LBJ School of Public Affairs, University of Texas;

Barry Bluestone, University of Massachusetts, Boston;

Robert Reich, JFK School of Government, Harvard University;

Robert Kuttner, Author, *Business Week* columnist, and economics editor at the *New Republic*.

EPI Reports and Working Papers are distributed by M.E. Sharpe, Inc. For a publication list, or to order publications, call **1-800-541-6563**.

Shorter **EPI Briefing Papers** are available directly from the Institute.